Roja Singh

Spotted Goddesses

Contributions to
Transnational Feminism

edited by

Erin Kenny
(Drury University, MO)
and
Silvia Schultermandl
(University of Graz, Austria)

Volume 6

LIT

Roja Singh

SPOTTED GODDESSES

Dalit women's agency-narratives
on caste and gender violence

LIT

Cover art: Roja Singh

All images copyrighted by Kalaimagal Arumugam

Printed with support of the Lisbeth Linley Foundation

Published in South Asia by Zubaan Publishers Pvt Ltd.

Bibliographic information published by the Deutsche Nationalbibliothek
The Deutsche Nationalbibliothek lists this publication in the Deutsche
Nationalbibliografie; detailed bibliographic data are available on the Internet at
http://dnb.d-nb.de.

ISBN 978-3-643-90915-2 (pb.)
ISBN 978-3-643-95915-7 (PDF)

A catalogue record for this book is available from the British Library

©LIT VERLAG GmbH & Co. KG Wien,
Zweigniederlassung Zürich 2018
Klosbachstr. 107
CH-8032 Zürich
Tel. +41 (0) 44-251 75 05
Fax +41 (0) 44-251 75 06
E-Mail: zuerich@lit-verlag.ch
http://www.lit-verlag.ch

LIT VERLAG Dr. W. Hopf
Berlin 2018
Fresnostr. 2
D-48159 Münster
Tel. +49 (0) 2 51-62 03 20
Fax +49 (0) 2 51-23 19 72
E-Mail: lit@lit-verlag.de
http://www.lit-verlag.de

Distribution:
In the UK: Global Book Marketing, e-mail: mo@centralbooks.com
In North America: International Specialized Book Services, e-mail: orders@isbs.com
In Germany: LIT Verlag Fresnostr. 2, D-48159 Münster
Tel. +49 (0) 2 51-620 32 22, Fax +49 (0) 2 51-922 60 99, e-mail: vertrieb@lit-verlag.de

e-books are available at www.litwebshop.de

I dedicate this book to my late parents, my *Amma* and my *Appa*:
Suganthy and Andrew Sathiasatchy.
Their generous, compassion-filled life and faith in a spiritual essence in all,
taught me that *earthy humanness* as a way of life sustains peaceful family,
community, and global inclusion. Under their caring wings, they protected me
from being hurt by a caste-ridden society that they experienced.
I honor, thank and adore them both.

TABLE OF CONTENTS

ACKNOWLEDGMENTS

My book, *Spotted Goddesses: Dalit Women's agency-narratives on caste and gender violence*, is a creation of relationships. Thankful to my resilient parents for transgressing caste boundaries in claiming dignity and education. I greatly admire my sons—Nivedhan and Eklan—for courageously blooming where planted, rooted in values of justice, humanness, and compassionate living. Their unconditional love for me patiently tolerated long hours of writing. My loving life-partner, Prince, was my first teacher who exposed me to Dalit struggles and led me into a proud ownership of my Dalit identity. He has been my constant stromg support in an ongoing meaningful engagement with the bold lives in this book. I am grateful as he continues to inspire me with his compassionate engagement with and passion for social justice and human rights. My nieces and nephews—Hannah, Sathya, Sarah, Nishanth, and Vasanth—engaged in valuable seed discussions on social justice scattered in this work. I am thankful to exemplary individuals in my life who educate and inspire me through their dedicated work for Dalit rights as human rights: Paul Divakar, Annie Namala, Smita Narula, Ruth Manoramma, and Bama Susairaj. My friend, Lisbeth Linley Nedds, inspired me with her reminders: "Never give up on your research." Her loving voice prods me in fulfilling directions. My immense gratitude to Ivan, Duffy and Will Nedds of the Lisbeth Linley Foundation for sponsoring this publication. My surrogate parents, Ginny and Brain Bussey, are my consistent refuge. My god-daughter Manasa rejuvenates me with her sunshine presence. My Mentor Josephine Diamond believed in the strength of my research

I am grateful to Dr. Cornel West for his encouragement with this book, for engaging with my thoughts, and for his sincere solidarity with Dalit culture, history, and struggles. With the involvement of such leaders, the Black Lives Matter movement has emerged as a global human rights movement in intertwining voices of all oppressed communities such as Dalits.

I thank Silvia Schultermandl and Erin Drury with LIT Verlag for initially reading my proposal and connecting with the nature of this book, and for their consistent faith in its meaning and purpose. I am deeply grateful to all Dalit women who shared their lives through this book and who continue to give their lives to overturn soil for new sprouts of life among Dalit and any victimized communities: Kalaimagal Arumugam, Rani Periasamy, all singers, dancers, and those who fed me throughout my field work. Special thanks to Guna Dayalan for taking me into the villages on his moped scooter. Many thanks to Sathianathan Clarke and V.G. Julie Rajan who shaped crucial chapters in this book. Clarke introduced me to the abundance of meanings in Dalit culture by involving me in his fieldwork in Tamil Nadu. I am grateful to all writers on my Works Cited pages who enriched this work in their research on human life and value. Thank you to LIT Verlag for publishing this work.

I owe immensely to my chief editor Fionnuala Regan who spent a lot of time to carefully read and edit my manuscript while deeply engaging my writing. Above and beyond editing, she has been a constant source of encouragement in identifying meaning and strength in these narratives. Without Fionnuala this book would not be possible. My sincere gratitude to my readers—David Baronov, Erin Drury, Erika Murphy, Smita Narula, and Silvia Schultermandl—who took the time to provide valuable suggestions to weed, transplant, and organically bring this book to fruition. Thanks to Katylyn Adams, Elley Hickey, Melanie Duguid-May, Lori Vail, and Kellen Vail for helping me read, type, and edit specific sections. I thank all others who helped with technical aspects in the formation stages, especially Nikola Zilic and Jana Hauser. All my close soul-friends stood with me cheering me on: Veena Bunyan, Renu Joseph, Aparna Kharedulla, Joel Lee, Lorraine Knox, Maria Ribeiro, Arlene Holpp-Scala, Sonali Suvvaru, Susan Victor, and many more.

Both my brothers, Stephen and Suvisedagan, have encouraged me since my childhood to never let my identity as a woman be a cultural impediment to what I wanted to be. My sisters-in-law, Christina and Rebecca, and brother-in-law, Melville, blessed this venture. Thanks to my mother-in-law, Ida Singh for helping me with childcare during my field work, making my research possible. My cousins, Sarah and Christopher Solomon, caringly nourished me physically and spiritually. My cousins, Meena and Kirupakar Shodavaram, helped me with accurate translations and transcribing. I am thankful to my cousins Dorothy Akka, John Rajadurai, and Priscilla Joseph who provided me with interesting family facts. Paul Dayanandan generously shared his knowledge on Dalit Christian life and history. This wonderful circle of support keeps me moving.

PROLOGUE

Dalit and Woman

I grew up in India unaware that caste-based human gradation kept Dalits "untouchable." I was twenty-six when I embraced my Dalit roots. *Spotted Goddesses: Dalit Women's agency-narratives on caste and gender violence*, holds both oral and written narratives by women from Dalit communities in the Chengalpattu, Pudukkottai, and Puduppatti regions in Tamil Nadu, South India interwoven with my voice as a Dalit woman living in New York, USA. Voices from Tamil Nadu testify to suffering, cultural strengths, and change-seeking audacious leadership. I have the privilege of listening with specific communities of Dalit women in Tamil Nadu and Andhra Pradesh for over twenty-five years. Forced into a tradition of violence and punishment for daring to cross boundaries drawn by religion, society, and culture, Dalit women in these parts of India continue to boldly transgress sanctioned institutions and create social change to claim human dignity as theirs. They respond to a culture of violence through *earthy humanness* as a way of life—an unconditional Dalit ethics of care claiming human dignity for all.

The phrase "*Spotted Goddesses*" in the book title captures the reification of a Dalit goddess, *Mariamman,* in the life and transfigurative workings of Dalit women. They wield subversive strategies to change traditional practices of violent punishments meted upon their bodies for the "crime" of being an "untouchable," dismissing the fact that they are socially configured and religiously sanctioned as "untouchable." In chapter three, I discuss *Mariamman* as a spotted goddess—settling on bodies as smallpox—and Dalit social actualization of the ambiguous necessity of her diseased and healing presence. She thus provides a contrast in religious and social meaning to traditional gods and goddesses in dominant Indian cultural thought.

Dalit and Outcaste

Dalits are those who were formerly referred to as "untouchables" and continue to be kept apart as "unclean" under the three-thousand-year-old caste system, which is a social hierarchy primarily present in India but found in other Asian and African countries as well. Today over 260 million Dalits live worldwide, but a clear majority are in South Asian countries such as Nepal, Bangladesh, Pakistan, Sri Lanka, and India (International Dalit Solidarity Network). "Dalit" is a self-chosen Marathi term that situates Dalits more in their social condition as "broken people" who are ground or broken like *dal* (lentil) with a heavy pestle (Massey 15). I propose that in their brokenness, rising from within a mortar as splatter narratives dodging a pounding pestle, Dalit women's voices take root in experiential meanings. Bhimrao Ramji Ambedkar (1891-1956)—the pioneer leader of the Dalit movement in India and architect of the Indian Constitution—popularized the term "Dalit" as a counter term to the degrading stigma as "untouchable" (Narula 2). To respectfully engage in presenting human agency in its diverse sprouts in Dalit women, I hesitate using words such as "down" or "bottom" to refer to an undesirable social position. Instead, I adopt "broken" and "ground" throughout this book when I refer to Dalits in their continued social condition as one of the most vulnerable and violated communities in India. In their broken state, Dalits—especially Dalit women who are most subject to violence—desire, demand, create, and sustain positive changes that confirm human dignity.

Dalit and "Untouchable"

I witnessed the practice of untouchability and other specifically caste-based discriminations and violence for the first time in 1991 when I married and moved to the town of Karunguzhi about fifty kilometers south of Chennai in the Chengalpattu district of Tamil Nadu. In just a few days, I was jerked into a shocking realization of the ways in which my society dehumanized a group of people, and I came to know that such treatment is based on religiously sanctioned cultural behavior traditionally associated with Hinduism, but now practiced by members in all religions. On my bicycle, I rode alongside the recklessly alive boundaries between caste communities and outcaste communities who had separate living areas and social spaces in towns and villages.

In Karunguzhi, I observed that social segregation of Dalits was not as simple as living in separate settlements caused by poverty; they are forced to live in socially dictated spaces as the ostracized "unclean." Dominant caste members severely punish Dalits if they dare transgress assigned spaces laden with all their indicative boundaries (untouchable, territorial, cultural, social, and economic) irrespective of gender. They target Dalit women to punish a Dalit community, often involving sexual abuse as amusement. My husband and I knew Dalits working as slaves in harvest fields for landlords; we saw Dalit women brought from the neighboring villages to a rice processing mill in front of our house late at night at the demand of their masters; I held mothers in my arms devastated by loss of children due to abuse, heat, snake bites, and suicide; we comforted parents whose daughters were raped; families took their lives due to shame of rape and debt; young Dalit girls and boys gave up hopes for education and stayed where they were told to stay in their state of servant-dependence on the mercy of caste communities. I was enraged by these atrocities and my own ignorance, but at the same time I was deeply muddled in my inability to act immediately. I had to learn more about the reasons (or lack thereof) behind such normalized injustice and cultural expressions of violence and punishment.

The beginnings of my education and activism were in partnering with my husband and local grass roots workers to address the injustice in the lives of Dalits victimized by a social malaise that I had become a part of in my blindness to caste realities. It is among these Dalit communities who embraced me where I learned of my Dalit roots when an elderly Dalit man, sipping a glass of tea in the courtyard of our house, said that he knew my grandfather. I probed into the history of my ancestral living spaces in Dalit communities and constantly questioned my parents who had managed to hide a Dalit identity from their children. In the last section of this book, I present my narrative on the tensions between an immediate sense of shame and guilt, and later an acceptance and continuous grappling with my Dalit identity as both a cultural impediment and a bonding enabler with Dalit women.

My close interactions with Dalit communities in Karunguzhi led me to anthropological research on narratives of Dalit women. The rich cultural aspects in these narratives drew me into responsive relationships as organic literatures conveying social analytical meanings. No South Asian Studies-based programs in the US (mostly headed by scholars from caste communities) and in India were receptive to this research focus; Josephine Diamond, however, chair of the Comparative Literature Department in Rutgers University (New Jersey, USA), saw the value of such research and I successfully completed a Ph.D. program in 2004.[1] In that research process, I was and still am shaken by the fact that the complexity of caste structures as a social hierarchy that is layered with more complex intersectional nodes coagulated by religion, power, class, gender, culture, traditional discourses, and much more could remain intact as normalized daily operational bodies of authority. As I read, argued, and grappled with various theories and academic discourses around these social conundrums, deep within me I was and continue to be more impacted by close relationships

---

[1] In 1996, Columbia University's Comparative Literature Program headed by South Asian "scholars" from the dominant caste in India, rejected my research focus. Ambedkar studied here, but Dalit research was not encouraged.

with Dalit women. After I moved to the United States in 1993, I consistently returned to Tamil Nadu continuing my engagement with Dalit women.

I built relationships with more Dalit communities in Pudukkottai District in Tamil Nadu since 2005, primarily to meet with Kalaimagal (Kalai) Arumugam (1971-) who is the founder and director of Dr. Ambedkar Women and Children Regeneration and Development Program popularly known as Dr. AWARD (hereafter referred to in this book as DA). This non-profit organization works towards self-sustenance and advocacy with Dalit communities, specifically among women and children. A major portion of this book is a result of the many forms of oral narratives on life experiences that emanated during these times of relationship building with Kalai, her co-worker Rani Periasamy (1981-), and the Dalit communities with whom they work. In three chapters of this book, these voices testify to the co-existence of violence and agency leading to changes in Dalit communities for physically safe and economically sufficient spaces.

In addition, this book bears the voices of many other Dalit women who relentlessly strive to claim basic rights to human dignity and privileges. They are opposed to the ideological rendering of their minds and bodies as nullified dispensable objects that could be ruthlessly violated as a cultural norm. I have the privilege of finding friendship and strength in the written narratives of Faustina Susairaj (1958-)—popularly known as Bama—a pioneer Dalit woman writer raised in the village of Puduppatti, who now lives in Uthiramerur in Tamil Nadu. In chapter nine, I discuss Bama's honest depictions of her Dalit community and Dalit identity as a *Parachi*—a woman of the *Paraiyar* community of Dalits in Tamil Nadu—choosing a positive identity over a negative one.[2] Bama lifts her pen inked with a fire for change to remind Dalit women that their strengths can break through stereotypes.

Dalit and Voice in this Book

I primarily engage with desirous voices in change-seeking and change-making bold leadership in women from Dalit communities. Since caste practices are rooted in dominant religious narratives, it has epistemologically seeped into the politicization of a fundamentalist expression of Hinduism in India as an indom-

---

[2] *Paraiyar* are Dalits in Tamil Nadu who traditionally play the Dalit drum, *Parai* which is made from the skin of cows (Tamil=to announce), to carry the message of death. Usually played by Dalit men, it was traditionally considered a symbol of death itself. Dalit communities, however, are choosing to subvert the negative meaning by playing the drum at communal celebrations as well. Some Dalit women have taken to drumming the *Parai* as a symbol of Dalit culture, especially those trained in the Dalit women cultural troupe of *Sakthi* (Tamil=power).

itable power structure that terrorizes those at the bottom of that systemic hierarchy. Today, explicit expressions of rigid caste identities are present in every religion in India. Given the immensity of power in the caste system and the almost impossibility of dismantling any aspect of that power, it is therefore vital to hear significant voices of testimony in this book by Dalit women in various forms of oral and written narratives telling their stories of suffering, punishment, and change-making rebellion.

Ethnographic in nature, this book honors the distinctive natures of experiences of Dalit women. My primary resources include oral narratives— interviews with and published memoirs from Dalit women in the state of Tamil Nadu belonging to various Dalit communities—since such personal discourses are markers of distinctive Dalit female thought. These narratives are fragile, passionate, responsible, responsive, and hopeful in the voicing of their life experiences as vigorous forms of protest and activism. Dalit women are active agents in change-making, sustaining culture, and strengthening relationships. At the core of these organic expressions are various tones, tunes, gestures, movements, purposes, spaces, and times. As participants in such an ethos of spontaneous lived expressions as Dalit and woman, they innovate strategies to transgress boundaries of mainstream cultural expectations into trans-cultural spaces despite punishments. These are spaces that have been culturally forbidden for Dalits because rights such as education, basic amenities, land, profitable work, economic freedom, safe spaces for women, and freedom to enter any space of worship are part of the privileged cultural world of caste communities. Some others like Rani and Kalai choose to be culturally rooted and to physically remain in their allocated living spaces while demanding justice from within those spaces. Subversion, however, turns into various forms of expression by Dalit women who take on different tactics of liberation to cross boundaries depending on the context of encounters with authoritative powers.

I bring attention to voices of Dalit women mainly because they are in the forefront as change-makers in their respective communities. They strive to gain basic needs such as clean drinking water, which is otherwise denied in their living spaces due to social segregation. Women identify the need for schools so that their daughters and sons have the tools to defy power structures that deny basic human rights. The fear of being sexually abused may be minimized if they could provide their daughters with an education that would remove them from spaces of vulnerability. When I hear and read about Dalit women who are raped or beaten by men in positions of power, it reiterates that violence against Dalit women is unmistakably a culturally normalized practice (Narula 30). This reality exists alongside the norm where Dalit women are cultural voices bearing and demanding a recognition of positive identities within their respective communities.

I see activism in Dalit women—in the regions I mention—grounded in *earthy humanness* that speaks to their awareness of both their vulnerability and strength mingled with a passionate determination for change. They live in a simplicity of belief of what is right and wrong as it relates to their everyday life where physical safety of an individual and of communities is of utmost importance. They are, however, aware of all the ways in which dominant powers intersect, camouflage, and attack at predictable and unpredictable moments, at surprising and unsurprising times and spaces. Dalit women look for every possible gap to protest and demand social change, surprising the dominant power bodies.

Chapter Contents

In chapter one, I lay out a herstory of the recognition of the strong presence and voices of Dalit women in India. Chapter two traces theories around the creation and sustenance of a caste system in India. In chapter three, I present discussions on ideological dominance gained through traditional figurations of the "Other" woman in Indian ethos as evident in excerpts from three traditional texts: *Manusmriti, Ramayana,* and *Mahabharata.* The purpose of this exploration is to expose the nature of set patterns in traditional practices of punishing those who are "different" as an ideological force. Wealthy communities made such narratives dominant in dictating the stereotyped images and spaces within which "Other" women need to stay. I do not in any way attempt to critique the religious piety that these texts elicit in specific faith communities that revere them as sacred texts. Instead, I emphasize the significance and necessity of narratives from Dalit women that explode hegemonic, ideological, and habitual perceptions. In chapter four, I place narratives by young Dalit girls about violence against them in villages of the Pudukkottai District in Tamil Nadu, in a framework of the Universal Declaration of Human Rights. Thus, I illustrate that oral narration is a form of resistance to victimization that reveals social agency as these girls refuse to accept a life of persecution.

Chapters five and six contain conversations and a discussion with Dalit leaders Kalai and Rani who pursue changes for their community through transgressing boundaries. Both these women have brought about significant changes through a movement of resistance involving processes of linkages, articulations, collaborations, and proactive measures drawing upon inherent cultural traits of rebellious determination and resilience. I present and discuss songs from Tamil Nadu in chapter seven as I highlight unique characteristics that emerge in these songs in a communal context within which imagination is an active boundary crossing in itself: elements of unlimited possibilities, desire for change, a normalization of the supernatural, reverence for nature, and significance of relationships.

Sangati, a 1994 novel by Bama, celebrated as a Dalit feminist novelist from Tamil Nadu is central to chapter eight as a testimonial narrative that presents the necessity and potential of Dalit women to forge positive identities despite limitations and punishments they endure. I detail her use of literary skills to subvert the traditional image of Dalit women as imperfect objects in a national caste imagining. I present a situation of *selective visibility* of Dalit women's bodies sought after as sexual prey by those who at the same time reject them as "untouchable." This chapter contains excerpts of my personal interview with Bama.

In the last section of this book, I narrate my life journey and discuss my ancestors' necessity to grab anonymity as a means to hide Dalit identity for gaining social acceptance. I grapple with my Dalit identity as a strategic practice of a constant "hide and seek" game in switching among the Dalit, dormant Dalit, and non-Dalit identity roles as I deem it convenient and safe for myself, family, and friends. I describe the missionary movement as considerate to Dalits in providing viable options, while not losing sight of the fact that some missionaries favored dominant caste communities as a better catch.

INTRODUCTION

Sprouting in Transnational Feminism: *Earthy Humanness* in Dalit Women

> If through my life I cannot bring dignity to other Dalit girls,
> there is no point to my life. I will never give up.
> –Kalaimagal Arumugam, Dalit activist.

> I am not desirous of my life even as a thread measure. My children are
> small, but I know that somehow they [village community] will save
> them and bring them up. I said that and I dared.
> –Rani Periasamy, Dalit activist.

> We believed what they told us repeatedly, that we are useless chicken,
> scratching about in the rubbish—and now we have no confidence in
> ourselves. At least from now on we must stand for ourselves.
> –Bama, Dalit writer, *Sangati.*

In this book, I establish that narratives of Dalit women in Chengalpattu, Pudukkottai, and Puduppatti regions in South India reveal an *earthy humanness*—an inherent way of life for Dalit women—as a natural projection of their agency and activism in their various forms of desires, voices, and action-based demands for equality and human dignity. *Earthy humanness* as a way of life is an unconditional ethics of care for the physical, spiritual, and economic wellbeing of a community, person, self and/or nature where identification with another is a mode to claim human dignity, and relationships. This *earthy humanness* grounded in lived experiences reveals inner tensions and struggles of daily lives where a meshing of submission and resistance forms the core of a *change-seeking restlessness* to counter a culture of violence and punishment leading to result-based activism. Spaces of restlessness lead to a kinesis of deep desires and actions to instate claims to human rights into their daily lives as a rightful way of life.

An activist subversion of stigmatized characteristics as "different" is an integral part of restlessness where "differences" become tools of battle. I provide an analytical comprehension of ideological perceptions of "different" women rooted in traditional dominant discourses as the basis of violence on Dalit women that continues. Violence is meted as punishment for transgressing into forbidden spaces while subversion becomes imperative to personify social change within inscribed spaces of submission. The practical organic incarnations of humanness are what feminist realms should be; legal rights and human rights fit into Dalit women's ethics of care for one another. In characterizing activism as *earthy humanness*, I identify transgressive strategies by which Dalit women in villages in Tamil Nadu activate social change: subverting "difference," claiming voice in self-representation, and directly targeting for removal of blocks to social and economic progress.

A Preview of this Book

As a brief preview, I offer the reader an opportunity to enter a relationship with two Dalit women leaders—Kalaimagal Arumugam and Rani Periasamy (whom I hereafter refer to as "Kalai" and "Rani")—in their various strategies and methods to demand and activate changes. They rebel, fall, rise, and continue to demand human rights and dignity, speaking the language of protest and doing what they have been forbidden to do—organizing for social change. They "trans" or cross caste boundaries in every possible and impossible way and manner of expression as they move with various modes of action. As a preview of narratives of social change in chapters five and six, an example of the explosive leadership of Kalai and Rani is their successful social movement to eradicate the selling in their villages of *saaraayam*, which is a locally brewed alcohol. They experienced the internal devastation that caste communities caused in their families by selling *saaraayam* to their men. Dalit men would abuse their wives by forcefully taking their hard-earned wages for buying *saaraayam* and would further physically and verbally abuse them under the influence of that alcohol. In purchasing this alcohol, Dalit men were fattening the purses of those caste men who exploited them yet again by causing the psyche of humiliation in Dalits who sought solace in such consumption: their sense of worth itself was commodified. *Saaraayam* destroyed peace in each Dalit family which led Kalai and Rani to initiate a movement to eradicate the presence of this alcohol; they succeeded. In Rani's words:

> *My husband would come home drunk, and when children were studying he would come and beat them up. ...I would say, "How can we educate our children? How can we have a home and live well?" I suffered a lot. After suffering so much, the day I came to DA* [Dr. Award organization founded by Kalaimagal], *from then on I became courageous. I thought that either the saaraayam should be destroyed or my husband should rectify his ways. I was determined to do both. Now my*

family is doing well. Otherwise, this used to be my only big problem.

Rani continued:

> [*Saaraayam* is a] *BIG problem, big problem. Such a big problem that you can write a movie story based on this. ... We gave importance to this problem; why? Even in the Collector's* [district government official] *office, they were not giving importance to this issue. To that extent, they* [arrack brewers] *are giving them* [government officials and police] *money, and they are not supporting this issue. We went in front of the temple and protested and the SP and DSP* [Superintendent of police and District Superintendent of Police] *could not stand our rebellion anymore. ... We were not desirous of our lives at all. People are desirous of money and are doing all this injustice. They all join together to do this business. Is it right if the government takes money and asks to kill someone? We called for a meeting in Annavasal and called all the local officers and DSP as well. ... We eradicated this* [*saaraayam* brewing and selling]. *We called a meeting here, and we made him* [police officer] *say that this was true.*

Dalit women led by Kalai and Rani demanded with bold voices the change that they wanted immediately. In totally eradicating *saaraayam* from their district, they could attain the quality of family and community life that they desired. Rani specifically mentioned that her husband stopped beating her, her children were able to focus on their studies, and she could seek a positive relationship with their father. Dalit women could go out after dark without the fear of being attacked by men under the influence of *saaraayam*, and they could rely more on the family income to feed and take care of the family.

The hegemonic power structures that Kalai and Rani were up against include: thug-like businessmen from various caste communities, abusive Dalit men who turned against their wives and children when acting as intermediary business men in finding clientele for the caste men, police officers who received a cut in the share of profit, larger *saaraayam* brewing companies, local politicians who were shareholders in these companies and altered state policies to their monetary favor, and the state government itself! All these representatives of social institutions caused curdling terror as those in authority, but Kalai and Rani opposed them with determination and fear as well which I describe in chapters five and six. The benefits of eradicating arrack occur at several levels: stopping the economic exploitation by the upper caste arrack business owners who target Dalit men; breaking through the cultural stigmatization of Dalit men as useless drunkards; revealing that Dalit families can aspire to save money towards higher goals than survival; debunking the myth that Dalit women are powerless silent victims; establishing the norm that Dalit women will institute new modes of life and laws into place; and creating bold spaces where these women will transgress into to claim identity and dignity. Furthermore, a Dalit women's movement brought the domestic problem to the public forum at various intersectional nodes. In this particular case, Dalit women combatted hegemonic structures of patriarchy, caste, and class at all levels: in the domestic realm, within the community of dominant caste men who owned liquor stalls, and in the larger state government.

Dalits in the Caste System

In chapter one, I present written narratives and theories on origins and practice of caste which are essential for a historical and cultural contextualization. Here, I provide a synopsis of the caste system for readers who are not familiar with this still existing social hierarchy. India is on the world map today for its mammoth role in globalization, rapid movement in technology, and increase in population to over a billion, but only few pointers highlight the ever-widening canyon between the worlds of caste and outcaste communities.

The caste system originated in the region we now call India and is the oldest living systemic social hierarchical structure (Narula 24). Theorists on castes trace the earliest mention of this hierarchy in the "Purusha Sukta" hymn in the *Rig Veda,* one of the earliest scriptural oral narratives that is traditionally associated with Hinduism and written in Sanskrit circa 1200-900 BCE (Khilnani 18). These narratives came to be established as dominant narratives by the then ruling class which unfortunately set the norms for a culturally rooted social stratification patented through religion to ensure the permanency and rigidity of graded inequality. It is in the *Rig Veda* that one reads of the creation story of humans along with a social gradation originating out of god Brahma's body (the creator god in Hinduism). Gradation of humans formed out of Brahma's body is based on one's work: Brahmin originated from the mouth, and they were priests and teachers; Kshatriya, who were the royalty, rose from the shoulders; Vaishya were those involved in trade and originated from the thighs; and Shudra, who were manual laborers, came out of the feet (Khilnani 18). In this creation story, Dalits are those rejected by Brahma and "outcaste" from the social order: the primordial evil fallen people (*Rig Veda* 9, 73.5). The hierarchy rose from the level of the purity of the work involved, and therefore, those who perform the work embody such gradation of purity: pure Brahmin, less pure

Shudra and polluted Dalit. I discuss the social and cultural ramifications of such a gradation on purity and pollution in detail in chapter two. Mostly, I use the term "caste communities" instead of "upper caste" since Dalits are not "low caste" but "outcaste," and hence every caste is socially deemed "higher" or "upper" in comparison.

The *Manusmriti* (circa second century BCE) or *The Laws of Manu* is a code of laws in Sanskrit that designates the social place of each caste and the culturally ingrained social behavioral rules that each person should strictly adhere to within their caste (Roy 269). In this code, Dalits are referred to as the *candalla* or "the paradigmatic fierce untouchable" (as historian Wendy Doniger provides in the Sanskrit–English translation, 1991) who are relegated to the socially ostracized place of living outside the margins of the rest of the society because they are unclean and therefore untouchable (Doniger 68). *Manusmriti* states:

> 51 But the dwellings of fierce untouchables and 'Dog-cookers' should be outside the villages, they must use discarded bowls, and dogs and donkey should be their wealth. 52 Their clothes should be the clothes of the dead, and their food should be in broken dishes; their ornaments should be made of black iron; and they should wander constantly. 53 A man who carries out his duties should not seek contact with them" (Manu qtd. in Doniger 242).

Dalits are polluted because they touch decaying matter considered unclean: dead bodies, animal and human feces, skin, and all other decaying matter that is thrown out of a body, and out of homes and communities (Manu qtd. in Doniger 105, 108, 113, 114). Such sanctioned delegation of roles, living spaces, and body dispensation has kept Dalits apart socially along with denying their human and civil rights. In chapter three, I specifically address Dalit women's degradation through perpetual stigmatization and violence as ordered by the *Manusmriti.*

Dalits Today

Most Dalits continue to remain stagnant at the bottom of India's social hierarchy branded "outcaste," "untouchable," and "polluted Other," and Dalit women are the most vulnerable and most victimized population in India today subject to constant physical abuse and rape. The National Campaign for Dalit Human Rights (NCDHR), a national Dalit human rights organization based in New Delhi, India, reported in 2000:

> Over one-sixth of India's population, some 170 million people, live a precarious existence, shunned by much of Indian society

because of their rank as "untouchables" or Dalits—literally meaning "broken" people—at the bottom of India's caste system. Dalits are discriminated against, denied access to land and basic resources, forced to work in degrading conditions, and routinely abused at the hands of police and dominant-caste groups that enjoy the state's protection.

NCDHR consistently documents such discriminations targeted on Dalit communities today as part of a normalized Indian cultural behavior. To add to these forms of injustice, physical abuse ranges from physical harm to rape and murder of Dalit women and girls who are most affected by caste-based violence (Narula 30-31). The intersectional dimensions of violence are meshed in class, caste, religion, and gender. Dalit women are the deviant "Other" among Dalits for not just being poor, woman, and Dalit, but for reifying the casting of them in dominant scriptural narratives as ugly, immoral, fierce, loud mouthed, violent, quarrelsome, and lustful. Violence as punishment against Dalit women is primarily about control to remind Dalits of being outcaste and to terrorize Dalit communities so that they would not dare cross their place of servitude. In chapter four, I place narratives of violence against Dalit women in the panorama of human rights violations that could be prevented if only the nation would consider Dalits as human beings deserving justice. According to the *All India Dalit Mahila Adhikar Manch* (AIDMAM)—a national forum on Dalit Women—on average, 27,000 incidents of violations on Dalit women are registered annually under the Scheduled Castes and Scheduled Tribes Prevention of Atrocities Act (1989). Sadly, the country turns a deaf ear to public forums organized by AIDMAM where Dalit women testify to atrocities committed against them.

In chapter four, I discuss the role of the United Nations (UN) and several nationally based organizations in India working to address such violations against Dalits, and especially Dalit women. Despite such efforts, the nature of cruelty has become worse and the number of violent incidents has been increasing. In her press statement from May 2013, the Special Rapporteur of the UN on violence against Dalits, Rashida Manjoo states that "Dalit women experience some of the worst forms of discrimination and oppression, and that there is a culture of impunity for violations of the rights of Dalit women in the country" (IDSN).[3] The Indian representatives to the UN accuse such reports of hav-

---

[3] IDSN is the International Dalit Solidarity Network founded in March 2000, based in Copenhagen. This network comprises international human rights groups, social development agencies, Dalit organizations and forums from Europe, and several caste-affected countries. IDSN advocates for Dalit human rights and raises awareness of Dalit issues nationally and internationally. Since its formation, this network speedily internationalized a focus on caste discrimination as human rights issue.

ing a "lack of full objectivity, oversimplification, absence of detail, unsubstantiated claims and sweeping generalizations" (IDSN). Such reactions are direct pointers to the lack of seriousness towards violations of human rights upon Dalits among a cadre of those who occupy positions of power as has always been the case in India.

Feminism in India and Dalit Women

Tracing the history and comprehending an active role of feminism in India is highly complex because women in India are the essential cultural beings on whom culture formulates vindictive norms, strong religious ideals and sentiments, and highly visible differences. When Indian feminism gained public visibility, it was the late 1970s and early 1980s as the movement had to be founded and ushered into the public arena in the midst of numerous urgent needs. Historian Radha Kumar, in tracing the history of feminism in India in *The History of Doing,* states that women in elite circles earlier in the twentieth century such as Sarojini Naidu, Nellie Sengupta, and Rajkumari Amrit Kaur were rebelling against men in their elite circles who excluded them from major actions and discourses regarding nationalism and the Indian independence movement. The elite feminists in a pre-independence India in the mid-nineteenth and early twentieth centuries demanded education and property rights; the next wave of educated elite women wrote about dealing with a loss of identity, feeling depressed and imprisoned in a marriage relationship, and feeling left out of the nationalist discourse on freedom and the independence struggle. These were overridden a decade later by the rising voice of middle-class women whose lives were at risk if they did not take action against strong fundamentalist religious forces that endorsed child marriage, *sati* (the traditional practice of an orthodox sect of Hinduism forcing a widow into her husband's funeral pyre to be burned alive with him), discrimination against widows, and the practice of dowry (where a bride should provide a large amount of money and materials to the groom's family). The salt *satyagraha*[4] marches and demonstrations held in pre-independence India in the early 1900s as peaceful protests on British taxation laws marked the beginnings of mass participation in protests by women from rural and working-class communities. Kumar details the birth of different forms of Indian feminism in the 1970s illustrating the development of the participation of rural women in demands for more wages in

---

[4] *Satyagraha* (Sanskrit=affirmation of truth) were peaceful demonstrations that Gandhi led by foot throughout India as a major strategy of protest to British authority, mainly taxation. Salt *satyagraha* were primarily marches along the shores of India in 1930 against British salt monopoly.

factories and the textile industry and in raising a voice against prostitution and alcoholism.

It is important to note the parallel timing (1970s) when the Dalit Panther Movement was gaining momentum in Maharashtra modelled on the Black Panthers in the USA (Zelliot 180). This movement among Dalits started as a militant group dedicated to stop violence against Dalits, but gained various forms including Dalit literatures as voices of anger rebelling against caste-based discriminations and violence, notes Zelliot. Ambedkar, who was the architect of the Indian Constitution, fueled the movement and sought to abolish "untouchability" and afford Dalits legal protections and social welfare programs. He launched an era of claim for equality, and set in stone a normative framework with which to challenge the continuation of dominant caste-based practices. However, one of the major notable facts regarding the very limited participation of Dalit women in feminist discourses since the feminist movement began has a lot to do with the beginnings of Indian feminism itself. A need to actualize women's power as mothers of the nation and the Gandhian way of elevating women's sacrificial and enduring aspects had to be broken through since they affected the lives of elite and middle-class women from caste communities. Kumar writes about these aspects and provides the rationale for the origin of feminism in India among elite caste circles where self-preservation concerning body, mind, and economic security in marriage were of utmost importance.

Women leaders such as Prabhavati, educated in the 1920s and 1930s, dared to step outside their elite and religious circles and acted within a communist framework that included the struggles of working class women, prostitutes, and scavengers, which involved Dalit women. Public demonstrations with the visible participation of Dalit women were happening but only as rare occurrences. Prabhavati was considered a threat by politically prominent figures who felt the onset of the power of the peasant mass (cf. Kumar 66). Salt *satyagraha* demonstrations proved to be a vehicle wherein the participation of Dalit and tribal mass was needed for the sake of numbers, and this seems to be a starting point for the active involvement of rural populations in political demands. Even though basic needs involving education and health were beyond the reach of the rural population, India's independence brought with it a surge in the realization of the power of the masses, and soon individuals and political entities started using that power to question existing practices that were non-favorable to the poor, and especially to Dalit women. Specific regions such as the Telangana, Himachal Pradesh, Bihar, and Gujarat saw demands made by Dalit women in the 1980s protesting against alcoholism, the rise of food prices, low wages, deforestation, and several other issues. Soon, the issue of dowry deaths swept the nation and became the main agenda for feminist groups from the early 1980s until now.

Sati, the outlawed cultural practice of forcing a widow into self-immolation, re-emerged in Roop Kanwar's incident in 1987 in Rajasthan and caused public outrage. The Rashtriya Swayamsevak Sangh (RSS), an extremist Hinduist wing, mobilized a national movement in support of *sati,* which made it a necessary issue to maintain the solidarity of feminist voices across the nation. Indian feminism, on the one hand, was setting itself up against a national religious ideology—in trying to secure a national identity by eradicating the imposition of a fundamental religious national identity on the bodies of some women—that was sweeping across the nation. On the other hand, feminists were on the streets, attacking religious ideology with street jargon and street theatre; women from all faiths held placards and screamed out for justice (Kumar 115–126). This painted a picture of feminists in India as those leading a radical national movement on a rampage to uproot traditional practices; collective action was imperative. However, Dalit women were significantly absent from all these expressions of overt feminist activity against specific practices that deeply affected women's lives and the future of women in India who were caught between the tensions of modernization and tradition. Even though the needs of the slum-dwelling communities in the cities were recognized by feminist organizations, the women in the villages were left unnoticed. Kumar remarks that by the end of the 1980s, many organizations and women's groups sprung to address specific issues, but soon organizational adherence to their own belief systems and preoccupation with defining and defending their own identity gained precedence over what Indian women as a whole actually needed (157). A bourgeoisie feminist culture evolved that moved further away from social issues concerning villages where Dalit communities lived.

Dalit women deal with violations very different from those affecting caste women. Dowry was not a part of Dalit culture for the most part, and the killing of women for dowry was not a common occurrence in Dalit communities (Bama, *Sangati* 89). Nor was s*ati* a Dalit village-based practice; it was more of a suburban issue that was ordained by orthodox Hinduism, and such rigid ideological and social practices fortunately rarely seeped into Dalit cultures (Gosh 14). The unique struggles of Dalit communities such as slavery, bonded labor, denial of wages, rape, physical violence and torture, untouchability, hazardous and menial work, and more were not brought into public view until the mid to late 1900s. The ideological imposition of the polluted state of Dalits, based on Hindu religious texts such as *Manusmriti,* meant that their ostracized life was accepted as a destined fact, and the struggles of the Dalit community had to be kept as segregated as their dwelling spaces. Raping Dalit women is a culturally accepted norm throughout the country which is not addressed in public forums led by mainstream Indian feminism. Comparable to feminism in India, the Dalit movement rose by opposing an ideological belief in ways that were not based on theoretical or counter-ideological suppositions, but based at the ground level involving real people with day-to-day struggles; they demand denied human dignity. Colonialism brought with it a complexity of some missionaries functioning as social reformists seeking to change the social condition of Dalits. Leaders such as Phule and Ambedkar started their own movements towards social reform and emancipation of Dalits leading to the visibility of self-expressions of Dalits and particularly Dalit women.

Earthy Voices of Dalit Women

I adapt the term *earthy humanness* as a human character to the kinds of activism in Dalit women I know. The term "feminism" would restrict the scope of Dalit narratives that stem from experiences of "difference" (I explain this idea later in this section), an idea that feminist theorists have grappled with since the 1970s as Sharmila Rege (2005) points out (Chauduri 212). Rege believes that the word "feminism" demands adherence to existing feminist practices and solidarity with existing mainstream feminist practices (Chauduri 225). As I describe this approach of humanness later in this Introduction, if I were to adopt only feminism as a theoretical field that effectively describes Dalit women's experiences, I would exclude collective experiences of Dalit communities involving the "doing" of intersectionality in efforts to dismantle dominant structures such as caste, class, gender, and religion.

Advocating for multiracial feminisms to include all forms, colors, and regions of activism, feminist activist Becky Thompson asserts, "Here I am using the term 'feminist' to describe collective action designed to confront interlocking race, class, gender and sexual oppressions (and other systemic discriminations)" (qtd. in Kirk and Rey 41). In the same "lentil," inter and intra cultural specific collective action for change—as seen among Dalit women—is collective activism and should be recognized as such. There should be such "grain" spaces for this liberation of breaking terminological borders in understanding or engaging with those who actively seek and make change. Thompson further stretches her thought asserting that, "those organizations [whether church, art, or friendship groups] that confront gender, race, sexual, and class oppression, whether named as 'feminist' or not, need to be considered integral to multiracial feminism" (qtd. in Kirk and Rey 41). I apply her thought further in a move away from "feminism" as a theory-bound term but bonding with the in-grained character of it as seeking and making change for all against all forms of injustice. A host of change-makers such as Bama, Patricia Hill Collins, Barbara Smith, Gloria Anzaldúa, Elisa Avendaño, Paula Gunn Allen, Kimberlé Crenshaw, and many more have urged the recognition of culture-specific strategies of leadership and agency.

It is crucial to dwell on the significant relevance of applying an intersectional lens to Dalit feminist responses and practices of social change. Dalit women assess, and demand changes based on denial of basic human rights and what they rightfully deserve as citizens. Within their understanding of life-situations lies ingrained an analysis of how power structures converge upon them. As social activists Sumi Cho, Kimberlé Williams Crenshaw and Leslie McCall affirm, it should matter how intersectionality takes on a social movement of change as an action-verb rather than a theoretical nomenclature: "Rather, what makes an analysis intersectional—whatever terms it deploys, whatever its iteration, whatever its field or discipline—is its adoption of an intersectional way of thinking about the problem of sameness and difference and its relation to power" (795). It is in this interrogation of social injustice that intersectionality gains kinetic momentum as a social movement. I stay consistent with my premise that Dalit women interrogate their state of difference and subvert that very difference as energizing cultural tropes of change rather than aspiring a replication of sameness as power. Although Crenshaw particularizes intersectionality around black women's lived experiences of various dimensions of power, attacking them from several angles, she blesses the multiplicities of intersectional analysis for change in each unique cultural context that do not fit the traditional dominant molds of understandings of oppression. Crenshaw agrees with Carbado et al. who acknowledge that "Intersectionality has moved internationally both to frame dynamics that have been historically distinct within other domestic spheres and as a way to contest material and political realities that are, by some measures, part of global and transhistorical relations of power" (307). Normalization of power can only be dismantled by such active expressions of response to particularized critical social analysis in a common framework of oppression. Gloria Anzaldúa provides similar insights into the actual work of feminism as she perceives it from the experiences of Chicana women. In chapter six, I adapt Anzaldúa's thoughts in *Borderlands/La Frontera: The New Mestiza* on women's assertion of unique experiences leading to bold actions of transgression. I acknowledge that Kalai and Rani are in this bold space as fearless leaders stepping into dangerous territories of dominance. *Earthy humanness* in Dalit women draws forth multiple natures of response to punishments of those labelled "different" by dominant discourses driven by historical processes of political doings.

I nestle my thoughts on activism among Dalit women, however, in transnational feminist praxis where intersectionality thrives. Transnational feminism frees a wide array of possibilities in not dragging diverse voices to fit into a box of thought or theory, but instead tills the ground to find new spaces and language where feminism can be experienced in its real unique natures and characteristics. This kind of a ground encourages thoughtful bonding across national, cultural, ethnic, and all other identity borders around these lived narratives and expressions of change-making.

Money, social status, work, salary, voice, tasks performed (work that could be willfully avoided or rejected by some), places of visibility, company kept, recreational privileges, and positions of power (including power to perform violence) are of mercantile value in the world of gender differences that establish and empower one's actualization of subjectivity where women are sidelined and violated. I will bring into consideration the case of Dalit communities who, in addition to those conditions mentioned above, are impacted by nationally normalized practices—untouchability, economic exploitation, rape, physical abuse, denial of entry into places of worship, and social ostracization, for example—that include specific demeaning cultural practices specific to the location, economic, and social standing of Dalit peoples. Both Dalit men and women are locked within drawn boundaries, denied the mercantile mentioned above, and are equal victims of the larger nationalist phenomenon of effective terrorization of the minority. Dalit *earthy humanness* reveals methods by which identities are asserted and affirmed as they are not dependent or dictated by a duality of categories. The multiplicity of their categorizations based on location, descent, and work, and the multiplicity of the powers of dominance work to their advantage by capacitating their narratives to rise above such notions as "monological patriarchy" or the concept that they have "little intellectual room" as Maya Goldenberg states (141). Dalit women share a collective knowledge through their lived experiences; they celebrate bodies and culture and rise above rules on caste, gender, food, space, socio-economic status, marriage, work, and domesticity.

Birthing this Book with the Aid of Transnational Feminists

I wish to place this book in a larger flora of discourse that transnational feminism opens, close to where women's experiences are felt in their earthy forms bereft of conditional strings attached to conditional feminist frameworks. In chapter one, I lay the rationale for the importance of recognizing the voices of Dalit women as distinct from feminism voiced and practiced by women from caste communities in India. I selectively draw upon synchronistic possibilities in transnational feminist thought and praxis that foregrounds the relationship between nation state as a power and its vulnerable citizens who bear the impacts of both colonialism and post colonialism. Most importantly, these discussions recognize the existence of transnational feminist practices that form alliances and are creatively subversive as well in responding to human rights violations caused by multiple power structures. My book rests on the premise that a transnational lens points to intersectionality in its various incarnations to break and punish targeted groups unsurprisingly as a naturalized social convergence of coercive forces. In this Introduction, I link my thoughts to transnational feminist scholars who are relevant to this book in specific areas: linking activism and theory, borderless representation, and ideas of "difference." These areas of dialogue are significant to be able to value actions as texts of agency to detangle representation from alleged identities to testimonies of lived experiences. Purposeful as agency, these experiences are valued as cultural markers beyond and within a state of being different from those valued and recognized by dominant culture.

Seeking grounds in transnational feminist practices allows me to situate Dalit voices in a supportive space that allows for a wholesome understanding of meanings of women's narratives. This engagement brings out the reality of the effulgent visibility of these narratives that are spoken, said, sung, and written in spaces traditionally branded invisible and silent. This invisibility and silence exists only in relation to those who choose not to see and hear these narratives. However, when these narratives are removed from the conditions understood and defined only by dominant cultural voices and mainstream academia, they exist as visible and audible to their immediate community, and this is what matters to the narrators; they could care less otherwise.

Theory and Activism

A focus on connecting activism and academic theory is especially significant due to the boom of the visibility provided by social media of the outcry and changes that women in the "margins" have made possible. I insist that the notable change is the transformation in recognizing marginal spaces as significant spaces in themselves. In *Critical Transnational Feminist Praxis,* Amanda Swarr and Richa Nagar bring together scholarly voices of eclectic experiences that testify to bridging the gap between what we read, what we experience, and what we witness in various global grounds. These essays tell the stories of women who are change-makers treading danger with sure footing, adapting to methods that are cleverly creative. They provide thoughts on the relevance, significance, challenges, and possibilities of transnational feminism. In their discussion of the postcolonial boom of theorization, Swarr and Nagar point to a celebrity culture in American academia assuming elite positioning as they "abstract and generalize" an understanding of the experiences of those "oppressed" (2). This process of abstraction submerges the voices of those who continue to be ground down into masses of "the subaltern," and scholars have set themselves "in opposition to those immersed in grounded struggles" (2). My book is rooted in such individuals and communities in explicating processes of activism and agency among Dalit women in Tamil Nadu. They participate in a constant and necessary momentum of being actively involved in creating and recreating a sense of self-worth and human dignity expressed in narrative tropes.

It is necessary to take note of Dalit communities presented in this book from the Chengalpattu, Pudukkottai, and Puduppatti districts of Tamil Nadu as those who possess agency and are not essentialized as immured communities. Such an approach calls for a substitution of pathos in the only *almost* engaged onlooker. Sangtin writers[5] Surbala Singh and Richa Singh present the social changes brought by collaborative efforts among poor farmers and manual laborers in the Sitapur District of the Indian state of Uttar Pradesh, primarily comprised of Dalit communities (Swarr and Nagar 124-43). The breaking-to-build work of these women and the inclusion of this essay in *Critical Transnational Feminist Praxis* is a benchmark to the coming together of social change, change-makers, witnesses, and theoretical analysis. As the writers claim—in their work with Dalit communities—what emerges is the realization that there are no discreet compartments when it comes to social change; women's issues are human rights issues and vice versa. In such emergence, gaps cease to exist between theory and praxis of social change: agency is an *earthy humanness* that extends to all demands for human rights and dignity.

The essays by the Sangtin writers testify to the active ways in which Dalit women take leadership in bringing about social, economic, and political changes in their communities, contending directly with authoritative power structures. Kalai and Rani are examples of such direct encounters with dominant structures, ensuring that their demanding voices are assertive. They are persistent in their dealings with the police force to truthfully record the reports of atrocities against their people. In my personal interview with Pugalenthi who

---

[5] Surbala and Richa Singh are activists working in about forty villages of Sitapur District in Uttar Pradesh, India. They are members of the Sangtin Writers Collective and work in alliance with *Sangtin Kisaan Mazdoor Sangathan* (SKMS), a people's movement in the Sitapur District formed as a result of *Sangtin Yatra: Saat Zindgiyon Mein Lipta Nari Vimarsh,* a collective form of activist-based writing. A merging of action, theory, and practice and holding conversations with women in rural India who create changes in their communities is their priority. This is an activist collective movement serving as an example of a ground-based feminism.

served as a senior police officer for fifteen years in the region where Kalai works, he stated:

> *Kalai amma used to come to the police station and would go*
> *without food for two to three days just waiting by sitting on the*
> *front stairs of the police station until she made sure that we had*
> *the correct facts recorded in our police report. She is so fear-*
> *less and determined. She would make sure that the Dalit people*
> *that we would arrest were not brutally beaten up. There were*
> *several dharnas in front of the police station led by Kalai am-*
> *ma.* (Pugalenthi)

Dharna is a protest marked by a mass gathering of people who would sit in visible public spaces and oftentimes cause disruption to traffic to demand justice. I elaborate on this strategy of protest in chapter five as well. A direct addressing of abuse and violence by such earthy leaders provides a contrast with a privileged position of feminist activism rising out of theory. Feminism resides in Dalit communities as a way of life with nothing to hide behind; there is a bare stripping of who they are and what they want as they "pierce" oppressive structures using tools of unique local strategies. In Dalit women, activism is survival and not just a method or expression of feminism; the call into being the inner will to change social conditions.

Only in seeking multiple spaces that foreground activism can one adapt personal experiences as learning grounds: various knowledge bases, teaching activism, and a social-action centered academia. In such adaptation, methods of change mirror theories and vice versa as both reflective and refractive of the tangibly real experiences; techniques of "doing" gain prominence over verbal articulations that are premised in bordered disciplines. These disciplines are otherwise pursed and zipped, alienated from the organic nature of lived experiences and orature of those living in simple social communities. I consider a merging of individual/collaborative knowledge, academia/activism, and theory/method (that Swarr and Nagar spell out) through activism that bring them to act upon and with each other to (2). The narratives in this book are both oral and written in various textures that include songs, folk tales, narratives of violence and of activism, memoirs, and communal autobiographies. I present practical and imaginary ways in which these communities of women who are forced to live within boundaries that are maintained within state and national borders dare towards "performance intersectionality." They name, target, and chip out caste, gender, socio-economic, religious, and other cultural inlays that forbid and punish self and communal development thereby chiseling changed social conditions.

Borderless Representations

In this section, I engage with ideas around representational politics primarily with two other scholars of transnational thought: Inderpal Grewal and Caren Kaplan. They introduce new ways of rooting and unrooting women's discourses and experiences by seeking new grounds of sprouting. Their propositions in "Postcolonial Studies and Transnational Feminist Practices" tie into the immense possibility of linking local representation of women's voices and experiences to an interdisciplinary study of relationships between various communities of women in different parts of the world. Representational politics is concerned with the purpose and meanings embedded in narratives of identity, change, and action: Who speaks, from where, and why? When women represent themselves through a communal bonding (as is the case of women in this book), it brings to the forefront their subjectivity grounded in an ethics of caring that far exceeds the traditional "feeble" notion that has been forced upon such practices.

Addressing the question of "How do we represent women's human rights?" in a conversation on transfeminist rendition of life experiences, Wendy S. Hesford and Wendy Kozol authenticate "truth-telling discourses as cultural narratives that articulate historical processes of oppression, resistance, and collective action" (9). Whether self-representation is seen in a local police station or in a multinational space of a women's forum where a woman can share her story, it ceases to be an event or a happening, and it is not a product. Wherever and whenever the affected presents or lobbies for human rights in relation to self-protection or communal protection, she is a participant in the continuum of the sacred rite of protest in testifying to herself and her people. The picking up of herself after being victimized and moving to a desired safe space is a part of the continuum of representational presence where she *denies power to power*. She is then able to disempower the politics in representation through her sole purpose and will to survive and claim justice in spaces that could be local, national, or transnational. Even if she succumbs to violent death, her story continues to activate undaunted resilience.

In *Between Woman and Nation*, Caren Kaplan, Norma Alarcón, and Minoo Moallem establish freeing of representation referring to Angie Chadram-Dernersesian's term of "de-colonization of representation" (13-14). Grewal and Kaplan point to diverse expressions of agency defying formulaic definitions, and through de-colonization are contingent on the reality of multiple expressions because of the very reason that women's responses to power structures are varied depending on the heterogeneity of dominant forces. They use both postcolonial and transnational feminist lenses to describe dominant forces.

Transnational feminism therefore dismantles border theories that seek to label feminism as a response to fixed dominant times, spaces, and targets. This allows for the recognition of power forces between and within communities and nations (Kaplan et al. 14). Grewal and Kaplan are concerned about freeing the institutionalization of feminism and foregrounding the subject's desire as of utmost importance (par. 9). Social agency is rooted in a strong desire to reverse situations. The interdisciplinary approach to human rights issues where women are active agents of change places representational speech, thought, and action on a plane of intersectionality where the notion of borders and compartmentalization of knowledge systems and products will disintegrate, and nodes of intersection will prove to be the spaces of "betweenness" (Kaplan et al. 14) as fertile zones of linkages that will produce diverse meanings and theories of nation, feminism, history, and social change. It is the desire of transnational feminists that a working together of disciplines of knowledge will accommodate a wholesome approach to decentering or isolation of racialization, sexualization, and genderization to include all aspects of social domination (Kaplan et al. 14). Such changed condition of institutions would open more critical avenues of analysis of dominant forces that have gotten away from scrutiny because they have camouflaged the connivance of times, institutions, structures, spaces, powers, and communities within and across national boundaries.

In the context of caste-based human rights violations of girls and women, it takes no schematic conniving or intentionality because of the effortless flow of the working together of historic, social, political, and religious processes. The beginning of apportionment of social responsibility paves the path into amassed wealth, privilege, and social status leaving a great number in a morass of social rejection. Grewal and Kaplan pose transnationalism as an ensemble of critical thinking that "signals attention to uneven and dissimilar circuits of culture and capital. Through such critical recognition, the links between patriarchies, colonialisms, racisms, and other forms of domination become more apparent and available for critique or appropriation" (par. 3). All these linkages stem from that allocation of social responsibility as to who is recruited to do what in a given society irrespective of who offers to take on responsibility as a social responsivity. Such exclusivity smooths the aligning of powers that essentially are patriarchal, colonial, and political including racist, caste-ist, heterosexist, and every other de-humanizing practice.

Transnational feminism provides the touchy reality to the slushy depth and sliminess of power structures that are camouflaged in their deeper workings. Drawing analogies from my life in the US as a mother of color with two boys, it is often quite interesting to note that signing up to volunteer for certain responsibilities in my children's schools, it is very rare that I will be called to carry out that responsibility; I am not allowed into that inner circle. This then leads into whose child acquires more visibility; furthermore, institutionally, the most socially privileged communities access better supportive educational tools. This accessing is apparent at the state level as to what kind of school districts gain more attention and resources.

Social responsivity is closely tied to access to social responsibility and privilege. I may have the education, but still structurally I remain an outsider where the grounds to prove myself are ensured to slip beneath me. When *I* take on leadership in initiatives to promote community relations and sharing educational resources, I face challenges of minimal encouragement and monetary support for civic engagement. I am thrown a bone here and there to be satisfied with while I should neatly shelve my expertise and desire to be a socially, communally, or academically responsive person. I am forced to hide my Ph.D. from aggravated social view that would judge my "social space" as a South Asian woman (of color), and therefore my children and I are "punishable" in whatever areas institutionally and socially possible as "outsiders."

Where does one sprout after being unrooted? I left India in 1990 angered by what I experienced as a Christian woman in my twenties—weighed as a marriage commodity and questioned on my caste identity. My marriage prospectors would leave once it became apparent that my family was against dowry and did not possess the same caste identity, but not before they ate the snacks provided (more in the last chapter). Soon I learned of similar processes of commodification and dispensation of women in the US as well and the discriminations against people of color, and gay, lesbian, transgender, queer, and differently abled persons. When I arrived in the US, I was shocked to learn about the history of African Americans and Native Americans in this country and more so at their current social conditions. An overarching question continues to haunt me: Is the politicking of representation so complicated and threatening that one cannot retain one's authentic voice? Responsivity through representation—whether social or otherwise—mirrors those in the front lines of privilege as a stagnant method of decisive blending in with the surroundings using age old encumbrances to religion that really created economic inequity to lock in rigid caste indentures. The reverse would be true as well. Such fluid inbreeding in power structures are articulated best in the unordered spaces acknowledged by transnational modes of social critique that transcend physicality and temporality. Dalit communities in India, and Black and Native American communities in the US are products of such apportionments of social responsibilities where their allocated social spaces make it dangerous to seek redress for what they rightfully deserve as citizens and as human beings. The stories in this book evidence a breaking out of bordered spaces imaginatively, culturally, and physically. Grewal and Kaplan lead social analysts to follow the trail into a dismantling of border theories in questioning the margin/center dichotomy that further thwarts boundaries as related to the nation and representation allowed to its women. In this between-ness of spaces of margin and center, the dismissed Other as the represented one can refuse to be identified through the nation's gaze and its definition of center and vice versa. Transnational feminism breaks through this traditional condition that has controlled any negotiations between those left out of nationalist discourses and those privileged to even debate on the woman burdened as the representative of tradition on her body. I consider it highly problematic that most South Asian scholars who participate in postcolonial feminist discourses do not engage the question of caste and Dalits, especially Dalit women and their invisibility in nationalist or feminist discourses. Indian feminists have participated in and perpetuated the subordination of Dalit women, even if by omission or a lack of self-interrogation.

I adapt avenues opened by transnational feminism in the possibilities of greening a major gap in representation of Dalit women. Scholars from caste communities in India, especially those residing in the US, have formulated theories and written volumes on the faulty nature and inadequacy of western concepts around feminism, colonialism, masculinities, gender, race, multiculturalism, fundamentalism, *et cetera*, but few discourses include the social reality of caste and untouchability as it relates to women or any gender identity. They are quick to point to external enemies because these South Asian scholars claim marginal status in the scholarly field dominated by western thought, while ignoring apparent caste-related social syndrome. There exists a normalized ignoring of earthy subversive voices by pushing them into spaces labelled "silenced" or "subaltern."

Subversive Living into "Difference"

Ideological discourses lead to social actions and attitudes that impose animations of notions of "difference" on bodies that carry them. Sedimentary habitual patterns of behavior become lodged in each time period and cultural context that continue to devalue groups of people as the "Other" based on several intersectional factors that include gender, religion, race, caste, sexual orientation, economic status, and more. No scholar establishes this cumulative dominant cultural imaging of those labelled "different" more effectively than the postcolonial studies scholar Edward Said in *Orientalism* (1978). Said proves through history, art, and literary representations by Europe of those who dwell in the East that such misrepresented knowledge of those constructed as "different" led to explorative exploitations (352). While colonialism constructed and represented the "orient" as a binary opposition to the West, Said was sure as well that it was directly linked to a comparative [de]valuing of cultural behavior (277). Such knowledge is exhibited as institutionalized illustrations of a cultural dominance (Said 6). Appropriating similar "lentils" of thought, I construe what is significant in postcolonial thinking in terms of the relationship of the narcissistic self of the dominant to that which is different in the lodging of those not dominant in the Indian cultural imagination and practice. Dalits and all other communities who are deviant to a power-based genealogy are products of cultural constructions dictated by dominant cultural discourses.

In the context of Dalit women, I adapt the term "difference" as a verb where lived experiential realities of Dalit women I engage with are a living into their "difference"—who they are—as they continue to be rebellious, hard-working, and resilient women valuing Dalit cultural strengths. "Difference" can be described as a state of being that already is in place and that which rejects an imposed, shameful identity and taps into a lived identity made real in its relationships built and sustained through specific, self-affirming cultural rituals. Instead of a stuck notion of "difference" as a negative theoretical exponent, I pose "difference" as a claimed positive identity that has gained life by demythologizing what has been imposed upon Dalit communities as glued identities stuck in a specific framework, nailed by ideas connected with religion, culture, and morale to dehumanize "Others." Dalit women's claims to positive identities should be recognized as an agency in itself to challenge traditional knowledges, constructions, and practices of "difference." As feminist theorist Marilyn Frye would confirm, "rather than 'essentializing' women, however, each woman and group of women acquires deepened and more complex and more fully experienced meaning/identity through the webs of likeness and contrasts built by communities and processes that are varieties of the practice of differences" (1007). Experiential knowledge bases where rituals, expressions, and responses are central to "difference" stand above the ordinary level of understanding these communities, which is usually only in relation to their suffering caused by superior power structures.

Transnational feminism provides a lens wherein I can focus on a praxis of "difference" as a positively subversive act that Dalit women live into as a way of life—a spontaneous cultural practice affirming Dalit female identity. Practices of "difference" can be both joyful and hurtful, depending on how they are lived into and are invigorated by shifting the notion of "difference" from a theoretical concept to a verb that is activated in an embodiment of difference; Dalit women live into the "difference" they are stigmatized with and propagate activities of protest. In claiming various capacities of beauty, talent, value, intelligence, and more, Dalit female identity thwarts hegemonic dictations of stigmatized images of the female "Other" that I describe in chapter three. I raise critical thoughts around the "different" figurations of two women and their punishment for transgression: Soorpanakha in the *Ramayana* and Hidimvà in *Mahabharata*. These two women do not fit into the pretty picture frame wherein Sita—the devoted wife of Rama—commands attention. Soorpanakha chooses to transform herself into an image acceptable as a pretty maiden but is defeated by Lord Rama's discernment; she is humiliated and mutilated by Rama and his brother Lakshmana who are taught by elders to follow cultural patterns of behavior. Dalit narratives provide alternatives to such dominant ideological narratives culturally appropriated to define beauty in a woman by embracing the very characteristics for which they are despised. In the ensuing chapters, I establish the grounds for chapter three as a rationale for the normalizing of punishment and the etching of cultural perceptions on Dalit women by dominant narratives. I further highlight the fierce battle that Dalit women engage in to change social perceptions and their living conditions by performing their very "difference," costumed as tools for change-making.

In a transnationalist comprehension, Kaplan et al. acknowledge Derrida's idea of *différance* as suspended moments and intervals of spaces that proves to provide spaces and opportunities for multiple analysis (14). It is in intervals of such spaces that Dalit women practice ideological combatting and customized subversive acts; they cleverly employ their very "difference" that they are despised for in dominant narratives and in daily practice of caste discrimination. These imposed differences as the "Other" etched in religio-ideological language identified within a Hinduist culture include but are not limited to their reckless morale, boldly rebellious nature, stubbornness, dispensable bodies, easy prey, and sub-gendered status. Since difference plays an important part in un-disguising, e.g the quarrelsome Dalit woman who will embrace that imposed denigrating difference as a tool of combat in truth-telling, honoring her voice as from beyond the margins is vital. Such honoring partners with decentralization and allows room to integrate the nuances and numerous interval spaces that she will find to squeeze into creating social changes she seeks, only to the surprise of her combatant—whether an individual or an institution.

At the time when Luce Irigaray's theories on "difference" and "sameness" were formulated and popularized (*Speculum of the Other Woman,* 1974 and *This Sex Which Is Not One,* 1977)—on the idea that female narratives are nullified based on social functions because women are relegated to their corners as mothers and keepers of nature—feminism in India was exploding with open demonstrations on the streets, and Hindu fundamentalist groups saw this as the rise of a radical movement and were making every effort to push women back into their corners (Kumar 103, 104). Women acting out of ideological differences far from popular fundamentalist practices was in itself a problem. In India, on the one hand, there are existent universal notions of differences around culture-specific gender roles and functions; on the other hand, in the 1980s and 90s, feminists and postcolonial thinkers rooted in India were finding their voices in intellectual and academic spaces outside of India. They heavily scrutinized colonialism, white Christian missionary movements, and western interventions upon social justice issues changing the lives of Dalits and other communities—especially women broken by internal colonizing powers in India. Postcolonial feminist theorists such as Gayatri Spivak highlighted "strategic essentialism" and stirred up academic conversations based on the "subaltern" incapacitated by external intervention and therefore stripped of the capacity to cross over from their "Other" condition (Ashcroft et al. 24-28). Several such postcolonialists interpret and use the "Other" as a cultural condition without considering when the "Other" ceases to be the "Other." Should dominant structures be duplicated by those in subaltern positions to reach a non-subaltern status? The term "subaltern" is problematic in its accommodation of social implications of the "sub" and the "altern" as secondary. I assert that experiences of those beyond the margins such as Dalits appear in postcolonial discourses mostly in relation to categories of dominance boxed into a subaltern theory. It has become fashionable for academics to appropriate postcolonialism as an academic stage for theoretical innovations where an engagement with active storytelling voices of the subjects themselves are mostly absent.

Theories such as the subaltern theory are in relation to an "altern" to dominant powers identified by South Asian scholars in the ramifications of colonialism. Antonio Gramsci (1891-1937), borrowing an analogy from the military, used the term "subaltern" to present the social condition of those in lesser rank or treated as the lesser being (Green 387-404). The subaltern theory in an academic context, for example, provides less opportunity for the "oppressed" to be understood and defined on their own terms and instead, postcolonial theories mostly encourage an understanding of the "oppressed" only in relation to dominant powers (Reed 562-63). While the "oppressor and oppressed" analysis could be a helpful lens to understand the systemic realities in oppression, it is inadequate to fully engage in the complex multiple layers of social, political, and religious workings and to understand the nature of "oppressed" communities. Unrooting the binary of oppressor and oppressed is crucial to decolonizing structures of social analysis freed to comprehend earthy organic forms of agency apparent in resistance, contestations, and actions of change that are a part of lived experiences of those labelled "oppressed."

Writing to alter feminist epistemology, philosopher Maria Lugones draws on a major belief that "travel" helps befriend pluralistic feminism freeing one from the arrogance of perception of women in "other" cultures as mere victims. She explains, "Through travelling to other people's 'worlds' we discover that there are 'worlds' in which those who are the victims of arrogant perception are really subjects, lively beings, resistors, constructors of visions, even though in the mainstream construction they are animated only by the arrogant perceiver and are pliable, foldable, file-awayable, classifiable" (432). This travel mode of re-locating oneself onto another is possible only when there is a willingness to find meanings. Lugones builds on her comments on the Aristotelian slave where she proposes, "We know the slave only through the master. The slave is a tool of the master" (432). She breaks a culturally arrogant notion where the oppressed are stagnant in that role existing only in relation to the oppressor. I claim that the "oppressed" have never ceased to live out and proliferate a subversive active role of agency.

Under a selective ignoring of the diversity of experiences lies a ready assumption that claims that positive identities are not already actively present among those stigmatized as the "Other." The notion of acknowledging the active, positive presence of "difference" in Dalit narratives is important to address its role in affirming both a specific, positive individual and a communal identity. In doing this, Dalit women diffuse traditional definitions and transfer the energy derived from such assertions into collective agency to demand rights as specific communities. Most authors of the essays in *Between Woman and Nation* point to the signifiers around racializing, genderizing, and sexualizing that uphold all analysis and challenge that through their work they will change the ways in which these prefabricated notions will be held accountable and investigated (14). In their list, they include queries on the relationship between woman and the nation. Kaplan et al. claim that "'[between] woman and nation' refers to a particular situated space of the performative and performativity where women and nation intersect in specific ways giving rise to the interval of *différance*" (6). This calls for an analysis of the absence of or non- or misrepresentation of what constitutes this interval of *différance.* Kaplan et al. bring attention to Homi K. Bhabha's position that this "performative" of and by the *différance* interrupts the "pedagogy of the nation" (7). If one does not conform to the standards of figurations within the rubric of the pedagogy, they should be punished; difference is an identification of the one to be violated.

In my discussion in chapter three on the figurations of women in dominant traditional discourses from India—Sita, Soorpanakha and Hidhimvà—I highlight that Sita's characteristics are arrogated by a nationalism where the submissive chaste woman is epitomized in her and wins the trophy as the one who truly represents national ideals and attains spiritual goals. Alternatively, Soorpanakha and Hidimvà enact "difference" and are punished for it; interrupting this pedagogy of punishment is necessary. Essentialization of what a caste woman should be or what a Dalit woman should be is broken by claiming agency and boldly living into the identity for which one is despised. On the one hand, the modern woman in India who has adopted "Americanism" as she appropriates it in her lifestyle and denial of a tradition-bound household interrupts the pedagogy of the nation at some level as a modern woman in the eyes of the nation state; but on the other hand, transnationalists lead us into a poststructuralist time, space, body, and mind (Kaplan et al. 5-7). While the rebellious modern Indian woman is in that space between modernity and tradition where compromises are sought by her and for her to accommodate her financial gains in a modern world, the ones who should be acknowledged are those who remain in submissive spaces and still interrupt the pedagogy of the nation—Dalit and Adivasi[6] (tribal) women. In activating Derrida's interval of *différance,* Dalit women bring together the real and imagined spaces of change. Transnational feminism provides useful tools to promote the credibility and visibility of the inherent agency that is present in that "double process of subordination and contestation" (Kaplan et al. 10). Dalit women leaders enact rebellion from submissive spaces and stigmatized characteristics. Therefore, their allies and subversive strategies are hard to identify, name, and predict which problematizes the nation's clear attack on their life-giving resources, and hence bodily attacks as punishment become the nation's easy weapon to terrorize. In their activism, Dalit women transcend temporality and physicality as they include the intangible and desirable through spaces they create and sustain. Subverting the "difference" that they are stigmatized for in order to represent themselves, they claim their place as agents of change in their respective communities.

Dalit Narratives in Transnational Feminism

I characterize Dalit narratives as *earthy humanness* bringing together all categories of experiences in a community as a whole entity solely concerned about human dignity. I restate: *earthy humanness* is an unconditional ethics of genuine caring for the economic, physical, and spiritual wellbeing of a community, person, self, and/or nature where identification with another is a mode to claim human dignity and relationships. This *earthy humanness* is grounded in lived experiences revealing ambiguous spaces of submission and resistance where *restlessness* caused by deep desires and actions for social change takes varied forms of transgression as protesting traditions of punishment.

---

[6] *Adivasi* (Tamil= earliest natives), referred to as Scheduled Tribe (ST) by the Indian Government, is a term used for communities indigenous to a region. The UN describes the ST as 'indigenous peoples' making up 8.08% of the total population of India.

Dalit women often self-locate in ways that allow them to take control of situations that are unchangeable in their minds. Therefore, their location is not confined to dictated spaces, tasks, or time; as Dalit women daringly transgress in their imagination, desire, voice, and action, they actively seek alternatives for themselves and mostly for their children. Kalai and Rani affect changes that ensure better living conditions for Dalits, removing them from confined spaces of demeaning work into new possibilities where a life of human dignity can be normalized. They are transcultural agents who actively seek to challenge and contest hegemonic forces. Dalit women annul cultural specifications as the "untouchable" in the crossing of boundaries from subliminal conditions into spaces that promise recognition of who they are.

Dalit women share a knowledge that empowers them to speak of lived experiences and ways to "trans" their living conditions. In chapter seven, I describe the borderless realms of singing where they can transform muddy or rocky pathways to concrete, accessible roads gilded with gold or tar; or unadorned bodies to figures adorned with jewelry and silk; or dependent slaves into liberated buttermilk sellers and more. For example, Ratinam, from the colony of Vallarpirai in the Chengalpattu district of Tamil Nadu joined by a chorus of women, sang this cyclical song as they danced in a circle:

> Lead singer: I took five plates of mud.
> Chorus: *Yellamma Yellam*
> Lead singer: And I laid a road of gold,
> Chorus: *Yellamma Yellam*
> Lead singer O you little boy who walks down that road,
> Chorus: *Yellamma Yellam*
> Lead singer: What is the reason for your snooty walk?
> Chorus: *Yellamma Yellam*
> Lead singer: Why do you have your hand on your hip?
> Chorus: *Yellamma Yellam*

In this lyrical excerpt and other songs described in chapter seven, there is an affirmation of changes that will happen because of Dalit women. Singers, Kalai, Rani, and many more women, men, and all gender identities involved in the movement for change are in partnership for change as each song and action is loaded with symbolic meanings on the strengths and capacities of Dalit women. Here, the singer owns her power to transform mud into gold to replace remote thorny pathways to her village with a road of gold. The Dalit deity *Yellamma* who protects the village will stand with her as the singer invokes her. Future generations will benefit from this transformation wielded in the partnering of *Yellama* and Dalit women; their words and spaces lead to transgressive transformations of bodies, culture, caste, gender, food, space, socio-economic status, and domestic position.

Transnational feminism opens deeper possibilities of exploring solidarities and collaborations where more spaces could be activated for a closer look at individual and collective subjectivity (as lived expressions of activism) and agency (Swarr and Nagar 5). In proposing and identifying ways in which "transnational feminisms are an intersectional set of understandings, tools, and practices," they highlight aspects where such praxis can "grapple with the complex and contradictory ways in which these processes both inform and are shaped by a range of subjectivities and understandings of individual and collective agency" (Swarr and Nagar 5). While transnational feminism can and will perform what it proposes and hopes for, it necessitates a redefinition of spaces where processes of intersectional grappling can occur that involve individual and collective agency. I emphasize a need for an inclusion of spaces where the desire for change as a mental space could be a form of activism and a boundary crossing of the mind, just as geographic, social, or economic boundaries are crossed. Heterogeneity of spaces should be preserved and acknowledged within nations, cultures, religions, and communities, and within processes and expressions of activism and agency. Voices, bodies, and minds coalesce to create a better understanding of the meaning of activism and agency, which are central to representation. Spaces within which representations happen are often confined into traditional categories such as political, national, feminist, or postcolonial. I suggest that the "trans" in transnational feminism should indicate a traverse of physical, economic, educational, religious, cultural, mental, and defined moral spaces. All these spaces can and will be constituted and reconstituted in both real and imagined mosaic freeing acts.

Humanizing narratives in an earthy way as a constantly growing and evolving praxis without an end goal is key to transnational feminism (Swarr and Nagar 9). Such humanizing problematizes the fact that the absence of an end goal often discloses a restless condition where narratives are tossed in and out of disciplines and institutionalized thought patterns without a home base where they could otherwise rest securely. On the other hand, they enrich the scope because this *restlessness* could break open encapsulated norms and strict disciplinary spaces. Adapting decentering as a characteristic makes a narrative explosive and eclectic in its capacity for a multiplicity of encounters with its expressions, meanings, and understandings that make them indomitable and pliable, rising above normative elucidations. Devoid of an ultimatum of experience, response, or criticism, these narratives illustrate that the potential constitutive elements of experience vary—listener, along with the narrator, is moved by the details of lived experiences. We cannot and must not judge such testimonies, but just allow our preset eager vitality to be altered by such narratives. Crossing over spaces and boundaries happens in both the narrator and listener, complicating coherent structural imaginations and definitions into which one is ready to shelve them. Both published and unpublished oral narratives possess this unique quality: to imagine spaces that may or may not exist, forcing us to reconfigure our idea of spaces and borders.

The possibility of liberating processes within expressions from a position of self-location that transnational feminism has opened for Dalit women is a social phenomenon that should be explored. Dalit voices that continue to speak to me come from physical locations such as school porches, shade of trees, harvest fields, Dalit homes, hostels, Dalit organization office buildings, stone quarries, and more. Such locations reveal a process of "trans-ing" into spaces imagined, entered, and lived, into which the listener could be invited or not. Effective collaboration is yet another key grain that transnational feminism highlights among change-making communities. Some women in this book choose to collaborate with social activist leaders, organizations, and global initiatives while most of them seek collaboration among their own family and community in daring to imagine alternatives. Therefore, Dalit women's agency is self-located and non-dependent on large collaborative structures. Their narratives exist independently as in their songs and life-stories—not waiting on approval, fearing no rejection, creating and dismantling meanings on their own, dialoging in self-located spaces, and mostly reaching only into their immediate community and surroundings as resources. In this positioning of self-location, these narratives are not bound by the confines of theoretical, national, or political boundaries, as they possess a self-invested authority to move across intercultural boundaries. They hold on to characteristics that reinforce their voice and visibility with an autonomy that shatters the myth of the oppressed as silent victim.

Kalai and Rani exude a determination to create social changes and transform the lives of Dalit communities. As Kalai narrates:

> *During a college celebration, a highly ranked Government official, District Collector Sheila Rani Suganth, came and spoke to us about women's empowerment. So I walked up to her and told her about what had happened in the stone quarry* [a young girl was raped]. *She came and met with the family—of the girl who was raped—and invited me to her house. We developed a good friendship, and she helped me start a non-formal education* [a government-based education program] *in Pudukkottai District. She encouraged me to start my own non-profit organization and guided me through the process. She provided me*

with all the training I needed; and I traveled with her, observ-
ing her work. (Kalaimagal)

This excerpt of Kalai's power-filled narratives in this book testify to her determination to form allies, stand for the rights of Dalit women, and effect social
changes in her community on her own initiative. Today (2017) Kalai, who is
forty-six, continues her social transformation work providing viable avenues
for Dalit women and children through her own non-profit organization—Dr.
AWARD (DA)—which she founded when she was twenty. Dalit female narratives are therefore proactive resources in themselves since they provide multi-
textured dimensions of Dalit culture along with Dalit female agency.

Transnational feminism is a practice of agency that goes beyond the process
of recovering or reconstructing a female identity as interpreted by a global description of liberation (Swarr and Nagar 4). The unique praxis of *earthy humanness* is about the impenetrability of an agency located and practiced collectively that is uncorrupted by dominant world knowledge systems. Ingrained is a
great amount of originality, artistry, extemporaneity, and autonomy revealed in
Dalit narratives that engender an unconditional humanness without the necessity to gauge literary or semantic value. These narratives exist as they are and as
they will be in their raw meanings through lived experiences of the narrator and
the immediate participant/listener. I wish to borrow from transnational feminist
praxis and push further the recognition of an audacity among those who literally and otherwise live on the fringes of dominant communities. The voices in
and beyond this book exist in an independent state; they do not seek recognition of applied practices. If transnational feminism is about boundary-crossing,
the voices in this book cross boundaries of authority, culture, location, and
difference.

The fact that Dalit women are prominent in their voice and visibility should
not be ignored, just as much as we cannot ignore the fact that they are targets of
physical and sexual abuse by their own men and men from caste communities.
Their voices and bodies intertwine not only as carriers of cultural self-
expression but as carriers of danger as well. They are visible targets of attack,
and their cultural voices reveal that pain and anguish. In the eyes of the larger
Indian society and global community, these women are tucked into invisible
spaces as invisible bodies, yet they continue to live into a reality of a transforming power of their voice and visibility as agents effecting positive identities and promising changes within their own communities; such realities remain
invisible for the most part. Dalit women's cultural invisibility, however, sets
them up for a *selective visibility* to those with power who seek them out as
sexual prey and, at the same time, allows them to maintain a cultural visibility
within their community as sustainers of their traditional cultural identity. I dis-

cuss this concept more in chapter eight with the aid of Bama's story of her cousin Mariamma who is a victim of sexual harassment. It is therefore essential to (re)conceptualize the voice and visibility of Dalit women as they establish and maintain Dalit identity in their own cultural context in relation to their understanding of humanness as lived experiences of relationships, kinship, intimacy, beauty, nature, motherhood, womanhood, agency, overt and covert activism, and much more. The multiplicity of expressions of humanness in these narratives diverts us from a singular theoretical stance into plurifarious construals of identity and agency.

As much as the experiences of Dalit women are not homogenous, neither are the presence and expressions of power. Dominant powers are more than just caste-, class-, or gender-based. The "less than human" social position that Dalit men and women are subject to cannot be formulized into the tradition-based, feminist generic categorization of dominance identified in patriarchy. Boundaries and frameworks of dominations in the lives of Dalits are in a static condition of rigid traditionalism of dominance while subject to the constancy of the shifting and anomalous nature of dominance itself as in hegemonic masculinity. As Moallem states, transnationalism should include intersecting social relations acknowledging multiple patriarchies, thus aligning herself with Grewal and Kaplan's claim to a malleable claying that transnational feminism always moves towards as opposed to a fixed framework (341). Such multiplicity of what patriarchy denotes is due to the variety and nuances of dominant powers in all castes and all religions. Changing economic and social conditions among Dalits have created layers of dominance amongst us according to type of work, privilege of education, land-ownership, and residential places; privileged Dalits will dominate over those not privileged. Living in such varied expressions of dominance calls for multiple notions of identity since this dominance is both amalgamated and separated as power anomalies that cannot be clearly isolated within specific gender, caste, or class categories. As an educated land-owning Dalit woman, I do experience intersections of power at war internally and externally: gender, race, caste, class, color, language, and religion. I discuss my identity journey along with my parents' in the last section of the book where I identify the infectors (including my family and me) of those intersecting loci that involve all gender, caste, and race categories.

In my book, I sway a transnational flame that brings to light otherwise hidden crevices in the lives of Dalit women where multiple ways of representation, diverse strategies of resistance, and overt and covert strategies of protest have taken root and are bearing fruit. This search brings to focus the active and creative responsivity to social responsibility among Dalit women in local spaces to such power structures that cause violation of human rights. The reader will seek meanings in the local responses and what these could offer to the larger understanding of human response to a violation of rights. The women in these villages in Tamil Nadu are transnational as evident in the ways in which they creatively protest by being able to find ways to cheat and transgress boundaries marked on their bodies and their living spaces by a nationalism grounded in fundamentalist discourse. Through this book, the reader will gather what Dalit women offer to this kaleidoscopic lens of feminism where borders are stretched, spaces of escape created, and frames unhinged in their own formulations of submission and resistance in their *earthy humanness* approach to change. Agency is a way of being that is cradled by songs, dances, spaces of work, testimonies, protest methods, desires, gathering of firewood, lighting a fire, gathering of water, mourning, and in the will to live.

As noted earlier, Alarcón et al. argue that women and nation intersect in a space of performative and performativity giving rise to the interval of difference (6). It is a space of becoming and rising above the settling for a cultural projection as an object of derision. Dalit women in this book are exemplary subversionists in whom subalternity is reconfigured in the diversity of their bodily and mental spaces as sites of conversion of their suppressed bodies into performances of protest. In heeding the command of a master will lurk a hidden strategy of resistance. They employ their "difference" and their "untouchable" state to strategically surprise and thwart looming bodies of authority. Their political efficacy is seen in the community and individual allies with whom they choose to share their stories and testimonials. As evident in this book, Dalit women usurp the negative pan-Dalit identities and adorn a new dismantling of those very identities by constantly re-ordering those and throwing the "powerful" into a state of confusion. Submission becomes camouflaged rebellion, and visible protest itself takes on the hyper-visibility that their victimized bodies would normally reflect.

CHAPTER ONE

Claiming Places: Herstory of Dalit Women's Narratives in India

Historically, few key persons and movements within India were responsible for the emergence of the visibility of Dalit women today. In *Dalit Visions* (1995), historian Gail Omvedt highlights the role of Jyotirao Phule (1827-1890) from the Shudra caste community as one of the foremost voices against Brahmanism who worked for Dalits in claiming equal opportunities in education and jobs (20). Phule established schools for Dalits and for girls from the upper caste communities, and combined social reform with literature in his plays, poems, ballads, and books. He worked to bring together the Shudra caste and Dalits to work in solidarity against Brahmanical domination while initiating the idea of seeking international solidarity with African Americans and Native Americans in the USA. Phule viewed Marx's class theory as applicable to some extent to explain the power of the wealthy Brahmins and Kshatriyas over Dalits, especially women (Omvedt 21). While Phule was the first prominent spokesperson for Dalits, it was Ambedkar (1891-1956) of the Mahar Dalit community from Maharashtra who stands out as the first Dalit voice against caste. Ambedkar's powerful political and social analytical writings and speeches gave rise to a national surge of Dalit social consciousness to demand their human, social, and political rights. His writings include *Castes in India—Their Mechanisms, Genesis and Development* (1916), *Annihilation of Caste* (1936), and *Who were the Shudras?* (1948). Ambedkar was born into a Mahar community; his father, who worked for the British army, gained access to education for his children in local government schools. Still, Ambedkar recalls experiences of being treated as "untouchable" and having to sit outside school classrooms. He proved to be a successful student despite such discriminations and graduated with a college degree in economics and political science from the University of Bombay in 1912 (Keer 8-10). He was awarded a scholarship to study economics and law at Columbia University in New York in 1913. Upon his return in 1917, he was appointed as the Defense Secretary to the King of Baroda. Later, he was professor of economics at the Sydenham College of Commerce and Economics in Bombay and went on to further his education in London and Germany; in 1927, he was awarded a doctoral degree by Columbia University (Keer 9-10).

Educated in London and New York, Ambedkar equipped himself as a skilled lawyer to represent the cause of his people. His knowledge of English and his proficiency in Marathi proved to be his greatest assets in establishing an effective counter-movement to an internal colonization of caste. Significantly, Ambedkar continually called for the involvement of Dalit women in his movement against caste. He gained inspiration from Phule in creating positive changes in the Dalit community, and in speaking out and writing against the Brahmanical caste system.

Omvedt observes that as early as the 1940s, "Mahar youth organizations were also started in many areas, and a 'woman's wing' came into existence in the sense that women's conferences were held concurrently with general Dalit conferences" (202). She refers to the All-India Depressed Class conferences that were held in Nagpur. These conferences used red flags to announce a pan-Indian "radical identity" (Omvedt 202). The flags were used a great deal during the festivities surrounding "Ambedkar *Jayanti*" (Ambedkar's birthdays), though Ambedkar himself shied away from such occasions. Women played a major role in these festivities, taking part in large numbers. These celebrations became major Dalit cultural events where Dalits celebrated their collective identity. Ambedkar *Jayanti* celebrations became the origin of various forms of literary expressions including writing (Omvedt 203). Dalits staged poems, plays, and songs based on Dalit experiences, and such literary expressions became the key inspiration for the Ambedkar Movement to assert its identity as one driven by rebellion and demand for justice. As it spread, the Ambedkar Movement that involved the participation of Dalit women formed alliances with lower caste communities; however, it grew more as a peasant movement than as a political force that could form alliances with existing political parties. Dalit women continued to write and stage their cultural expressions at public events (Omvedt 203).

On April 14, 1942 at Ambedkar's fiftieth birthday celebration amidst a mass of Dalits gathered from all over the country, Ambedkar challenged the Congress Party which was made up of caste Hindus by asserting: "I make only one condition. Tell me what share I am to have in the Swaraj. If you don't want to tell me that and you want to make up with the British behind my back, hell on both of you" (qtd. in Omvedt 216). Omvedt says that in July 1942 Ambedkar was made the "Labor Member" for the government of India. Following this appointment, a Dalit Federation was formed at a gathering of over seventy thousand people, about one-third of whom were women from all over India. Ambedkar continued to strongly emphasize the education of Dalit women and started educational institutions for Dalits: the Sidharth Science and Arts College in Bombay in 1946-47 and the Milind College of Arts and Science in Aurangabad. In 1946-47, there were about 119 Dalit male students, and by 1973 the number increased to 7,185. Over four hundred Dalit women had enrolled in these colleges by 1973 (Omvedt 202). The education of Dalit women became one of the major factors behind their involvement in Dalit social movements. These educated young Dalits began to criticize openly the fact that Dalits continued to be socially deprived despite constitutional amendments that condemned discrimination based on caste. For the first time, young educated Dalit women questioned the authority of Hindu scriptures.

It is significant that the first expressions of protest from Dalits against established religious and political orders came in the form of writing. Young Dalits started writing poetry and fiction based on their experiences of suffering and discrimination. The first Dalit literary conference was held in 1970 in Mahad, Maharashtra. Dalit literature became an expression of revolt and rejection of the caste legacy of Hinduism (Omvedt 33). Soon after the conference, several Dalit women started writing about their condition of double oppression as Dalits and as women—the sub-gendered. Dalit women have continued to transgress boundaries and are increasingly aware of their vulnerable outcaste state. They respond by subversion to a social demonizing of them as the "Other," and assumptions that they are immoral and lack a capacity for positive action. Their process of expressions includes oral narratives, dances, street theatre, agitations, political participation, and education. Dalit women find such processes to be self-asserting as well as self-protecting—offering both physical protection and moral protection of human dignity. Educated Dalit women have formed organizations for Dalit peoples: Ruth Manorama (National Federation of Dalit Women), Kalaimagal (Dr. Ambedkar Women and Children Regeneration and Development Program, [DA]), Asha Kowtal (All India Dalit Mahila Adhikar Manch [AIDMAM] and National Campaign for Dalit Human Rights [NCDHR]), Fatima Bernard (Tamil Nadu), Jhansi Geddam (Stree Shakti), Grace Neela (Mehboobnagar District, Andhra Pradesh), Beena Pallickal (NCDHR), Vimal Thorat (NCDHR member and Professor, The Indira Gandhi National Open University, Delhi), Manjula Pradeep (Navsarjan, Ahmedabad), and Deepti Sukumar (Safai Karmachari Andolan, Tamil Nadu). These are a few examples of prominent Dalit women who actively create and sustain leadership initiatives, networking opportunities, and new programs that empower Dalit women to be self-sufficient.

Dalit women writers are key change-makers in establishing and propagating alternative ideologies that contend with traditional stigmatizations. Bama's *Karukku* (1992) and *Sangati* (1994) are voices of a Dalit woman narrating life stories of a community of Dalit women who have been integral to the formation of a desire in her to own and declare her Dalit female identity. She writes about the ways in which Christianity has brought complex dynamics into the caste paradigm; for example, Christian converts—including nuns from all dominant caste communities—look down upon Dalit Christians. Poems written in Marathi by Jothi Lanjewar (1950-) speak of an experiential reality coming forth from her own life and a calling for Dalit women to take pride in their bodies and minds as sources of life and energy. Urmila Pawar and Kumud Pawde are writers inspired by the speeches and writings of Ambedkar who led people to believe in alternatives to Hinduism, illiteracy, and poverty. Dalit women writers like Pawde extend their efforts beyond writing to social action. Pawde delivers fiery speeches on the necessity for Dalit women to claim their rights and involves herself in proactive strategies for change.

Urmila Pawar is yet another pioneering writer inspired by the teachings of Ambedkar who started writing in 1975 emphasizing the need for justice for Dalit women. She emphasizes Dalit cultural strengths upheld by Dalit women. Eleanor Zelliot notes the several biographies and autobiographies of Dalit women as "fascinating accounts" of a combination of "courage and despair" (322). The historic movement of writings by Dalit women led to the first Dalit women's literary conference held in Bombay in 1986: the Dalit Stri Samwadini (Dalit Women's Dialogue). The first anthology of Dalit writings translated into English was published in 1992, which included several Dalit women writers. Education of Dalit women is key to the propagation of Dalit ethics of care and claiming justice.

A shift occurred in the Dalit mindset and culture as some Dalits have gained education; it is noteworthy that the first generation of Dalits who had access to education and jobs during colonial rule in the early 1900s left their colonies in a hurry, fleeing social degradation. Many adapted the social passing as the Shudra (categorized by the Indian Government as Backward Caste) or Vanniya caste in other towns or cities as a way to promote themselves and to erase a shameful past. The emergent Dalit wave now has an infrastructure due to the collaboration of various Dalit organizations. The second and third generations of educated, economically viable, and socially conscious Dalits in the latter part of the twentieth century up until now are fearlessly claiming their Dalit identity because they understand the workings of India's social stratification, and they have tools to protect their pride in a Dalit identity.

While discourses from South Asian scholars such as Gayatri Spivak are on target in naming the enemy and critiquing the West for assuming the role of the savior in social mediating roles, they are off target in not naming the concrete changes that have been made possible due to western interventions in individual lives and communities, as well as nationally with demands for policy changes that are now taking place. Dalit leadership and major Dalit organizations in India today are sustained by an international community; this is a necessary reality that will continue to haunt the minds of the South Asian postcolonial elite in American and other academic circles who raise questions and initiate debates on who is authorized to "redeem" a social condition, while Dalit women are raped and killed every day. Statistics reveal that at least three Dalit women are raped every day, and thirteen Dalits are murdered every week (International Dalit Solidarity Network).

Visible Changes through *Earthy Humanness*

Currently, there are national and international solidarity groups working specifically with Dalits, as well as other human rights organizations throughout the world that are now aware of Dalit struggles. In 1999, and under the leadership of human rights lawyer Smita Narula, the international NGO Human Rights Watch published its groundbreaking report, *Broken People: Caste Violence Against India's 'Untouchables.'* The report—which Narula researched and wrote in collaboration with Dalit activists from across the country—drew international attention to the subject of caste-based discrimination and helped spur the formation of India's National Campaign on Dalit Human Rights, and of the International Dalit Solidarity Network. These groups in turn helped focus the attention of U.N. human rights bodies on caste-based atrocities, despite all attempts by the Indian government to silence Dalit voices and sweep the caste issue under the proverbial rug. Following UN involvement, Dalit women have gained more confidence and have found ways to establish their own organizations and representatives locally and globally. Only in the past two decades, national solidarity initiatives have taken root among Dalit leaders and Dalit communities. Several decades later many Dalit organizations are still monetarily and structurally dependent upon international support. Those culturally labeled as "untouchable" would not have challenged those notions in the first place if not for such interventions.

However, Dalit women act on their own as well with necessary training provided by Dalit organizations, as the story on the eradication of *saaraayam* led by Kalai and Rani proves. Another example is the concept and practice of *sangam* which is a major breakthrough in the visible changes among Dalit communities of women taking charge of change-making. *Sangam* is a self-help group modelled on the indigenous essence of the humane economy of sharing resources. Kalai and Rani have served as heads of the women's *sangam* in their respective villages. These *sangam* promote the concept and practice of saving money by and for Dalit women. Some colonies have a pool that they draw from when a colony or a particular individual is in need. They have a monthly membership fee in these *sangam;* through membership in a structured women's organization, these women negotiate with the local and state government to establish schools, lay roads, and meet other demands that would decrease the isolation of Dalit villages. They report that the state government only allows about twenty members in the *sangam*, and so they start multiple *sangam* to accommodate more women! I discuss these *sangam* in chapter six as a major self-made financial resource that is central to a Dalit economy of shared resources in which women gain an economic security that the capitalist world outside their village denies them. Both Kalai and Rani served as village *sarpanch* (village council leaders) who share their stories of leadership in chapters five and six. They both testify to a resilient determination to change situations to make Dalit women self-sufficient by creating alternatives to working and living conditions that make them sexually and economically exploitable.

In my conversations with a group of *jogin* women (those dedicated to temples, referred to as *Devadasi*) in August of 2002, in the colony of Hadkomandalam about fifty kilometers from Hyderabad, I learned of an urgency for change from this early cultural practice of enslaving Dalit girls. These women were proud to be a part of an organization called the "Mahila (Women's) Action Centre" (MAC), where they have gained the confidence to even sit on chairs and not be afraid of being indicted. Mariyamma, who served as the dedicated secretary of the MAC organization, asserted: "We will not accept the vicious cycle for our children anymore. They need to be educated and find jobs. We want a better future for our children." Journalist Meera Shenoy reiterates this in her interview with a *jogin* woman who said, "My father made me a *jogin* to make his ends meet. I will do everything possible to make sure my daughter does not go through the hell I have experienced" (qtd. in Shenoy, *India Abroad*, February 28, 2003). These women have claimed the right to education and sent their children to school. They introduced me to their high school graduates, some of whom attended engineering and polytechnic colleges, and others who even took jobs in Hyderabad, a city that is India's equivalent of Silicon Valley. In May of 2012, I met with Grace Neela, the director of MAC who runs a hostel facility, *Aashray* for the daughters of *jogin* women and young Dalit girls who have been rescued. She reports that several years later, each of the *jogin* women who belong to MAC have broken the cycle, and their children have been educated and have moved into better jobs and better economic conditions.

Several organizations led by Dalit women are in place in the state of Andhra Pradesh; these women serve as community organizers, lawyers, trainers, community leaders, surveyors, and monitors of atrocities. Most notably, the Dalit Bahujan Shramik Union—an agricultural workers' union—was founded by Dalit women leaders representing cases of violence against Dalit women. They expose discriminations in schools, demand disaster relief efforts, and take part in political election processes and state budget allocation thereby facilitating economic enterprises and business management among Dalit communities. Such leadership among Dalit women provides motivation among them to invest their time, energy, and money into organizing around specific issues even as basic as clean drinking water and electricity. The organization *Dappu* is an organizationally structured collective of NGOs in Hyderabad, founded and run mainly by Dalits and non-Dalits for Dalit Bahujan (people's) empowerment. Dalit rights activists Paul Divakar and Annie Namala were key forces behind this initiative, and now it is self-sufficient as the Dalit Bahujan Shramik Union working in partnership with other local NGOs and labor unions across various states. Dalit women taking on battles with local officials as well as state and central government power structures speaks to their capacity for individualized and collective choice and action. Such focused concentration of determination to create sustainable changes has prevailed in continuously contending with inimical forces. This provides spaces for Dalit women to function in their leadership roles as mentors to Dalit women in their respective and neighboring villages.

Political participation of Dalits is increasing significantly. On April 25th, 1999, *The New York Times* published "Ideas and Trends: Why Governments Tumble; India's Poorest are Becoming its Loudest" where Celia W. Dugger observes:

> The percentage of people from formerly untouchable castes who said they were members of political parties rose from 13 percent in 1971 to 19 percent in 1996, while the percentage from upper castes who said they belonged to a party declined from 36 percent to 28 percent. The percentage of very poor people who believe voting makes a difference rose from 38 percent in 1971 to 51 percent in 1996 and jumped from 42 percent to 60 percent for low caste people.

At the "World Conference against Racism" in Durban, South Africa in August-September 2001, Dalit women demanded the inclusion of caste as a form of discrimination, even though representatives from the Indian Government did everything possible to stifle these efforts. Over two hundred and fifty Dalit men and women from all over India participated in the conference speaking at NGO sessions. *Sakthi* (power) is a Dalit women's group that succeeded in drawing international attention through their art of drumming the *parai*, a Dalit drum traditionally played only by Dalit men to announce death. Such a symbol of death and mourning is now subverted into symbols of celebration by Dalit women as an internal symbol of collective power.

The NCDHR, which is the first national coalition of Dalit movements (with a strong presence at the WCAR in Durban), consists of Dalit women in its national programs as board members and directors. The NCDHR identifies itself as "a democratic secular platform led by Dalit women and men activists, with support and solidarity from movements and organizations, academics, individuals, people's organizations and institutions throughout the country who are committed to work to protect and promote human rights of Dalits" (National Campaign for Dalit Human Rights, 2015, n. pag.). Vimal Thorat who is one of the program directors is a scholar and researcher who speaks at the UN and other international summits impacting policy changes. Movements such as REDS (Rural Education and Development Society) headed by Jyothi Raj work at two general levels: producing publications to reach the educated mass and organizing mass Dalit gatherings to reach the common Dalit population (I attended one such mass gathering in January 2000 in Tumkur, Andhra Pradesh marking Ambedkar's birthday). REDS organizes protests, literacy programs, and training task groups with Dalit men and women, as well as coordinates independent committees headed by Dalit women to promote education, self-employment, and labor unions. AIDMAM is a forum of solidarity of Dalit and non-Dalit women and men committed to the protection of the rights of Dalit women. It reports that "89.5% of Dalit women contribute considerably to economic production in the country as rural agricultural labor, unorganized industrial workers and as self-employed workers in the informal sector.... Dalit women's knowledge and skill in sustainable agriculture, irrigation techniques, animal husbandry and other artisan productions have critical value and contribution for ecologically sustainable development" (National Campaign for Dalit Human Rights). Similarly, several other organizations such as "Prajwala"— facilitated by Annie Namala, a woman from a dominant caste community— train Dalit women to take up leadership in representing issues related to sexual abuse, economic abuse, and temple prostitution in the areas surrounding Chittoor in South India.

Mari M. Thekaekara, in *Endless Filth* (1999), writes about the battle for justice among Dalit communities who clean public latrines and are labeled "manual scavengers" by the Indian Government. They are known by several local terms such as *Bhangi* in Gujarat *or Thoti* in Tamil Nadu. She mentions that seven hundred Dalit women who protested in the state of Gujarat in 1996 were arrested and brutalized for demanding better wages for the dirty work that they are forced to do. The women were persistent in their demand, and even after the police brutalities, they did win their case and secured more wages (Thekaekara 13). Organizations such as *Navsarjan* unite Dalit women and men to eradicate the work of manual scavenging which further brands them "polluted" and "untouchable." Committed Dalit women and men are working tirelessly towards creating rehabilitation programs to find alternative jobs for Bhangi. Martin Macwan, Founding Director of *Navsarjan*, strongly believes that even if efforts are going into eradicating manual scavenging, people's attitude regarding the impurity of Dalits must be changed. Macwan narrates how a *Bhangi* woman with her child has to beg for her food and receives the same food given to stray dogs that would walk away from the spoilt food that a *Bhangi* has to eat (Thekaekara 65). Manjula, a participant at the Global Women's Leadership Program of Rutgers University in 2002 who leads "Navsarjan," spoke of her work specifically with Dalit women who are sexually abused in harvest fields and plantations. Dalit women who were afraid to talk about their plight, now speak up when they are wronged and are eager to be educated on the prevention of sexual assault. In addition, Bezwada Wilson, born into a family that performed the task of manual scavenging, founded the Safai Karmachari Andolan in 1994 which has grown to become a national movement to end the practice of manual scavenging.[7] Kalai and Rani have both partnered with this national movement to organize Dalit women to eradicate the practice of manual scavenging in their district.

Several movements such as the one led by Kalai and Rani against alcohol took place in South India. In 1992, Dalit women in the village of Dubagunta in the southern state of Andhra Pradesh demanded that the state government ban the selling of liquor in the entire state. The women involved in this movement were participants in the National Literacy Mission that was started by the Government in the Nellore District of Andhra Pradesh in January 1990. This is an example of self-location because these women chose to cross over into the terrain of literacy training and gain access to formal education by enrolling in the mass literacy program. It was because of this program that women had opportunities to form a collective to discuss their problems. As part of the process, they identified alcoholism as a major common social issue and decided to take up a fight against liquor selling and consumption, which led to spearheading a major campaign against bureaucracy, the police force, and the state.

Liquor contractors remain a powerful presence in villages because they form alliances with local politicians and the police force. They have local thugs on their side who protect these contactors from local protests against them. The

---

[7] Bezwada Wilson, whose parents had to work as manual scavengers, is one of the six recipients of the 2016 Ramon Magsaysay Award by the Philippines-based award foundation in Manila for his efforts to eradicate manual scavenging.

state government made a profit of over 390 million rupees in 1970-71 (1 USD = 25 INR) which rose to 8.12 billion rupees (1 USD = 45 INR) in 1991-92 on the sale of arrack. This was one main reason why the state government did not prohibit the making and selling of arrack. The government started a program *Varuna Vahini* that allowed the possession of arrack sachets in homes. According to *Economic and Political Weekly*, the average family income in the state of Andhra Pradesh in 1991-92 was 1,840 rupees per year and of this, 830 rupees was spent on liquor! The women wanted an answer as to why their villages did not have basic amenities such as schools, drinking water, or proper wages but had a regular alcohol supply. The government in its defense stated that the revenue was spent on providing welfare benefits to the villages. The women then said that they would sacrifice a day's wage to cover the government's cost for welfare programs. This movement spread across all of Andhra Pradesh, and soon the government issued a ban on making and selling arrack in the state of Andhra Pradesh. Under the ordinance of the "Andhra Pradesh Excise Act," the manufacture of liquor is illegal and punishable with fines up to 100,000 rupees. Dalit women acted collectively to get to the root of the problem and fought the power of alcoholism through public protests and by recognizing the needs of their men (87-90). Dalit women addressed the need for an assurance of emotional and psychological security for their men, and worked towards securing better economic conditions so that the men would not be drawn to momentary alcoholic escape from misery. This is an example of where the women's strength lies; they are willing to risk losing their honor and life by breaking through systemic power structures rather than just trying to find gaps to squeeze through to survive.

In chapter seven, I present songs by Dalit women as their cultural strength that promotes trust, values relationships, and encourages creative ways to sustain a positive collective identity. Dalit women gather to create and share rituals songs, stories, and dances; such cultural aspects were passed on from ancestors as voices of foremothers that provide assurance of the value of life, love, relationships, and specifically the beauty of their bodies. The voices of Dalit women have always existed, but were never heard or recognized by the outside world except as those of poor untouchables who had to be pitied or exploited. The politics of being seen and heard is closely linked to the politics of who is seeing and hearing, or to be more precise, who is not seeing and who is not hearing. Dalit women, however, continue to draw strength from their cultural elements where assertions of positive identities happen in the most spontaneous and organic ways. Today, Dalit women claim their voice and visibility by demanding political, social, cultural, and academic recognition. These women who are generally only known as those who clean polluted matter have traditionally been involved in the process of trying to overcome an internalization of victimization by employing effective strategies from within their culture.

In the expressions of Dalit female identity through songs that I highlight in chapter seven and in chapter eight on Bama, I establish that such narratives thwart traditional dominance in their traditional figurations as evil "Other" women. I establish the fact that Dalit women as "Othered" women are self-representational where their voice and visibility are their self-chosen states of cultural presence. In most chapters, I discuss the state of pollution in the *Manusmriti* that Dalit women are made to embody and now counter through their self-presentation; almost all Dalits I interact with in the villages have no knowledge about the *Manusmriti*, but live the reality of the "dirty untouchable" and the "polluted Other." The proclamations of this religious text relegate Dalits to inhabit separate cremation grounds, reifying the reality of polluted matter that these ancient writings define them to be. Statistics reveal that in India more than one million Dalits, mainly women and children, are involved in the demeaning work of manual scavenging (Narula 9). This work requires Dalits to clean unsanitary public dry latrines with their bare hands; hence, they are further ostracized as polluted. This is clear evidence that age-old traditional beliefs exist even today as Dalits perform "dirty" work because they are polluted beings (Safai Karmachari Andolan, n. pag.). Here lies a glaring reason to closely consider the impact of appropriations of traditional religious discourses by dominant communities on the larger Indian ethos today. Such concretizations are normalized by dominant narratives as part of the Indian epistemology and cultural paradigm; thus, a large part of the Indian population is blind to the existence of over a hundred and seventy million people who live in segregated spaces subject to dehumanization and violence every day.

In the past twenty years, the growth of Dalit movements in India and especially the expansion in leadership by Dalit women have been tremendous. The post Durban impact is seen in many parts of India; at state levels, several changes have taken place. A commission on untouchability has been made public in Andhra Pradesh, twenty-two orders have been set against caste discrimination in the state of Madhya Pradesh, and a few other states such as Rajasthan, Tamil Nadu, and Maharashtra have experienced similar impacts. Due to all these positive changes, international and national agencies have provided funds to Dalit development programs throughout the country. Most notable is the "National Center for Dalit Studies" in New Delhi headed by Sukhadeo Thorat. This center produces publications and academic councils leading to the formation of a recognizable Dalit intelligentsia including Dalit women. Most recently, a bill was passed in the state of Andhra Pradesh: The Andhra Pradesh Scheduled Castes Sub-Plan and Tribal Sub-Plan (Planning, Allocation and

Utilization of Financial Resources) Bill, 2012. This ensures the proper allocation of funds for Dalits and tribal communities. In the USA, Dalit American
transmedia artist and activist Thenmozhi Soundarajan along with other Dalit
women in the US and in India helped lead the #DalitWomenFight campaign
and started Dalit History Month in April to exemplify Dalit history and resistance. [8]

The battle for justice becomes harder as there is no distinction between public and private realms in the lives of Dalit women because they are constantly
caught in anomalous, socially conditioned spaces: visible and invisible, touchable and untouchable, undesirable and sexually available. Patriarchy is not only
a part of public life, but it is both public and private as it is manifest in religious, cultural, social, and political niches that operate out of public institutions
with private, self-fulfilling agendas. This is made possible through the operative machinery of power between both male and female that allows amalgama-
tion, transference, transgression, oppression, and the vague boundaries of binary oppositional identities and practices. Such conditions make it difficult for
Dalit women to find a long-term strategy for change. They must decide whether to start with religion, politics, patriarchy, or economy! To be able to begin
moving beyond defensive paradigms of survival, it is essential that trans-
authoritative, trans-cultural, and trans-nationalist practices of voice and visibility which are evident among Dalit women through expressions of *earthy humanness* be popularized as day-to-day practices in Dalit communities. Dalit
female expressions are significant in their action for resistance and in their
refusal to actualize concepts of purity and pollution as defining markers of their
identity as "untouchable." Instead, they reject de-humanization imposed upon
their lives in being tossed in and out of identities.

---

[8] www.dalitwomenfight.com

CHAPTER TWO

Criminalizing Dalit, "Dirty" and "Different": Ideological, Historical, and Political Casting

Caste structures would be fractured if not for their strong grounding in the dualist ideology of whether one is "clean" or "dirty." Dalits are considered dirty and relegated to the most unclean and often hazardous tasks: handling dead bodies, cleaning human feces in public toilets and streets, gathering and carrying garbage to the dumps, laboring in the fields, and working as domestic servants, among others. Brahmin caste communities are considered "pure" as they could narrate scriptures, mediate prayers, teach, and learn. Since these tasks are delineated by traditional scriptures associated with Hinduism, such a paradigm purports a strict religiously defined difference that ordains a dichotomy which separates communities of people. Today, however, one cannot strictly confine caste to religion, for the inequity of the structure lends itself to provide spaces for the legitimized realization of political maneuverings using religion. Under caste-based discrimination and exclusion, those who seek to escape an "untouchable" status through education, conversion, or entrepreneurship are punishable. There is fierce resistance to change of social status of Dalits from those vested in the religious, political, economic, and social status quo, and dominant forces target Dalit women to punish rebellion.

People's Watch, a Dalit human rights organization in Chennai, Tamil Nadu, documented 1,346 cases of rape of Dalit women and 4,410 specific cases of physical violence against Dalits in 2009; only 268 of these cases made it to the courtrooms. A multiple disownment by state, society, and religion posits Dalits as one of the most vulnerable groups of people in India today. The state especially denies them their basic rights as citizens of the country by failing to protect them from violence, disease, and death. They are subject to dehumanizing violations and discriminations: not accepted into Hindu temples; relegated to separate living spaces; forced to use separate glasses in local restaurants; subjected to specifications for the work they can and cannot do; forced to eat human feces; subjected to physical attacks and rape; treated as untouchable; and denied education and health care, to name a few.

Dalit women are often subject to sexual exploitation since most of them are submissively dependent on their work in the fields or other "space" owned by caste groups who abuse them for mere egotistic pleasure. The interesting question that often arises is with regard to the overarching, glaring ambiguity of the "untouchability" of the Dalit woman. When does this "untouchable" woman become "touchable"? The dominant caste male possesses the ultimate power to decide that raping is not touching since it is his caste and gender privilege towards a dispensable body. She is "untouchable" because she is "polluted," but becomes "touchable" as ordained by the power of caste, class, and gender that is attached to a caste status of "purity" that authorizes the "touchable" caste male to violate the "untouchable." Writing about the mindless rape of Native American women, Andrea Smith declares that in the Christian colonial imagination Native bodies are polluted with sexual sin. She claims, "Because Indian bodies are considered 'dirty' they are sexually violable and 'rapeable.' In patriarchal thinking, only a 'pure' body can really be violated. The rape of bodies that are considered inherently impure simply does not count" (qtd. in Kirk and Rey 275-76). Similarly, an act of violence—in the caste principle—does not count touching the "untouchable" as transgressing holy orders; instead, it further denigrates the "untouchable" and is therefore acceptable, cheered, and condoned as it is performed on dispensable bodies. The dominant caste male plays out this role of an *ordained rapist* whether done in secrecy or in public.

Linking Ideology and Practice

Phule, who worked against the dominance of Brahmanism in claiming equal opportunities for Dalits, most importantly expounded the image of the Aryan in Hindu mythology as the cruel and violent invader who destroyed the egalitarian life of the natives of India. He made heroes of the *Raksha* (ogre) figures, traditionally portrayed as evil in scriptures associated with Hinduism (Omvedt 17-24). As one of the first exponents of Marxism in India, Phule made a clear demarcation between Brahmins as exploiters and peasant communities as the exploited, and exposed the causes and consequences of poverty. As Omvedt sums it up, "Phule's theory can be looked at as a kind of incipient historical materialism in which economic exploitation and cultural dominance are interwoven" (21). Phule extended Marx's theory based on class to a sociological interpretation of the opposition of peasant Dalit communities to Brahmanic bureaucracy and religious separatist ideology of "clean" and "dirty."

Ambedkar wrote extensively on the separatism based on purity and pollution as the base of a Brahmanical caste system. He painfully writes that he was discriminated against as "untouchable" by dominant caste Indians abroad and in Maharashtra. In his autobiography, *Waiting for a Visa* (1935), he recalls:

> I knew that in the school I could not sit in the midst of my
> classmates according to my rank [in class performance], but

that I was to sit in a corner by myself. I knew that in the school I was to have a separate piece of gunny cloth for me to squat on in the classroom, and the servant employed to clean the school would not touch the gunny cloth used by me. I was required to carry the gunny cloth home in the evening, and bring it back the next day. … While in the school I knew that children of the touchable classes, when they felt thirsty, could go out to the water tap, open it, and quench their thirst. All that was necessary was the permission of the teacher. But my position was separate. I could not touch the tap; and unless it was opened for me by a touchable person, it was not possible for me to quench my thirst. In my case the permission of the teacher was not enough. The presence of the school peon was necessary, for he was the only person whom the class teacher could use for such a purpose. If the peon was not available, I had to go without water. The situation can be summed up in the statement—no peon, no water. *(*Ambedkar qtd. in Moon 661-62)

Ambedkar writes about these and many more experiences of hate and discrimination that continued into his life as a lawyer. The intricate and open ways in which caste power plays out among individuals and institutions are ruthless upon Dalit children in schools who continue to be treated "dirty." Children of the toilet cleaning community of Dalits clean toilets in their schools instead of sitting in the classroom (*Navsarjan*). According to Kalaimagal, teachers favor caste children and force Dalit children to sit outside the classrooms. Such circumstances are punishment-based cultural practices wherein being an untouchable is criminalized, and therefore a Dalit should be dehumanized while dominant castes are entitled to privilege.

In *Annihilation of Caste* (1936)—Ambedkar's undelivered speech—he records the discriminations upon the *Balais*, a Dalit community in Central India: no fancy clothing, messengers of death, forced servanthood, and more (215). When they refused adherence, they were further punished by being denied access to drinking water, and having their crops and homes destroyed. Any attempts to cross over into forbidden territories was severely punished. Ambedkar writes about a Dalit community in Gujarat that was punished for sending their children to school, which he points to as a civic right to education that they claimed (216). He exposes such incidents as examples of the reification of pollution upon the bodies of untouchables that led to such treatment. Denial of equal rights came out of the strong belief that they are polluted beings and are lesser humans. Ambedkar lists the imperative needs for change:

that the Hindu society must be reorganized on a religious basis
which would recognize the principles of liberty, equality and
fraternity; (5) that in order to achieve this object the sense of
religious sanctity behind caste and varna must be destroyed; (6)
that the sanctity of caste and varna can be destroyed only by
discarding the divine authority of the *shastras*. (334-335)

Ambedkar's personal encounters and experiences of untouchability primarily
aid in the concretization of apparent connections between social rejection and
religious sanctions.

A continuum of the effects of the dichotomous ideology of pollution and purity is central to the practice of social dismissal of Dalit communities, especially Dalit women. Voices of Dalit women in this book testify to this reality as
they experience it today; the solidified, reified links between religious discourses and normalization of inhuman social practices become evident.
Ambedkar questions:

How do you expect to succeed if you allow the *shastras* [Hindu
scriptural writings] to continue to mold the beliefs and opinions
of the people? ... Reformers working for the removal of untouchability, including Mahatma Gandhi, do not seem to realize that the acts of people are merely the results of their beliefs
inculcated in their minds by the *shastras,* and that people will
not change their conduct until they cease to believe in the sanctity of the *shastras* in which their conduct is founded. (287)

Ambedkar's desire was to see a reformation in the foundational thoughts that
shoulder the daily practice of untouchability: *chaturvarnya or varnashrama
dharma,* the division of society into the four major caste groups. This speaks
directly to those who strongly hold the view that caste originated out of class
and cannot be pinned on religion. Ambedkar takes great care to establish the
fact that the uppermost class identified themselves as the purest caste in the *Rig
Veda* (Hindu scriptural hymns, c. 1500-1200 BCE). He exposes the marriage
between *chaturvarnya* and *Manusmriti* (Hindu codes of law, c. 250 BCE)
where the transgressor is nevertheless punished: "Unless there is penalty attached to the act of transgression, men will not keep to their restrictive classes.
The whole system will break down, being contrary to human nature. *Chaturvarnya* cannot subsist by its own inherent goodness. It must be enforced law"
(268). Ambedkar notes this penalty as a codified method by which the
Manusmriti upholds the condition of punishment for those who transgress their
limits set by codes of law.

There are consequences for those in the purer social groups who do not
abide by what is expected of them; they need to carry out their religious duty—

it is *dharma*. Ambedkar views Rama's (incarnation of Lord Vishnu) acts of punishing transgressors in the *Ramayana* (Hindu epic, c. 400-200 BCE) not as a personal reaction but violent acts that had to fit into a set of cultural laws. According to Ambedkar, "That is why the *Manusmriti* prescribes such heavy sentences…. The supporters of the *chaturvarnya* should give an assurance that they could induce modern society in the twentieth century to re-forge the penal sanctions of the *Manusmriti*" (270). The necessity of fitting into regimented religious patterns of thought and action is imposed upon Dalits (and Shudras, the lowest caste) and those who are obligated by religion to uphold and fulfil the scriptures and preserve their social status.

Louis Dumont, one of the early theorists on caste, argues that the markings of "clean" and "dirty" in the orthodox Hindu religion are necessary in the constitution and maintenance of social harmony and balance. In 1966 he states:

> The Brahmans being in principle priests occupy the supreme rank with respect to the whole set of castes. The untouchables as very impure servants are segregated outside the villages proper in distinct hamlets. The untouchables may not use the same wells as the others, access to local Hindu temples was forbidden to them… (Dumont 47).

The same social conditions of separate spaces and forbiddance of Hindu temple entry for Dalits exists today. In 1999 Narula reports:

> Despite the fact that untouchability was abolished under India's constitution in 1950s, the practice of "untouchability"—the imposition of social disabilities on persons by reason of their birth in certain castes—remains very much a part of rural India. 'Untouchables' may not cross the line dividing their part of the village from that occupied by higher castes. They may not use the same wells, visit the same temples, drink from the same cups in tea stalls, or lay claim to land that is legally theirs. Dalit children are frequently made to sit in the back of classrooms, and communities as a whole are made to perform degrading rituals in the name of caste. (2)

Reports of this nature testify to the long sustenance of ordinances of space, identity, and social roles attached to being impure. Social isolation is a visible manifestation of a debilitating structure that denies social mobility for the "untouchable."

Angana P. Chatterjee, in her cultural anthropological research, expounds the impacts of Hindutva[9] as a dangerous fundamentalist incarnation of Hinduism

---

[9] Hindutva is a nationalism that has evolved in India since the institutionalized solidification of Hindu ideals as the *Arya Samaj* founded in 1875. The current expressions and

on the state of Orissa (55-60). The Sangh Parivar in its various incarnations, such as the Rashtriya Swayamsevak Sangh (RSS), is a fundamentalist group that has usurped Hindu ideals to claim supremacy and prerogative to threaten and use violence against those who do not follow a Hindu faith based on the notion of grounded privilege. Chatterjee makes clear connections between social rejection of peoples, religious ideals, and violence perpetrated upon those in Orissa. The powerful testimonies she presents from various minority peoples in Orissa speak to unimaginable horrors that non-Hindu communities experience daily. She points to the fact that "Gandhian secularism" questioned untouchability but not caste as a systemic power that saturates the national imagination: "[Caste] relegated the practice of religion to the non-state sphere but advocated and infused Hindu morality in defining civic practice for India" (Chatterjee 58). Especially in Orissa, one of the economically struggling states, dominant caste communities terrify vulnerable groups to mark a position of authority. Raping women; burning homes, churches, and mosques; and opening fire on innocent women and children are some of the methods of terrorizing practiced by dominant caste communities in Orissa.

Dalit women are the most vulnerable as they are traditionally considered dispensable; however, they serve as the "necessary difference" in the construction of systems of authority qualified by gradations of purity. Specific characteristics are imposed upon Dalit women by caste groups to establish a contrast to the expected purity and chastity in caste women. Since caste determines social status and therefore economic status, the ideology of caste both defines and makes permanent a social identity of separateness indicated in their segregated hamlet called a colony or *ceri*.[10] In the separated *ceri*, Dalit communities are not only "dirty" and "untouchable," but invisible as well (Narula 2). They are cornered and helpless when attacked in their locked-in, isolated spaces.

Race Role in Caste Differences

Ambedkar believed that one could attempt to trace racial connotations in categorizations of peoples in the principle of the *chaturvarnya* that happened around the second millennium BCE. Current discriminatory acts came about

---

institutional bodies that are dedicated to establishing national identity of India as an essentially Hindu nation have resorted to extreme measures of violence upon minority communities that include Dalits, tribal communities, Muslims and Christians.

[10] Most villages in India have separate hamlets where Dalits live. A hamlet is called "colony" or "*ceri*" [pronounced as "chaeree"] in Tamil Nadu. These segregated spaces can be accessed only through rugged pathways. Caste people do not come into Dalit colonies, and Dalits come into the caste villages or town just to perform their cleaning tasks and are not allowed to touch a caste person.

after a time when racial mixing had already happened to a great extent in India (Ambedkar 268). One cannot, however, undermine the influence of racial identity on class identities that were locked in as solidified permanency as caste categorizations. It is important to note that the end of the eighteenth century saw the rise of many theories related to the origin of caste in racial supremacy.

Sanskrit, one of the ancient languages of India and revered as a sacred language, led researchers on caste to the premise of the possible migration of Aryans from elsewhere into India bringing with them a notion of cultural and religious superiority. In his book *Prehistoric India* (1950), Stuart Piggot mentions that Coeurdoux, a French missionary, and Sir William Jones, an English administrator, published theories (in 1767 and 1786) that there are connections between the Sanskrit language and Latin and Greek (246). These theorists suggest a migration from the regions of Greece and Rome that could have happened in the past to give rise to what was called Indo-European languages. This group of languages was divided into *centum* (Celtic, Germanic, Greek, etc.) and *satem* groups (Baltic and Slavic languages such as Armenian, Iranian, and Sanskrit).

Piggot believes that etymology makes evident that there was a group of people who originated these languages, labeled by researchers as the Indo-European group (246). Researchers came up with the possible homeland of the Indo-Europeans to be South Russia and the land eastward towards the Caspian Sea. This region stretched from South Russia to Turkestan, sharing cultural characteristics with regions in Asia Minor and Mesopotamia such as nomadic sheep and cattle owners and agriculturists, with particular burial rituals and unique weapons. Piggot notes that these regions suffered the attack of mountaineers from the north and were dispersed widely into various regions including the Indus valley (245).

The presence of the names of gods in ancient diplomatic documents, from the regions of the Caspian Sea and Mesopotamia dating to about the fourteenth and fifteenth centuries BCE, suggests the connections between the Gods of ancient India such as *Indra, Mitra,* and *Varuna* mentioned in the *Rig Veda,* the earliest Hindu scripture (1300-1000 BCE). The *Avesta* in Persia and the *Rig Veda* in India, which linguistically belonged to the same period, are the earliest documents that provide insights into these ancient civilizations. The *Rig Veda* is the primary source of information for historians and sociologists about the life and culture of the Aryans in the second millennium BCE or even prior to that because of the practice of oral tradition that was transcribed centuries later. It contains over one thousand hymns that are chants, praise, and prayers which are highly metrical. The main culture reflected in the *Rig Veda* is that of the Aryans or *Arya* ("pure") who "figure as conquerors in a newly won land" (Piggot 259). The narratives depict Aryans as heroic figures whose chief God is *Indra*, the leader of their conquest. It mentions the aspirations and the lifestyle of a society claimed as upper-class, which had a form of social stratification based on one's occupation or duty.

Historians such as Zenaide A. Ragozin (1835-1924) suggest that there were primarily two races that competed for survival in ancient India: Aryans and Dravidians. Some archeologists and historians state that the original inhabitants of the Indus area were the Dravidians. In his book, *The Story of Vedic India* published in 1895, Ragozin confirms that the Aryan settlers who spread widely into the northern regions of India lived very tightly protected lives guarding the race against the indigenous inhabitants (54). The *Rig Veda* serves as Ragozin's primary source of sociological information that the Dravidians lived in the Vindhya regions of India prior to the coming of the Aryans. The Dravidians were scattered throughout the regions surrounding the Vindhya and covered the entire Dekhan plateau region in the South. Writing on the features of Dravidian life and customs, Ragozin states that they lived in small communities in villages and were hardworking traders and farmers. The *Rig Veda* refers to them as *Dasyu,* or "demon slaves," while the Aryans are referred to as the *Arya* (Ragozin 55).

The *Rig Veda* describes the religion of the Dravidians as barbarous since they believed in goblins and spirits. They worshipped the earth as both male and female, and the snake was their chief emblem. The *Rig Veda* makes references to them as *Shishna-devas,* "whose God is *Shishna* or *Shesh* (snake)" (Ragozin 293). In the *Rig Veda*, the battle between the Aryan god *Indra* and the Dravidian snake god *Ahi* always ends with the victory of Indra. The *Rig Veda's* poetic rendering of the battle between the Aryan champion god and the Dravidian's sacred emblem is in fact a rendering of a battle of races that is repeated time and time again as seen in the epics such as the *Ramayana* and the *Mahabharata.* The snake god was soon absorbed into the Aryan religion.

Another aspect of the native religion that made it despicable to the Aryans was the ritual of human sacrifice offered to the earth god twice a year during seeding and harvest. The Aryans condemned this practice, and they portrayed the Dravidians as demons, cannibal giants, and wizards with supernatural powers who practiced the art of evil. This image grew into monstrous proportions in Aryan legends that were passed down through generations. The Dravidians were looked upon as people to be feared, despised, and avoided, thus producing the imaginative figures of the *Rakshas* or ogres in the scriptural epics of *Ramayana* and *Mahabharata* (400-200 BCE). These characteristics came to be associated with any group of people who were different from the *Arya.* As the disruptors of the peace and serenity of the Aryan sages, the inhabitants of the land where sages chose to dwell were depicted as monstrous beings who carried away beautiful Aryan maidens and opposed the peaceful existence of the good Aryans who called themselves the friends of the *Devas* or gods. Ragozin asserts, "The *Ramayana* is full of their evil prowesses; indeed the *Raksha* clearly stand out as the main obstacle encountered by Rama in his campaign against Ceylon, which embodies in heroic and epic guise the Aryan invasion of the South" (298). Such invasion has been mythologized as the battle between the non-human Dravidians and the gentle-souled Aryans. Ragozin affirms that it was in reality an "honest sturdy hand-to-hand conflict between bona-fide human, mortal champions," which the *Rig Veda* converted into a timeless division of gods and demons (303).

The *Rig Veda*, according to Ragozin, records a development of social institutions such as royalty, aristocracy, priesthood, and caste hierarchy. The Aryans advanced eastward into the River Ganges and spread into the River Jamuna regions "which became the center and headquarters of the race when the Vedic era had glided and merged into the Brahmanic period" (304). The warriors traveled to various places to protect their regions from attack, while some stayed home and engaged themselves in matters of advice and counsel to these travelers and evolved into spiritual leaders, who became the Brahmin caste. The bards or poets who were called *Rishis* are said to be the earliest of the Brahmanistic proponents who composed the *Rig Veda.* They dwelt in the royal households and were looked up to for counsel; they were the *purohitas.* These kinds of religious roles as advisors were transferred into a social diplomacy that sought to use religious power and counsel to rule the people. Ragozin suggests, "All this shows us the institution of the castes in a novel and most natural, convincing light as a reaction, on the part of the strictly orthodox worshippers (Aryans) of Agni (fire) and Soma (plant/earth)" (304). He proposes that the natives who converted into the Aryan spirituality were admitted only on the condition of occupying a subordinate position, that of the *Shudras*, the fourth caste. One could infer from this thesis that those natives who opposed the Aryan spirituality were the outcastes, who were forced to be the *Dasyu.* Ragozin establishes the position of the Dravidians as demons from the perspective of the Aryans, which suggest that good and evil were racial entities. A discussion of sections from the *Manusmriti* and the epics of the *Ramayana* and *Mahabharata* in the next chapter will elucidate the conflict between dominant groups and "different" groups.

Ragozin points to the fact that caste division is mentioned by name only once in the entire *Rig Veda,* but the distinction between the Aryans and the Dravidians is mentioned several times. The word for caste is *Varna* or color, which again is evidence that the social division was based on race. Ragozin points out that the Dravidians were dark-skinned whereas the Aryans were fair-skinned. The word *Dasyu* is an old Aryan word that the Persians used just to denote nations or peoples; it was used to refer to the peoples of the land that the Aryans came into and then took on meanings such as dark-skinned, fiends, evil demons, powers of darkness, and eventually, slaves or servants, signifying the completion of conquest (304-305).

Etymologist Gustav Oppert (1836-1908) researched and wrote extensively on Dravidians in his work, *On the Original Inhabitants of Bharatvarsa or India: The Dravidians* (1988). He argues that Dravidians were the original inhabitants of the Indus region and that Dalits are the descendants of this race (12-22).[11] He based his study on the origin and development of certain Telugu (a South Indian language) words used by Dalits and used earlier to refer to Dalits. Aryans who came into the land found the Dravidians to be physically remarkably different from them. They taunted the Dravidians for their color and their flat noses, and depicted them with faces that looked like they did not have noses. Oppert mentions that scriptures used the word *Dasyu* to refer to the Dravidians who proved to be rebellious and courageous against the Aryans.

Oppert uses etymology to prove the connection of the Dravidians to Dalits. For example, the word *Malla* now refers to a Dalit community in the state of Andhra Pradesh, and Oppert traces this word in the Hindu scriptures where it is used to refer to Dravidian communities. This name was used by Aryans to form a religious coalition with the Dravidians by naming their god *Marici,* a variation of *Malla. Marici* is said to be the predecessor of *Rakshas. Malla* translates as "the hills," and hence the Dravidians residing in the hills came to be called *Malla.* Oppert points out the reference to *Malla* in the *Ramayana* and the *Mahabharata* as territories in the North. In addition, he finds more than one hundred words that refer to Dalits today such as *Maadiga, Paraiah, Pallar,* and *Mahar* that trace their origins in the Indus valley among the Dravidian communities, and these words reveal Aryan relations and perceptions of the Dravidians.

The archeological surveys undertaken by Sir John Marshall and Ernest Mackay between 1922 and 1931 exploded the Aryan myth that the Dravidians were barbaric monsters. Dr. Sarvepalli Radhakrishnan (1888-1975), who represented Indian philosophy in the West in the mid twentieth century, states that the Aryans found the natives of India who opposed their advance to be uncivi-

---

[11] Gustav Oppert was born in Hamburg, Germany, and lived, learned, and taught in India in the Presidency College in Chennai. Oppert's research is primarily based on the use of language. The historical and social context for certain words has helped him track civilizations that used specific words. Oppert extensively engages with the social customs and practices of the Aryans and Dravidians as evident in his findings.

lized as they ate beef and indulged in goblin worship (1923, 118). However, the excavations undertaken by Marshall on either side of the Indus river, which empties itself in the Arabian Sea in the northeast of the Indian continent (now in the Pakistan region above Gujarat), revealed a civilization much more advanced than that of the Aryan nomads. These cities discovered were Mohanjedaro and Harrapa. Anthropologist Jeanene Fowler reports that these civilizations could be placed around 2500-1500 BCE. She argues that there were exchanges of ideas and lifestyles between the Aryan and Dravidian communities (1197, 93). Stanley Wolpert, writing on Indus culture, states that these names suggest a Dravidian origin of these civilizations. For example, Harappa may be derived from *Haran,* meaning Civan (god), and *Appa* is the supreme father. This *Civan* of the Dravidians later was transformed into *Shiva* of the Aryans (2000, 14-23). The Dravidians had organized forms of culture and society even though they did not have the weapons and diplomacy that the Aryans possessed. The Aryans' claim to supremacy was established through their religion, whose gods were shown to be more civilized than the fierce gods of the Dravidians, and through their advanced weaponry.

Based on his readings of the *Rig Veda,* Wolpert states that during the pre-Aryan days the Dravidian society had classifications associated with occupations. However, people could choose their occupations, and no one occupation was considered inferior to another; and, there was social mobility. As mentioned earlier, the Aryans adapted this into a social division based on occupation which evolved into a rigid and stagnant caste system. Later came the *Varnashrama,* the classification based on color (*varna* = color, *ashrama*=style of life). The four castes came to be established. The lowest caste Shudras were the Dravidians who did not oppose occupational hierarchy, and the ones who opposed were classified as the *panchamas* (fifths) who were subject to open oppression (Wolpert 14-23).

Furthermore, *Puran`an`ooru*, one of the eight ancient idylls of the Tamil language (another ancient language of India dating from c. 300 BCE), is a compilation of four hundred verses written by various authors of the time.[12] According to the English translation provided by Dr. V. Saminathaiya, a lyric written by Paandiyan Nedunchezhiyan says this about the society at that stage:

> Learning of letters is good notwithstanding the strenuous efforts involved. Among those born in one and the same family (of the low grade) it is only [the] learned one with marked intelligence is welcomed and respected by the society and he will be one who commands respect from his mother. Further, the

---

[12] *Puran`an`ooru* translated from Tamil to English by Dr. V. Saminathaiya in 1955 is the earliest translation and closest to the original ancient idylls.

> king himself would seek the sagacious counsel of the wise to
> run his state. (Saminathaiya 183)

Another poem from the same collection says:

> The Thudiyan (the herald), the Paanan (the wandering min-
> strel), the Paraiyann (announcer, drum player) and Kadamban
> (a flower found in the mountain regions used to worship the
> God, Murugan) are regarded as base members of the society
> and were thrown out of the society as outcastes. (Saminathaiya
> 335)

Thus developed the belief that a hierarchical caste system was in place which
excluded certain peoples as "dirty base members." To the detriment of the Dravidian woman in particular, this system was sanctioned in the *Manusmriti*. This
social hierarchy locked in by religion worked to the convenience of colonizers
who thrived on the social disunity among their subjects.

Religious and Political Colonialisms

Historians have pointed out that caste ideology as a system or structure
emerged after external powers of hierarchy such as the Portuguese, German,
Moghul, French, and British were present in India. The colonial presence
viewed caste as a phenomenon that could work to their advantage of defraying
a possible unified effort among the natives. Nicholas B. Dirks argues that the
ruling powers in India intensified caste-based stigmatizations. He employs
historical documentations of European and Moghul travelers and merchants
who mention caste as an anomalous phenomenon that describes people rather
than identifying them as a separate category. Dirks claims that it was the foreign interpretations of a loosely existent social pattern that made caste an emphatic orderly structure and gave it a politically autocratic characteristic (19).

Dirks provides information on Christian missionaries who used caste to
their advantage in promoting their propaganda for equality in Christianity as
opposed to the inequality in Hinduism. The British encouraged missionaries
such as Abbe Dubois to conduct more surveys and write more reports on caste
divisions. Dirks states that the strict divisions of the Hindu society were attested and propagated by scholars and British officials of his time and later times
such as A.D. Campbell and Max Muller (21-24). The distinction he made with
caste as a civil institution served as a base for the later political connivances or
fundamentalist approaches that certain sects of Hinduism saw possible in caste.
Dirks further points out that Dubois was highly impressed with the adherence
to the ancient scriptures in the civil society in India; he views this lack of as a
serious flaw in Christianity.

Dirks informs us that colonial presence made it possible for extensive research on caste and provided colonial archives on caste used by rulers. Castes that were scattered were numbered and assigned specific identifications based on empirical research. The objectification of caste ended up in a reification of caste as a structure of which even the Indians were unaware. Some examples Dirks provides are of historian Francis Buchanan employed by the East India Company who conducted his survey in the Mysore region in 1800, which was followed by Collin Mackenzie's survey in 1847. Dirks states:

> Colonial knowledge was far more powerful than the colonial state ever was (a very different balance of power from that which existed in metropolitan forms of governmentality); and thus the colonial documentation project encoded British anxiety that rule was always dependent on knowledge, even as it performed that rule throughout the gathering and application of knowledge. (123)

For Dirks, colonial knowledge was the foundation for linking epistemological and political power that happened in the mid and late nineteenth century due to colonial surveys. Each caste that now clearly placed a demarcation on rigid identities started claiming territorial power, and the anti-Brahmanic wave started emerging in the late nineteenth century. Community conflicts were on the rise along with colonial reports; political parties were being formed against those perpetrating Brahmanism as was evident in the establishment of the Justice Party in Madras in 1916, and they spread throughout India as a movement (Dirks 238). Dirks traces linkages between traditions, power, colonial ideology, native religious ideology, and history. The current Indian stereotyping of caste identities, however, is rooted in a traditional national imagination that colonists simply used to their benefit. I determine that the figurations of Dravidian women in traditional Indian thought are the main internal source of the current stigmatization of and violence upon Dalit women, and caste differences were further exacerbated by politicization of caste identities as colonial strategies. The devaluation of those different has been filtered through and affected by the objectification of Indian society by the imposition of ideas from external powers as well. National leaders like Gandhi, in turn, made use of colonial divisive conniving to settle for leaving caste structure and Dalits "untouched" in political discourses.

Christianity Attempts to Bridge "Difference"

The arrival of Christianity in India played a major role in questioning caste. Dalits were converting in large numbers to Christianity during the late nineteenth and early twentieth centuries as a result of colonialism, and at the same time—when modernity provided new ways of thinking—the West was deeply influenced by the writings of Marx and Freud. Marx's concept of alienation or estrangement spoke to the predicament of the common people under capitalism in the industrialized world and the colonies. The anti-caste movements in India increasingly adopted Marxist ideas. In her research on the Dalit movement, Omvedt makes the important observation that in the 1960s, the exploiters of the outcaste and the tribal communities identified the Naxalite movement in Bihar as a terrorist group for adopting Marxist ideas in demanding justice (Omvedt 11). Ambedkar, however, believed that class struggle leaves caste out, and he distinguished between the economic sphere and the religious sphere. Omvedt states that by the 1970s, caste was emphasized more as a "cultural/ideological factor" based on religion (25). And soon there developed a class-caste approach which examined the close ties between caste and occupation and the denial of economic rights within that structure.

The recognition of the ideological power of caste as vested in religion became the primary reason for mass conversions among Dalit communities, evident in the late nineteenth century as well. It was in the hope of embracing a new order of social life that Dalits converted to Christianity and other religions such as Islam, Sikhism, and most importantly, Buddhism (Kanmony 203). Christian missionaries who came to India even as early as the fifteenth century, however, came with little understanding of the complexities of an ancient structure of social hierarchy in Hindu epistemology. Their underestimation of the political nature of social stratification in India and their simplistic understanding of a complex structure proved to be major flaws in their attempts to convert Indians to Christianity. The assumption that providing Dalits with food, education, and—added into the bargain—a new religion would change a society proved to be wrong. Few Dalit communities benefitted from such social openings. While on the one hand, the British were opening schools for Dalits, they were relegating power to the already elite castes, thus maintaining an oppressive structure. Most Dalits readily accepted what they were offered through conversion: dignity and an escape from dehumanization. But, even the few Dalits who are able to move out of their segregated colonies due to their Christian education face structural hurdles, including being stereotyped as incapable.

Conversion was a means of western ideological and imperial conquest, but it provided to some Dalits a human dignity through education and acceptance into a religious structure. They learned to read and write in a language foreign to them and to their internal colonizer: Brahmin. They were able to interact with white missionaries, while they were forbidden to do so with caste people. Dalit women's contact with white women missionaries especially thrilled them because white women assumed superiority over Brahmin women. Holding a book—the Bible—in their hands and communicating with a culture associated with power seemed liberating from centuries of exclusion by Hinduism. Dalits understandably settled for this improvement in their situation, as they gained education along with room for courageous audacity (skipping the step stool of confidence) in their recognition as human beings through the missionary movement. This was a major factor in the beginnings of Dalit women's visibility (Govindarajan 155).

British rule in India thrived because of their alliance with the elite among caste groups who worked in collaboration with the British in setting up a regime that would allow privileges for the select few. One of the reasons why this acquiescence turned to antagonism was the direction of British policies towards open education for all and, therefore, open opportunities for all. The British did follow their own agenda of investing in such policies, but the Indian National Congress was formed in 1885 as a counter movement to prevent this open accessibility of privileges. Another major reason was that the British represented a western religion, another ethos that had started questioning some of the fundamentals of social practices related to the Hindu culture (Aloysius 105-106). While colonialism is subject to severe scrutiny from postcolonial writers who have claimed convenient social positions outside of India, nationalists who vehemently still practice the colonial paradigm thrive on an internally oppressive structure.

If colonialism proved to be destructive to a nation's ethos, the freedom from such colonial power for more than half a century now is resulting in massive self-destruction due to internal strife. The two religious cultures of Hinduism and Islam have developed extremely violent expressions of ideologies into strong counter powers claiming territorial and social identities. The bloodshed over Ayodhya in 1996 and the gory violence between Hindus and Muslims that erupted in Gujarat in 2002 are manifestations of a projected fear of an inherent power that might explode from minority communities. Writing on "Confronting Empire," activist Arundhati Roy alleges that this violence is the result of an imperialist empire in the incarnation of an "ultra-nationalist Hindu guild" (Roy, *War Talk* 104). She reports that during the Gujarat violence, the economic base of an entire Muslim community was destroyed (105). Both the Ayodhya case and the Gujarat case are examples of violence perpetrated by organized, armed, and politically powerful groups to achieve political ends and economic domination by punishing minority groups.

The minority religious groups comprise mostly tribal communities and Dalits for whom mostly mass conversion strategies are clear subversive social statements rather than just a religious conversion. The mass conversion of a whole Dalit village in Tamil Nadu near Tirunelveli in March 1981 to Islam, and the additional one hundred and fifty Dalits renouncing Hinduism near Ramanathapuram in Tamil Nadu shortly thereafter are concrete examples of such social statements claiming their human rights and freedom from an "oppressive Hinduism" (Venkatesan, *The Hindu*, Oct 20, 2002). If India claims to be a secular country, then certainly mass conversions to Christianity, Islam, and Buddhism should be viewed as a process against the denial of human dignity and social mobility within the conservatism of Hinduism.

As Dhananjay Keer records, Ambedkar professed, "I was born a Hindu but I will never die a Hindu" (252). He converted to Buddhism in 1956 along with a mass of the Mahar (Dalit) community in Maharashtra. Zelliott states, "Buddhism offered scriptural justification for worth achieved by mind and action, not by birth" (12). Of course, the gender-based and sexual orientation-based issues and self-righteous attitudes of the fundamental expressions of each of these religions are now questionable and does make it problematic to present them as counter movements to the evolved manifestation of Hinduism. However, one has to mention the mass conversions among Dalits from colonial days until now. While Hindu nationalists saw British authority as an overarching supremacy, Dalits saw it as an external power that created viable social and economic spaces for them. The much-critiqued railways and roadways of colonialism were in fact symbolically important new institutions that hired Dalits for "dignified" jobs as against their traditionally assigned tasks of dealing with polluted matter.

Whether Dalits were allured by education is not the concern here. Instead, the fact that for the first time, education was made available to them during the colonial rule is of great significance; the social and economic benefit was rightfully a central attraction for Dalits. The influx of white missionaries, who symbolized power, provided the first external voices against caste in the eighteenth century. In the late nineteenth century, a time when dominant-caste women gaining education was still a fashionable new phenomenon, Dalit women could access highly advanced education in British schools in India and could dialogue with British men and women. Caste as a paradigm was beginning to be questioned with such external intrusions of engagement with power and authority. Though a handful of Dalits did achieve social mobility with education and a dignified job during the missionary movement in colonial India, the mass of the population continues to live in such socially and economically degrading conditions (Narula 1). These conditions exist because structural changes did not happen, and those who eagerly converted out of Hinduism were soon disillusioned by the infiltration of caste discriminations in other religions as well.

Political leaders driven by fundamentalist ideals consider those who convert to other religions as traitors who allow themselves to be seduced.

Punished for Conversion

It is important to consider the cultural trend to punish transgression in any form, including conversion. Politicians today want to maintain the traditional structures of brand-naming India as a Hindu country where maintenance of differences should be nursed and threats to social and economic segregation should be rooted out. Therefore, ordinances against conversion from Hinduism have been implemented in several states at several points in time in independent India. The states of Tamil Nadu, Gujarat, Madhya Pradesh, Arunachal Pradesh, and Orissa specifically implemented such efforts against conversion in 2002. In 2014, India returned vehemently to the idea that such ordinances against conversion could reduce an oppositional political majority among the minority groups and stop the economic viability of Dalits within the religious structures they embrace. Dalits reject Hinduism and convert to other religions in large numbers. Radha Venkatesan writing for *The Hindu* newspaper in Tamil Nadu records a history of conversion as a form of protest. She quotes Dalit activists who raise the question, "When I am not given the right to offer worship in Hindu Temples, how can the government force us to remain? First, let the government stop the exploitation by caste Hindus and then prevent exploitation by religious fundamentalists" (Venkatesan, *The Hindu* Oct 20, 2002, 17). Despite the joint efforts of leaders from various minority groups, the abovementioned states implemented these ordinances. Jayalalitha, then the Chief Minister of Tamil Nadu and a Brahmin by birth, formed coalitions with the Bharatiya Janata Party (BJP), a Hindu fundamentalist nationalist political party. According to her ordinance, the penalty for conversion should be doubled if it involved a Dalit, whether converting or causing conversion (*The Hindu* Dec 17, 2002). Such ordinances are dangerous experimentations that most certainly sanction major communal violence and further damage vulnerable Dalit communities the most.

The Bharatya Janata Party (BJP, a political party associated with instating principles and practice of Hindutva), under the leadership of Narendra Modi as the Prime Minister of India, declared a national movement, *Ghar Vapsi* ("Return Home"). This a national call for those Hindus who have converted to any other religion to come back to Hinduism, assuring them safety and economic benefits. *The Hindu* has extensively covered news stories of nationwide responses to this call. People are reverting out of fear; the Government doles out welfare benefits to those who remain in their outcaste status as Hindu.[13] *The Hindu* reports that in the state of Kerala, a family in Alappuzha re-converted to Hinduism to acquire the benefits of reservations, which is allocation of job positions and placements in educational institutions for Dalits. This family converted to become Pentecostal Christians but have now been declared Hindus after a ritual in a temple. The Vishva Hindu Parishad (VHP), a sector of RSS, is helping them in the social and religious identity reinstatement process (George 1). In the same village, thirty Christians from eight families are reported to have reconverted to Hinduism from Christianity. The VHP declares that this was voluntary, and they were not forced or allured in any way (George 1). A few days later, says VHP, eleven Muslims reconverted to Hinduism.

Efforts to threaten those who do not conform to a dominant religious ideology and astute political measures to reinstate religious ordinances define a religious and cultural internment. It is imperative to take these nationalist religious movements into serious consideration as they repeat processes of punishments as impositions of religious and social power upon people who need to adhere to and remain within branded social and economic spaces and religiously sanctioned cultural identities. In "Purity and pollution: Dalit woman within India's religious colonialism," I state that Indian nationalism is a phenomenon that has "amalgamated political, historical, and sociological movements in building a nation founded on religious consciousness" (Singh 79-80). Social punishments as cultural rituals on women's bodies confirm the existence of a structure of exclusion and hostility towards specific groups of people within realms of culture and religion. Those considered "dirty" do not matter but are punishable if entering social and cultural spaces reserved for the "clean." Purity signifies power as that which is divine and can relegate meanings to practices, rituals, and interpretations of scriptures. Religion, as an institutionalized system of beliefs and the most powerful force in the world today which sanctions both creation and destruction, has become the machinery for masculinist sexual and gender politics. Within that spatiality of religion controlled by the male, that which is culturally private—namely the woman's body—becomes culturally public when religion and culture are kneaded together. The public sphere of politics, either social or cultural, becomes localized into private spheres to suit the needs of the dominant caste to execute ordinances of punishment.

---

[13] My caste identity in my high school leaving documents state that I am an "Indian Christian" under "Caste category" which otherwise would have remained "Scheduled Caste." Conversion from Hinduism to Christianity does not make a Dalit eligible for government "benefits" such as special quotas for Dalits in college admissions and jobs.

CHAPTER THREE

Spotted Goddesses Subvert "Difference": Traditional Narratives and Punishment Ordinances

The social position of Dalit women is a sub-gendered state that forces them into spaces where they are rendered invisible and powerless as women, Dalit, and economically poor. The expressions of *earthy humanness* I engage with in this book are embedded in Dalit women who claim positive identities, rich culture, and leadership capacities. However, the fact that women from several broken communities in India are subject to ridicule, violence, and rape in a continuum with traditional norms of punishing the "different" should not be ignored. Common habitual, cultural perceptions and treatment of the "different" woman were configured as sanctioned traditional figurations in oral traditions of storytelling and recorded in written forms as epics around the second millennium BCE, which later came to be associated with Hinduism. I write this chapter with no purpose to disregard religious values of devotees towards traditional narratives placed within Hinduism. I discuss three traditional narratives—*Manusmriti*, *Ramayana*, and *Mahabharata*—only in these aspects: informing the reader about cultural, representational paradigms of "different" women who are outside dominant communities and an appropriation of these narratives by dominant communities as sacred roots to a tradition of punishing these women.

It is necessary to explore self-presentational, positive images of Dalit women to consider ways in which their bodies, minds, and morality continue to be distorted by dominant appropriations of traditional narratives. Dalit women provide a myriad of Dalit cultural symbols in their narratives, demonstrating a need to acknowledge a positive image of the self as trans-figuration in the midst of centuries of social rejection. Trans-figuration is the social and cultural process by which women like Kalai and Rani live into the reality of "difference" as fierce rebels claiming justice in subverting traditional figurations as "different" women who had to be tamed to submission. They are women wild with passion for social change, blasting through dominant forces.

Sanctioned Figurations of "Different" Women

Skewed appropriations of traditional narratives have shaped cultural notions and behavior based on religious thought in countries like India. I explain how images of "different" women ensure normalization of violence against women and all those who do not fit into the caste-based cultural and religious norms of a good and pure woman.

"Untouchable" in *Manusmriti*

The *Manusmriti* or *Laws of Manu* originates in a belief in the primordial man, Manu, the first man after the world was reborn. In traditional belief, Manu is an avatar of Brahma who befriends a fish that saves his life in a deluge, ending in Manu starting a new life on a mountain top along with seven priests. His recordings of the revelations of Brahma are the origins of *Manusmriti,* as Manu is "the wise one" or "of the human race," and *Smriti* is "a memorized tradition or direct revelation" in the Sanskritized rendition. The laws were put into code around 250 BCE based on the belief that the world is destroyed and reborn every four billion years. In 2,685 verses *Manusmriti* lays tenets and laws for each caste to strictly follow for every single activity (Edmonds 24-25). Religious studies scholar Louis Renou characterizes *Manusmriti* as "Indian juridical theory … on religious rules, institutions, customs and ethical precepts which dominate an individual's existence" (116). The book draws rules for observances of specific practices and behavior for certain rites and relationships such as birth, death, puberty, marital relations, menstruation, social relations, eating habits, and much more.

Wendy Doniger and Brian Smith, who translated the *Manusmriti* into English as *The Laws of Manu* (1991), characterize the laws as "encompassing representation of life in the world—how it is and how it should be lived" (xvii). The *Dharma* (religious duty) of every human being stated in the text provides authoritative base for the evolution of culture and tradition. They emphasize that stratifications in the *Manusmriti* of what is pure are based on perfection—namely, the priest (Brahmin) is considered the purest paradigmatic human being and is therefore perfect. Doniger's introduction to her translation starts with two epigraphs, one from *Apastamba*—an ancient *veda* (scripture)—and the other by Friedrich Nietzsche. As seen in the epigraphs, while *Apastamba* qualifies the *Manusmriti* as the natural law of religious order, Nietzsche sees such religious laws of stratification based on purity being absorbed deeper into the unconsciousness of people who live out the ideals. The *Ramayana* and *Mahabharata*, the two great epics of the Hindu tradition that were written a few centuries later, are documentations that the people had to live by the rules of the *Manusmriti.*

Manusmriti sets moral and territorial boundaries for the "pure" and the "dirty," thereby separating categories of people wherein the outcaste is named *candalla* or "fierce untouchable" who just did not fit into Brahma's plans for creating humanity.[14] Dalit women are "polluted," the lowest creatures among the *candalla,* contaminating anyone who comes into contact with them. *Manusmriti* dehumanizes a Dalit woman in its references to the "fierce untouchable" woman as being on par with wild animals (referred to as derogatory). I discuss two objectifications of Dalit women as portrayed in the *Manusmriti*: pollution and curse. In relegating unclean work, the *Manusmriti* declares her "polluted" and hence, she embodies a curse; Brahmins should dread Dalit women as the cause of a curse.

Pollution and Curse

The comparison of the states of pollution of a caste woman and a Dalit woman is evident in the following passages from the *Manusmriti:*

> When there is a miscarriage, (a woman) becomes clean after the same number of nights as the months (since conception), and a menstruating woman becomes clean by bathing after the bleeding has stopped. 5.66. (106). If a man has touched a 'Notorious by day,' Untouchable, a menstruating woman, anyone who has just given birth, a corpse, or anyone who has touched any of these objects, he can be cleaned by a bath. 5.85. (107).[15]

A caste woman moves in and out of pollution and purity depending on the biological functions of her body. While the *Manusmriti* provides sanctions for the caste woman to be able to regain her purity once her biological functions are completed, a Dalit woman remains stagnant in her state of pollution. Furthermore, she is reduced to the polluted matter that renders a caste woman "untouchable" during that period of time, and a Dalit woman is not be touched at *any time.* Such transference between body, matter, and ideas is only made possible by ordaining traditional narratives as dominant discourses with unquestionable authority.

---

[14] The word *candalla* is often used as a curse word adapted into Tamil with a derogatory meaning of "traitor" or "betrayer."

[15] Quotes from the *Manusmriti* are cited from Wendy Doniger and Brain K. Smith's translation, *The Laws of Manu,* 1991.

The following passages from the *Manusmriti* describe the consequences of touching an untouchable woman:

> If a priest unknowingly has sex with 'Fierce' Untouchable women or very low-caste women, eats (their food) or accepts (gifts from them), he falls, if knowingly, he becomes their equal. 11.177. (268)
>
> A double fine should be imposed on a man who has already been convicted (again) and is accused again within a year, and it should be just as much for cohabiting with a woman outlaw or a "Fierce Untouchable" woman. 8.373. (192)
>
> A priest killer gets the womb of a dog, a pig, a donkey, a camel, a cow, a goat, a sheep, a wild animal, a bird, a 'Fierce' Untouchable, or a 'Tribal.' 12.55. (283)

In the *Manusmriti,* a Dalit woman will cause the downfall of a caste person as the reification of curse. The caste person who has intimate relations with her becomes "untouchable" because she pollutes their purity and destroys chances of salvation. Due to the perception that she is an active participant in making the curse effective, she is not considered a victim when raped. In the propositions of the *Manusmriti*, if a Dalit woman is a willing participant in sexual relations with a Brahmin, she disrobes and displaces him. Nevertheless, she is the brute whether she is the victim or not, and her body as the curse becomes the premise of victimization of which caste males need to beware. However, the *Manusmriti* does not state that the untouchable woman could gain redemption in sexual relations with a caste male embodying "purity." Instead, the "dirty" woman will pollute a priest and remain in a state of pollution as a permanent condition of punishment. A Dalit woman is stagnant in her polluted state as "a curse" and "the cursed" as she cannot recess into anything worse or become anything better.

Manusmriti equates the womb of a Dalit woman with that of pigs, dogs, camels, cows, goat, sheep, wild animals, and birds. She is considered doubly vile as she procreates polluted, vile creatures in her womb as the site of pollution. She becomes the banished wanderer—the woman in exile—the carrier of biological and spiritual plague who is to remain untouchable and unseen. A caste male is strong, but she is the lowliest monster awaiting to devour his purity. Such spiritual ambiguity is evident in the very rudiments of ordained practices with regard to the "clean" and "dirty." Her body and mind are negated as dispensable, and hence, violation of her body should not matter as it is a space of "nothingness": she holds nothing worthy of consideration, pity, or protection. *Manusmriti* carefully places a Dalit woman within constrictions that will break her to the point where redemption is not an option and she should accept her fate as "curse" and "cursed." Imprisoned within religious order boundaries, she is the "wanderer" with no particular place to stay, but paradigmatically, she is the "stagnant wanderer," with no external territorial movement or inner spiritual movement since there is no seemingly necessary reason for such movement. A Dalit woman is a fateful victim who should not be concerned with questions of loss of status or identity.

Similarly, Dalit women are the antithesis to everything that is pure, sacred, and redemptive churned into a formulation of religious tenets, the ground on which the pure should not tread; and, the grounds of her exile become spaces of danger and foreboding. Within those spaces of exile, she is expected to become weaker as her polluted nature will intensify. Her body and the territory of her exile become critical locations that should be pointed to as interchangeable and interdependent in any efforts to claim de-colonization from such a state.

The Epic Narratives in *Ramayana* and *Mahabharata*

The epic of *Ramayana* written by the sage Valmiki around 400-200 BCE, starts with a description of Ayodhya revered as the birthplace of Rama, an incarnation of Vishnu (the God revered in the Hindu tradition of faith as the one who protects creation). He is Kshatriya by caste, born to King Dasaratha of Ayodhya who banishes Rama to the forest and is later saddened by his own act. He submits to Rama's stepmother's claim to the throne for her son, Bharata. Rama, along with his new wife, Sita, and his brother Lakshmana live in the forest of Panchami. This forest is inhabited by *Raksha* (ogres), a popular portrayal of the indigenous people of these regions in traditional oral and written narratives. War ensues between the *Raksha* and the Kshatriyas because of the instigation of the Brahmin sages who consider the *Raksha* a hindrance to fulfill their *yagas* or penance. Due to the kidnapping of Sita by Ravana, a *Raksha* king, a battle ensues developing into a war between good and evil forces, with Rama representing the former and the *Raksha* representing the latter. The epic ends with Rama defeating Ravana, rescuing Sita, and becoming King; doubting Sita's chastity, he banishes her and returns to heaven as his god-self Vishnu.[16]

The *Mahabharata*, written around 500 BCE, is the longest poetic epic ever written. The authorship is attributed to the Sage Krishna-Dwaipayana Vyasa as a treatise on life inclusive of religion, family, politics, and salvation. The main theme is the rivalry between two families: the Pandavas (five brothers) and the Kauravas (one hundred brothers). The Pandavas are in exile in the forest be-

---

[16] The story is summarized from my reading of the Tamil rendition of *Ramayana* by Kambar popularly known as *Kamba Ramayanam.* He lived c. 1180-1250. The epic is said to be written in the 12th century BC.

cause they lose a gambling match. The episode of concern for discussion in this chapter takes place while the Pandavas are in exile near Indraprasta, a kingdom in the Northern regions of India. The whole epic is noted for heroic characters such as Arjuna, the third of the Pandava brothers and considered the protagonist of the *Mahabharata*, and Lord Krishna. Apart from establishing family loyalties, this epic is filled with a mixture of grace, piety, love, violence, and revenge moving towards the ultimate goal of peace and reconciliation. While the *Mahabharata* is acclaimed to be a sacred history containing traditions, ethics, and philosophy, it is about the struggle of "good" against "evil." Some aspects of "evil" are shown to dwell in human characters such as Dhu`shana, but the *Raksha* take on the personification of evil itself. The *Raksha* appear throughout the epic as the evil forces that the Pandavas encounter in the forest. Each encounter becomes a symbolic battle of good versus evil.[17]

Section CLIV of the *Mahabharata* narrates a story about a *Raksha* named Hidimvà and his sister Hidimvà as well. Vyasa describes Hidimvà as a cannibal who sees the Pandava brothers sleeping in his woods. He longs to eat them and sends his sister ("female cannibal") to slaughter them; she falls in love with one of the Pandavas—Bhima. She changes her body into a "beautiful" maiden and warns Bhima of the impending danger to his family's life due to her brother. She promises to save him if he will fulfill her "lust" for him; Bhima refuses and agrees to face the brother Hidimva. A fierce battle ensues, and Bhima kills Hidimva. Due to the persistent desire of the sister Hidimvà, he agrees to marry her in her human form under a time contract during which she bears him a son. I discuss more details on this episode later in this chapter.

"Difference" as Evil

Ramayana illustrates the existent paradigms of social relations between those who are made to fit into cultural molds of "good" and "evil" parallel to those considered "pure" and "dirty." The *Raksha* King Ravana's father was Brahman, and his mother was *Daitya,* whose traditionally identified evil characteristics come to stay in Ravana rather than admirable Brahmanical characteristics. In Hindu mythology, the *Daitya* are demonic spirits born to the gods *Diti* and *Kasyappa,* who follow the commands of the serpent dragon *Vritra* who opposes the Brahmin sages and their rituals (Mittal 65). The *Daitya* are equivalent to demons (Gupta 84). Valmiki depicts Ravana along with his brothers and sisters in demonic forms as those who are "evil" because they abandoned Brahman-

---

[17] My summary is influenced primarily by my reading of the English rendition *The Mahabharata* by Romesh C. Dutt (1911). In addition, I refer to the Tamil summary of *Mahabharata* by Chitra Krishnan (2010).

ism, possibly following images disseminated through a traditional oral narrative. Asuras' dark-skinned bodies and arrogant ethics serve as antithesis to Rama's defined grace and goodness, and make them a natural target for ridicule and animosity. For example, Valmiki depicts Ravana who is the villain in the story of *Ramayana* as physically strong, with ten heads, and twenty shoulders and arms. He rules one thousand and eight territories and is granted the boon to rule them for one hundred and eight *yugas* or eras. Ravana's sister, Soorpanakha, is described as the dark and ugly *Rakshasi* filled with lust (Raj 101).[18]

Valmiki took great care to reveal to the reader the popularized figurations of monsters through oral narratives as those without morals, beauty, virtue, or honor. One thousand years after Valmiki, Kambar, a Tamil poet, wrote a more elaborate version of the *Ramayana* in Tamil (ancient Dravidian language) as the war between the races. However, translators such as Chakravarti Rajagopalcahari establish the *Ramayana* as the "tale of the Lord and his consort born as mortals, experiencing human sorrow and establishing *Dharma* on earth…. And Brahma's words have come true…. As long as the mountains stand and the rivers flow so long shall the *Ramayana* be cherished among men and save them from sin" (Rajagopalachari 16).[19] The epic is considered holy, establishing the power and suffering of the divine as potent against demonic powers. Paula Richman, exploring the diversity of the *Ramayana* tradition in *Many Ramayanas,* comments on the influence of the epic on the religious sentiments of the people revealed in the worshipping of TV sets when the epic *Ramayana* was telecast as a TV series in 1987.[20] She quotes Philip Lutgendorf, a scholar of the *Ramayana* tradition narrated in Hindi, saying:

> The *Ramayana* serial had become the most popular program ever shown on Indian Television–and something more: an event, a phenomenon of such proportions that intellectuals and policy makers struggled to come to terms with its significance and long-range import. Never before had such a large percent-

---

[18] *Dalitology* by M.C. Raj (Tumkur: Ambedkar Resource Center, 2001) is a pioneering voluminous book, one of the first such consolidated discourses on the origins of Dalit consciousness and the future of the Dalit Movement in India. Raj is widely published and engages with western theories on oppression as proposed by Franz Fanon. Raj and his wife Jothi are the founders and directors of Rural Education for Development Society (REDS) in Tumkur, Karnataka.

[19] C. Rajagopalachari. *Ramayana* (Bombay: Bharatya Vidya Bhavan, 1990) is an English translation of the Tamil version of *Kamba Ramayanam* by poet Kambar.

[20] In her introduction, "The Diversity of the *Ramayana* Tradition," Paula Richman lays out the plurality of the epic in terms of the various versions available and the all-pervasive nature of the epic to control the minds of its readers, listeners, and viewers.

age of South Asias' population been united in a single activity;
never before had a single message instantaneously reached so
enormous a regional audience. (3)

The epic continues to succeed in pervading the ideology of "good" against
"evil," inevitably perceived as personhood related. After several hundred years
of such religious discourse, the *Ramayana* is deeply loved as a story filled with
adventures, battles, prince, princesses, kings, queens, and monsters.

In a postcolonial feminist analysis, Rajeswari Sunderajan specifies that "the
significance of the two television serials of the epics of *Ramayana* and *Mahabharata*, whose central female figures [Sita and Draupadi] became symbols of
'our' national culture" (134). They represent the valorization of tradition and
nationalism woven around religion, morals, and virtue. Nationalism targets and
highlights religious patriotism as a struggle against the "different" in the unfor-
gettable aspect of the *Ramayana* whether in the epic itself or in its adaptations
as folktales, television serials, and theatre. Implicitly, caste communities should
choose "good" over "evil," while demons, *dasyu*, and *asura* in their traditional
portrayal as the "evil" and "different" should be controlled by punishment.

In *Dalitology* (2000), Raj discusses in detail the plight of the indigenous
rulers at the connivance of the Brahmans and Kshatriyas (99). He claims that
the indigenous communities lived in peace and were interrupted by Rama's sojourn.[21] The Aryan sages approach Rama to save them from indigenous monsters referred to as ogres. Raj states that the sages were intruders too, but the
indigenous people allowed them to stay. He quotes from Canto VI of the *Ramayana* when Rama reveals the true purpose of his sojourn: "You should not
speak to me thus. I am at the command of the ascetics. I have to enter the forest
only for my own business. It is only to stop the persecution of ours by the ogres
that I have entered the forest in obedience to the command of my father" (100).
Raj observes that the *Rakshas* are disfigured in the story to evoke utmost horror, intensifying a fearsome appearance. E.V.R. Periyar (1879-1973),[22] a Dalit
scholar and influential politician from Tamil Nadu, states in his commentary on
the *Ramayana* that the *Rakshas* were trying to stop the sages from performing
yagas or sacrifices that involved the killing of animals (Raj 100).

---

[21] Raj bases this statement on the stories in Tamil literature about generous indigenous
leaders such as *Paari* and *Sibi* who sacrificed their wealth and body for the sake of
maintaining peace and harmony with one another and with nature. Their stories appear
in the Tamil epic of *Puran`an`ooru* (c.300B.C.).

[22] E.V.R. Periyar was considered the prophetic voice of the Dravidian race when he
called for a movement against the Brahmins and formed the political party "Dravida
Munnetra Kazhagam" in Tamil Nadu. He lost popularity among the majority due to his
adherence to atheism in a country founded on religious beliefs.

Valmiki's *Ramayana* provides a culturally specific portrayal of women in Sita, and particularly Soorpanakha, revealing their subjugation to religious dictates. Sita remains within her expectations of the *pativrata* (total devotion to her husband in any circumstance) which she considers her privilege, while Soorpanakha is imprisoned within her mold of the monstrous other. As the woman on the loose, she is a paradigmatic parallel to the wandering "fierce untouchable" described in the *Manusmriti*. The following section reveals the portrayal of Soorpanakha as *paisasikas* (devil)—the different one—in contrast to the cultured Rama and dutiful Sita:

> Indeed the *Ramayana* celebrates the rules of *Laws of Manusmriti*:
>
> Like the ancient monarch Manu, father of the human race,
> Dasa-ratha ruled his people with a father's loving grace,
>
> Truth and Justice swayed each action and each baser motive quelled,
> People's Love and Monarch's Duty every thought and deed impelled,
>
> Twice-born men were free from passion, lust of gold and impure greed,
> Faithful to their Rites and Scriptures, truthful in their word and deed.
> ……………………………………………………………………..
> Kshatras bowed to the holy Brahmans, Vaisyas to the Kshatras bowed,
> Toiling Shudras lived by labor, of their honest duty proud
>
> To the Gods and to the Fathers. To each guest in virtue trained,
> Rites were done with due devotion as by holy writ ordained.
> (Dutt 2-3)

The twice-born are those from the Brahmin, Kshatriya, and Vaishya castes who could or have moved up in their caste status depending on how rigidly they adhered to the scriptures. The people in the kingdom of Ayodhya lived by the tenets of the *Manusmriti* and with the hierarchy of castes where contempt on the *Asura* communities was prevalent (Raj 101).

Women Unlike Sita

In Valmiki's *Ramayana,* Rama is a Kshatriya caste settler on an inhabited land. Valmiki establishes conquest in the epic as an entitlement to dominance by communities vested with power: materially, spiritually, physically, and intellectually. This idea calls for a study of specific instances of conquest in the context of Rama's encounters with *Rakshasi* (female ogres).

Rama, with the help of the sage Agastya, chooses the forest of Panchavati, beside the river Godavari as his dwelling to spend the years of his banishment. Valmiki describes the land where Rama enters as fertile and filled with pleasing flora and fauna:

> Godavari's limpid waters in her gloomy gorges strayed
> Unseen rangers of the jungle nestled in the darksome shade!

> 'Mark the woodlands,' uttered Rama, 'by the saint Agastya told
> Panchavati's lonesome forest with its blossoms red and gold,
> ………………………………………………………………..
> Where the river leaves it margin with a soft and gentle kiss,
> Where my sweet and soft-eyed Sita may repose in sylvan bliss,

> Where the lawn is fresh and verdant and the kusa young and bright,
> And the creeper yields her blossoms for our sacrificial rite.'
> (83)

Soorpanakha, while wandering in her "verdant" territory, spots Rama, Sita, and Lakshmana whom she identifies as strangers in her land. She is curious about their fair-skinned physical appearance unlike her dark skin and desires their complexion. Valmiki unfolds the social condition in which Soorpanakha as the "different" un-Sita-like woman desires all that these strangers have, while they reject her for all that she is depicted to be: dark, big, and aggressive. After identifying Rama as the leader of the three, she immediately falls in love with him.

While Rama desires the beautiful land of the *Raksha,* Soorpanakha desires Rama for his fair-skinned beauty. Soorpanakha accosts Rama, Sita, and Lakshmana:

> And it so befell, a maiden, dweller of the darksome wood,
> Led by wandering thought or fancy once before the cottage stood,
> Soorpanakha, *Raksha* maiden, sister of the *Raksha* lord,

> Came and looked with eager longing till her soul was passion
> stirred. (89)

Soorpanakha is filled with desire for Rama, who is a "gentle husband," recounting the past to his "sweet and soft eyed" (89) wife. At this juncture of Rama's reminiscing, Valmiki inserts Soorpanakha into the story.

As developed later in the epic, a battle ensues with its inception in claims to territorial rights. Soorpanakha is driven with a desire for Rama and rightfully questions his presence in her territory:

> Who be thou in hermit's vestments, in thy native beauty bright,
> Friended by a youthful woman, armed with thy bow of might,
> Who be thou in these lone regions where the *Rakshas* hold
> their sway,
> Wherefore in a lonely cottage in this darksome jungle stay?
> (89)

Soorpanakha's recurring question, "Who be thou?" reveals her curiosity about Rama. The plot for the story of the battle of "good" and "evil" is shown to have its inception in this misplaced desire of Soorpanakha. Her attraction towards Rama tragically leads to her physical mutilation as punishment.

Soorpanakha accepts the settling of Rama and his family in her home, revealing a guilelessness that is evident in history where dominant communities settle into native territories and claim authority. Conquest is established not necessarily due to the superior power of the intruder, but rather because of the innocent welcoming by the natives as evident in the Christian colonial history including Native-American and Australian-Aborigine communities. Soorpanakha has no premade rationale to distrust the intruders and is immediately attracted to Rama, not knowing that she is lodged in his cultural judgement as the one to reject, humiliate, and punish. She does not attempt to chase away the new settlers from her habitat by harming them.

When Soorpanakha expresses her desire to marry Rama, both Rama and Lakshmana tease her as ignorant and humiliate her as an object of ridicule. Mockingly, Rama persuades Soorpanakha to turn her attractions towards Lakshmana as an eligible bachelor. Lakshmana only further mocks her: "I'm slave of royal Rama, woulds't thou be a vassal's bride? / Rather be his younger consort, banish Sita from his arms, / Spurning Sita's faded beauty let him seek thy fresher charms" (91). Lakshmana implores her to marry Rama and be his second wife. Soorpanakha is further agitated by this suggestion and threatens to slay Sita. Soorpanakha, who normally takes pride in her strength, is now a toy in the hands of these men and is angered by their ridicule and rejection: "Torn by anger strong as tempest thus her answer addrest: / 'Are these mocking accents uttered, Rama, to insult my flame, / Feasting on her faded beauty dost thou still revere thy dame?'" (91). Rama considers the reactions of the *Raksha* savage: "'Brother, we have acted wrongly, for with those of savage breed / Word in jest is courting danger, - this the penance of our deed'" (92). Rama refers to Soorpanakha as the "savage breed," not capable of humor and therefore angered by "jest" (Erndl 71).[23] He interprets Soorpanakha's anger as a lack of understanding his humor rather than a protest to his ridicule and rejection. The "chivalric" love of Rama and Sita is divine and counters the "guileless desire" of Soorpanakha for Rama which is ridiculed as "savage lust."

Renouncing "Difference" as Deviance

Kambar's version of *Ramayana* known as *Kamba Ramayanam* in Tamil narrates the story of Soorpanakha adopting the human form of a beautiful maiden to appear in front of Rama (quotes are from the English translation by Rajagopalachari). This decision is surely based on an internalized notion that her body is undesirable:

> So she stood there wondering, watching, unable to turn her eyes away. She thought, 'My own form would fill him with disgust. I shall change my appearance and then approach him.'
>
> She transformed herself into a beautiful young woman and appeared before him like the full moon. Her slender frame was like a golden creeper climbing the Kalpaka tree in heaven. Her lovely lips and teeth were matched by her fawn-like eyes.
>
> Her gait was that of a peacock. Her anklets made music as she came near. Rama looked up and his eyes beheld this creature of ravishing beauty. She bowed low and touched his feet. Then she withdrew a little with modesty shading her eyes. (141)

In Kambar's story, where Soorpanakha changes her form to suit Rama's desires, she is aware of her inferior color and stature in comparison with Rama. Kathleen Erndl, in her social-analytical commentary on the "The Mutilation of Soorpanakha" (in *Many Ramayanas),* discerns: "The construction of Soorpanakha as 'Other,' as non-human, is particularly appropriate, since she really *is* other than human" (71). Soorpanakha's self-renunciation in exchange for another accepted image of attractiveness could reflect a tragic submission to

---

[23] Kathleen Erndl writes on the mutilation of Soorpanakha and quotes K. Ramaswami Sastri who says, "Rama and Lakshmana crack jokes at her expense. The poet says there is no humor in her mental composition (parihasavicaksana). He probably suggests that the cruel and egoistic *Rakshas* were not capable of humor" (71).

standards of beauty, grace, and wisdom imposed by a dominant group. Soorpanakha affirms Rama's supposition that she is a "female of the forest" and that she is a *Raksha*. Valmiki describes the dominant social imaging of her as "poor in beauty and plain in face" (91). In Kambar's version, she is dark and big in contrast to the fair and slender Sita, and so Soorpanakha rejects her body and transforms into a body acceptable to Rama. When Rama wonders who she could be, public judgment controls her self-identity as she submits to his culturally informed, dominant iconography of definitions of beauty. Similarly, Hidimvà in the *Mahabharata* indulges in this process of transforming her image on seeing Bhima:

> And on going there, she beheld the Pandavas asleep with their mother and the invincible Bhimasena sitting awake. And beholding Bhimasena unrivalled on earth for beauty like unto a vigorous Sala tree, the *Raksha* woman immediately fell in love with him, and she said to herself—this person of hue like heated gold and of mighty arms, of broad shoulders as the lion, and so resplendent, of neck marked with three lines like a conchshell and eyes like lotus-petals is worthy of being my husband…. Thus saying, the *Raksha* woman capable of assuming any form at will, assumed an excellent human form and began to advance with slow steps towards Bhima of mighty arms. Decked with celestial ornaments, she advanced with smiles on her lips and a modest gait, addressing Bhima, said–O bull among men, whence hast thou come here and who art thou? ...Who … is this lady of transcendent beauty sleeping so trustfully in these woods as if she were lying in her own chamber? … Ye beings of celestial beauty, I have been sent hither by that *Raksha*sa – my brother…. (Roy 312)

Having internalized the dominant conceptualization of beauty, Sister Hidimvà acknowledges her lack thereof and assumes the form of a human female to be desired by Bhima. Both Soorpanakha and Hidimvà masquerade and reject their natural body, transforming themselves into "desirable" women.

Both women attempt to bring about a reconciliation of desire by a renunciation of their bodies. The writers present cultural perceptions which underlie the text, exposing the notion of the woman who is "different" as treacherous, vulgar, and threatening to the sanctity of the religious code of marriage. In Kambar's version, Rama—on seeing Soorpanakha in human form—assumes that she is a ravishing visitor from some distant place. Ironically, he demands, "Which is your place? What is your name? Who are your kinsfolk?" (141). She promptly establishes her identity: "I am the daughter of the grandson of Brahma. Kubera is a brother of mine. Another is Ravana, conqueror of Kailaasa. I am a maiden and my name is Kaamavalli [woman filled with lust]" (141). While Soorpanakha takes pride in her family and her rights to the territory, she hides her true physical identity. She subordinates herself to Rama's vision and perception of who she might be.

In the society that Valmiki describes, Soorpanakha stands in stark contrast with Rama and Sita:

> [Soorpanakha]
> Looked on Rama lion-chested, mighty-armed, lotus- eyed,
> Stately as the jungle tusker, with his crown of tresses tied,
>
> Looked on Rama lofty-fronted, with a royal visage graced,
> Like Kandarpa young and lustrous, lotus-hued and lotus-faced!
>
> What though she a *Raksha* maiden, poor in beauty plain in face,
> Fell her glasses passion-laden on the prince of peerless grace,
>
> What though wild her eyes and tresses, and her accents counseled fear,
> Soft-eyed Rama fired her bosom, and his sweet voice thrilled her ear.
> ………………………………………………………………..
> Fawn-eyed Sita fell in terror as the *Raksha* rose to slay,
> So beneath the flaming meteor sinks Rohini's softer ray,
>
> And like demon of destruction furious Surpa-nakha came,
> Rama rose to stop the slaughter and protect the helpless dame.
> (91)

Such images of contrasts instate physical appearance as a determinant carrier of traits of wisdom, grace, and power. The *Rakshas*, depicted as dark with strongly built bodies, are stereotyped as demons with no right to gain respect and branded as lustful, threatening savages without mercy. Soorpanakha's "wild eyes" are filled with lust and anger as opposed to Sita's "fawn eyes" which are filled with fear, grace, and devotion. Rama is "lotus-hued" and "lotus-faced," while Soorpanakha is "poor in beauty, plain in face." She lacks character in her looks, and is de-faced and effaced in comparison with Rama. The process of Soorpanakha's mutilation is well on its way before it is consummated because violence is initiated as an internalized process of mutilation of the self.

"Difference" as Immoral

Kambar places Soorpanakha's assessment of her incapacitated beauty in a conscious realization of her moral inferiority to Sita as well: "Would he look at me as well, I who am so impure? ... / That woman is all purity, she is beautiful, and she is the mistress of his broad chest" (qtd. in Erndl 74).[24] Erndl draws attention to these words when Soorpanakha contemplates getting even with "purity" by banishing its perfection in Sita. While the narratives exemplify Sita as the chaste woman, they cast Soorpanakha as the impure woman led by thoughts and feelings of lust and violence. Erndl notes in Kambar a more sympathetic portrayal of Soorpanakha compared to Valmiki, but he heightens the "Other" in Soorpanakha as well. In the Tamil version, Soorpanakha is said to be impure or the one who has lost her virginity: "[...] her purity waned like the fame of a man who hordes up wealth and gives nothing with love as his reward for apprise!" (73). According to Erndl, Kambar suggests that if she lacks *karpu* (chastity), all her other powers will be in vain as well. Similarly, Vyasa's character of Sister Hidimvà in the *Mahabharata* marvels at Bhima's purity: "Who also, O sinless one, is this lady?" (Roy 312). In addressing him as the "sinless one," she places herself in contrast to the Kshatriya. She is able transform herself externally to suit him but is unsure about her capacity to match his inner beauty. Placing her physical strength on par with Bhima's inner sanctity, she promises to preserve his body and soul if he will marry her.

In Kambar's version of the *Ramayana*, the punished Soorpanakha still negotiates with Rama to accept her, and she will prevent the war that will now ensue because of the insult against her. She is cast as a woman whose self-interest clouds her loyalty to her community; she promises to help Rama win the war over the *Rakshas*. This act undermines her part in the collective identity of her community. Similarly, Hidimvà abandons her kin for desire; her speech and actions are guided by passion in which she not only loses herself, but her brother as well. While family honor is the basis of the battles in this epic, the *Rakshasi* are either shown to be devoid of honor or ready to abandon family honor for desire. Hidimvà becomes a victim of her brother's anger leading to mutilation and death.

Valmiki holds a mirror to Soorpanakha and Hidimvà as cultural representations of "bad" and "dirty" women who are punished; they choose to follow their desires, transgressing religious boundaries and betraying their men. While the dominant male perceives the bold and persistent "different" women as deviant, the women qualify these traits of "difference" as the very rudiments of their strength. Rama and Lakshmana assume positions as protectors of a tradi-

---

[24] Erndl uses the translation of Kambar by Hart and Heiftz.

tion where the woman is servile, virtuous, and gentle. Feminist philosopher Simone de Beauvoir writes of this binary opposition between the "good" and "evil" woman in *The Second Sex* (1953): "Men have tried to overcome the bad by taking possession of woman; they have succeeded in part.... But just as Christianity, by bringing in the idea of redemption and salvation, has given the word damnation its full meaning, just so it is in contrast to the sanctified woman, that the bad woman stands out in full relief" (192).[25] Rama and Lakshmana carry out a similar ideology of opposition where women should be submissive to be "good" and not be allowed to express physical desires whilst pleasing the male. Both Sita and Soorpanakha provide mythical ideals, the former as the ideal female, and the latter as the archetypal evil woman. Soorpanakha's attempts to abduct Sita further vilify her as the "deviant Other" to be feared, who will separate "good" women from their husbands, carry them to a distant land, strip their identity, and—by her magical powers—transform them into non-human creatures.

Erndl observes certain comparative aspects that are evident in the casting of Sita and Soorpanakha in the several versions of *Ramayana* that she discusses. She divides them into two types of women: good and evil. Sita's goodness derives from her purity and her servility, while Soorpanakha's evil stems from her impurity and insubordinate character. Erndl points to the *Manusmriti* that a woman should obey and be protected by her father in youth, her husband in married life, and her sons in old age; a woman should never be independent (83). While this woman gains her identity as *sakti* (power) from her purity, a power controlled by patriarchy, Soorpanakha—cast as the "demon"—is not bound by such laws and is free to roam. The *Ramayana* narrative reveals perceptions of her as a loose woman, a widow without a husband who wanders as she pleases, uncontrolled. The role of these dominant narratives in making permanent such norms of "good" and "bad" behavior is integral to understanding the ethos that punishes women who do not fit into dominant strains of thought as submissively "good" and "beautiful" to the "sacred" social eye.

Ethnologist Gloria Raheja provides information on the depth of the impact of the emulation of the Sita figure in India that has pervaded the minds of Dalit women. She quotes from an interview with a Dalit sweeper woman, Kalaso from Gujarat. Raheja reports that on being asked about the importance of the emulation of Sita, Kalaso insisted, "… the women of her family and caste did indeed strive to model their behavior according to the image of Sita" (qtd. in Kumar 74). She states that the impact of the Sita image has led to its internali-

---

[25] De Beauvoir goes on to state that two facets of "good" and "bad" are imposed upon women by men who want the good woman to serve him obediently and the bad woman to satisfy his carnal desires, both imaginative and real (192).

zation by Dalit women as the "ideal woman." Raheja raises the crucial question, "And should we then regard Kalaso's words not simply as evidence of penetration of female subjectivity by the terms of male discourse on patriliny, but as a strategic presentation of self in a social arena? And should we regard many of the words of our interlocutors not as fixed and reified and essentialized mirrors of consciousness, but as shifting and purposeful negotiations of identity and relationship?" (73). Sita's chastity is parallel to her beauty which is revealed in the female aspect of spirituality, and blessed by and gaining significance through servitude to masculinity. Soorpanakha's emulation of Sita is proving to be influential even today in such internalizations by Dalit women of standards of beauty and virtue; this demonstrates an acceptance of the presiding norms set by traditional perceptions. Dalit female voices in the ensuing chapters reveal such inner tensions of claiming Dalit female beauty while struggling to ignore nominal beauty models provided by patterns of traditional thought.

"Difference" Deserves Punishment

Soorpanakha returns after being dispensed by Rama to carry away Sita, whom she sees as her only hurdle to marrying Rama. Kambar narrates, "Lakshmana shouted and sprang on the *Rakshasi*. Catching hold of her hair, he kicked her and drew his sword. Soorpanakha when attacked resumed her own shape and attacked Lakshmana. Lakshmana easily caught hold of her and mutilated her and drove her off" (142). According to Kambar, Lakshmana cuts off her ears, nose, and breasts. Erndl comments that in Tamil culture, the breasts symbolize woman-power as life-giver and therefore the mutilation of the nipples signifies a harsh insult to the woman. Soorpanakha is wounded, and she runs into the forest, bleeding and loudly appealing to her kinsfolk: "Oh brother Khara! Oh Brother Ravana! Oh Indrajit! Oh kings of the Raksasaa race! Are you all asleep? A mere man has insulted me and cut off my nose. Do you hear my lamentations?" (142). Commentators extensively discuss this event of physical conflict between Lakshmana and Soorpanakha as a crime against a helpless female by a powerful male. The mutilated and incapacitated woman—who has physically and psychologically sacrificed her body and sense of identity—seeks help to reinstate her conscious will, awareness of her strength, and self-worth.

In *Kamba Ramayanam*, the mutilated Soorpanakha, laments and narrates her tale of woe to her brother Khara: "Surpa-nakha in her anguish raised her accents shrill and high, / And the rocks and wooded valleys answered back the dismal cry, / Khara, the doughty Dushan heard the far resounding wail, / Saw her red disfigured visage, heard her sad and woeful tale" (142). In the cry of calling attention to her violation is Soorpanakha's lament of revenge, reversing her own rejection of her strength and appearance rather than a passive cry of self-pity. Soorpanakha mourns the loss of her honor and that of her people as she runs defaced and frenzied, carrying the scars of her victimization. Losing parts of her face and breasts renders her emblematic of a faceless, androgenic demon punished for transgressing boundaries. Ironically, it is Rama who is the trespasser, and Soorpanakha is punished. Erndl states that mutilation as a punishment for women stands out as a major feature of this episode in the various versions of the epic. What is expected from her punishment is acceptance and compliance. Such punishment is sanctioned by the *Manusmriti*, enacted in the religious epics, and carried out on the lives of subjugated women who might desire a liberating change. This culture of punishment has travelled through time and is carried out upon the bodies of Dalit women or any woman who dares to cross boundaries drawn by religion and cultural norms.

Deified Subversion of "Difference" in *Kali*

Contrary to victimized "different" women in traditional epics, the local gods and goddesses in Dalit cultures are almost always armed with weapons to protect their people; in their appearance, they resemble figurations of deviant women in traditional epics—enormous and fearsome with large protruding eyes, dangling tongues, and huge bloody teeth. Associations made with appearances and character undergo transgressive transformations in Dalit spirituality as mythical, traditional representations of evil take on concrete, subversive meanings of goodness. A humanness that connects with real, suffering people is reflective of goodness that should be lodged in monstrous appearances. In that spiritual tradition, as much as purity could be located in polluted identities, celebrative spaces should be found in those shunned as invisible and dispensable, and strength identified within broken and mutilated people.

The representation of Soorpanakha calls to mind the *Tantric* tradition: the non-orthodox Hindu tradition that leans towards animism with Dravidian roots and worships female power. Soorpanakha foreshadows this tradition, conceptualized only later than the *Ramayana*. *Kali* is one of the goddesses of the Tantric tradition (origin is traced to circa 200 BCE-AD 300) who demands devotion to herself and symbolizes liberation for those who are subdued by oppressive powers. The indigenous origin of *Kali* is suggested by her absence in the sacred text of *Rig Veda,* which is dated around 1500-1200 BCE; and only in the scripture *Upanishads,* composed around 800-400 BCE (Mundaka 1.2.4), does one see traces of her. This mention suggests the influence of native goddesses in Aryan religion and the inclusion of *Kali* in the pantheon of goddesses. The physical appearance of *Kali* could place her origin among the Dravidians because she is dark with a lolling tongue, fanglike teeth, disheveled hair, and numerous arms holding deadly weapons—an epitome of terror, resembling the Aryan portrayal of *Rakshasi* as fearsome.

David Kinsley in *The Sword and the Flute* (1975) notes that *Kali* is mentioned in the *Mahabharata* but only as the peripheral non-Aryan deity who lives in the cremation grounds and carries the dead away. Kinsley points out that in the *Devi-Mahatmya*, a part of the *Markandeya Purana* (c. AD 400), she is provided full prominence as a goddess. In this text, she appears as the female force that kills threatening male forces or demons (Kinsley 81-90). She claims for herself the supreme power and position in the realm of divinity. She represents death, destruction, and chaos in creating a universe for herself where she is in control and chaos rules against order and stability. Her physical appearance is meant to remind the devotee of her/his egocentrism as she is fearful to look at, compared to prime Aryan goddesses. Her body parts are depicted with extra prominence such as her elaborately adorned nose, ears, and voluptuous breasts. Mookerjee and Khanna explore the tantric tradition in *The Tantric Way*, describing *Kali* as one who embodies birth, death, creation, and destruction (9). They suggest that as a dark goddess, she signifies unmixed pure consciousness, who provides and preserves in the endowments of body parts. She has four hands to be able to counter the Aryan image with the two hands that slew the Dravidian woman (9).[26] This appearance suggests the state of the world grounded in self and on the consequences of an uncontrolled self.

Soorpanakha, with a fearsome appearance as the one who wanders freely—dark and deviant—provides an image of *Kali*. There is a subversive transformation in the image of *Kali* who holds body parts in her hand with her tongue sticking out, far from being muted or mutilated. Soorpanakha's reliance on the power of action and speech is evident in the *Kali* figure who provides the impetus for women to be dark, aggressive, out in the battlefield, and having the right to fend for herself.[27] As the elucidator of *maya* or illusion, *Kali* exposes the vanity of self and promotes the essentiality of self-knowledge that invokes one to recognize the positive force within oneself. As Kinsley observes, the self is referred to as the negative overpowering force, and knowledge is referred to as the positive discerning force within oneself (86-90). *Kali* defies the tradition of

---

[26] Ajit Mookerjee and Madhu Khanna explain these ramifications in *The Tantric Way*. They provide a clear description on *Kali*'s unique characteristics concerning birth and death, creation and destruction as a positive energy.

[27] In *Hindu Goddesses*, Kinsley engages with the concept of the world as illusory and Tantric Goddesses such as *Durga* and *Kali* elucidating the necessity to rise above illusions to a knowledge of where one's origin and destination lies: the self. *Kali* demonstrates the importance of self.

beauty inherent in the fair-skinned and projects her dark-skinned self as the revelation of truth in her beauty.

Archetype and Myth

Jung explains that archetypes are manifestations of the external opponent to whatever seems to be right and good (Jacobi 66-73). Since there is no one primary god in Hinduism, forces of good need to be counteracted with forces of evil, and demons help with concretizing the understanding of evil forces that should be rejected in order to establish forces of good as the ruling power. The definition of what is good and evil is controlled by those who assume the powers of good; preconceived ideas about a particular group of people lead to a devising of images that manifest such preconceptions. Here, based on the historical evidence of the social dynamics that already existed between the Aryans and the Dravidians, demonic images that would etch *Dasyu* (mentioned in the *Rig Veda)* in a cultural imagination and religious praxis were necessary to affirm the superiority of Aryan culture and religion. *Dasyu* had to be dissolved into inhuman archetypal images that justified Aryan conquest and dehumanization of certain Dravidians by classifying them as primordially evil. The Aryan ethic of conquest needed an opponent of demonic proportions in order to celebrate its victory in successful punishment. The defeated "different" become the demons; such imaging of "good" and "evil" as the conquering and the conquered helps formulate the principle of inclusion and exclusion. Hidimvà and Soorpanakha become the archetypal images of "different" women to be punished and defeated as they are deviant in appearance and behavior.

According to French anthropologist Claude Levi-Strauss, figures of evil that are presented in myths reflect social structure and relations. The unique characteristic of myth in which the past, present, and future are held together, however, is the timelessness (209-210). Hence, the enactment of the *Ramayana* and *Mahabharata* in its many translations and versions around the world attests to the timelessness of the myth. As linguistic discourse, it travels through time and pervades all cultures (209). The religious discourses of the *Ramayana*, the *Mahabharata,* and the *Manusmriti* establish themselves persistently in the psyche of individuals and in the culture of a country. They are reinforced through the legends, the values, and the archetypes of good and evil. The archetypes of the *Rakshasi* in the *Ramayana* and the *Mahabharata* disguise the historical realities of conquest and provide an apparently essential basis for a cultural stereotype based on religious status. The images of *Rakshasi* and "fierce untouchable" women are signifiers of polluters and pollution, evil and the perpetrators of evil, demons and perpetrators of monstrosity that are essential to the sanctioning of a higher moral order. Dalit women, along with other women considered different from the norm, have been burdened with this image of demons of mythical proportions. A coming together of subversion and "difference" in the lives of Dalit women would permit epic possibilities of a spirituality from within oneself, especially the self that embodies difference.

Mariamman, the Spotted Goddess subverts "Difference"

Mari, Mariamman, or Mariyaatha is a goddess particularly worshipped by Tamil Dalit communities as their chief protector and granter of wishes. Mari is rain, and amman is mother; in these terms, she is venerated as the provider, protector, and nurturer of her people. Dalit villages harbor various kinds of shrines and temples for her, ranging from elaborate temple structures to just a stone with a cloth wrapped around it that one could find under a tree. To them, she is an incarnation of Kali in her fierce appearance, usually depicted with four to eight arms bearing weapons and objects used in her worship rituals to protect her people. Placing Mariamman in the evocative pantheon of goddesses associated with Kali calls forth an empowering convergence of an identity formation process wherein the one who suffers is consoled by Kali, the incarnation of the all-encompassing presence of female power—sakti.

Mookerjee and Khanna designate sakti as the primordial female power that birthed the rigidified religious principles and gods associated with the traditional practices of the Hindu doctrines. They identify Kali as an incarnation of that sakti in whom "creation, preservation and annihilation" are encapsulated. This sakti belongs to the tantric tradition of religious thought; tan in Sanskrit is to "expand" (9). Mookerjee and Khanna suggest that the tantra synthesizes "spirit and matter" (9). In this convergence, the divine being and the human are on an equal plain of relationship, contrary to the ideological premise of a hierarchy of peoples propounded in the Rig Veda. They explain tantra as "not a withdrawal from life – but the fullest possible acceptance of our desires, feelings and situations as human beings" (9). Kali bridges the gap between the forbidden divine realm for Dalits and the ambiguous physical reality of experiencing pain and communal celebrations as the matrix of their lives.

The idea of dissipating gaps among different realms comes close to the endearing ways in which Amman or Mariamman is claimed and held close by Dalits in Tamil Nadu. There is a merging of identities of Kali in her variations in different parts of the world and her devotees who please her through worship rituals and offerings. She is fierce in her black color, almost nakedness, full-breasted appearance with disheveled hair, and adornment with a garland of human heads. In this traditionally "undesirable" appearance, she is most powerful: she is an out-of-the-norm female figure (in the dominant cultural imagination) who is loyal, fierce, and at the same time gentle in her love for her devotees. Mookerjee and Khanna explain, "She inspires awe and love at the same time" (75). She provides meaning to ambiguity, and an enigmatic aspect of embodying paradoxical power within the *earthy humanness* of her existence positions her closer to Dalit lives. I place *Mariamman* in this tradition of spirituality as she is said to be a popular form of *Kali* appropriated in South India, especially in Tamil Nadu. Lourdusamy propagates this idea of *Mariamman* as the Dalit *Kali* who resembles the difference that Dalit women have been criticized for and celebrate her for the very reason that she embodies their women in her audacious earthy human character (4).

In its essence as a non-Brahmanic tradition, the priests in *Mariamman's* temple are non-Brahmins, whereas in an orthodox Hindu temple, only Brahmins would serve as priests. Cultural anthropologist Paul Younger in his research essay on social meanings in worship of *Mariamman* in the famous temple in Samayapauram in Tiruchirappalli, Tamil Nadu (very close to Pudukkottai, one of the locations of my field work), observes a challenging of religious ideologies and cultural practices. He describes:

> The people of Tiruchirapalli see the Goddess as a deity who like themselves did not enjoy the respect of the learned Brahmanas or kings of old, and does not win the approval of the missionaries or the support of westernized civil servants today. Because she stood up to this disrespect, they feel that she alone can understand their individual problems, can provide a sense of unity and identity by tying together the jumble of lower caste which make up their society, can give them a sense of continuity with their village roots they still carry with them [those who moved to the city areas], and through those roots can tie them to the larger order of the cosmos. (*The Journal of the American Academy of Religion*, 1980, 501)

Devotees are consoled by this sense of identity with her rejected self, and in that oneness, they show their empathy and a reciprocity in their care and protection of her image as she dwells in and among them.

The *Mariamman* temple in Annavasal near the Pudukkottai region in Tamil Nadu that I visited in June 2014 depicts her with four arms, each carrying either a weapon or a conch. Four Dalit priests in the temple along with devotees were preparing for the *Maraiamman* festival to happen the next day when they would prepare *kuj* (rice porridge) and serve it to all who come to the temple as an offering made to *Maraimman* herself. Each person who comes to the temple is well fed as if they were *Mariamman* herself. One of the priests, Marudai, informed me that they make sure that no one leaves the temple dissatisfied because they do not want *Mariamman* dissatisfied.[28] This is one of the ways they ensure protection provided by their goddess who would otherwise inflict punishment. He mentioned an important fact that some devotees inflict pain on themselves to gain her sympathy and favor, some others roll on the temple grounds to get her attention to grant a wish, and some carry pots of turmeric water or burning hot coal adorned with margosa leaves with which to please her. In the months of October and November, her devotees walk on burning coal embers to express their deep devotion to her. Traditionally, in the past, he said, those inflicted with smallpox believed that she had descended into their bodies. She refused to leave such bodies unless these kinds of offerings were made, including the sacrifice of goats. He pointed to a woman under a *neem* tree beside the temple who was selling coconut and banana in a small plastic bag that I could buy and offer to *Mariamman* along with prayers that will surely be granted; I did so.

Worship rituals for *Mariamman* are varied depending on the specific region in Tamil Nadu. Younger records that in the Samayapuram temple, the worship involves a fast and frenzied dancing in which one chief worshipper is identified and carried into the temple by the dancing devotees and is presented to *Mariamman*. He or she could self-inflict physical torture to gain *Mariamman's* sympathy, attention, and admiration for the courage displayed. Younger identifies the worshipper as one who is a bridge between the devotees and the goddess: "The Worshipper brings together a natural worldly order (*samsara*) and the highest release of the self (*moksa*) are clearly marked out; as is the action (*dharma*) that flows between them" (513). The special moment of transcendence in his dance and trance serve as a bridge:

> The worshipper, as he moves through his roles in the festival, recognizes in turn his identity with all others in samsara through his participation in the 'audience,' the special transcendent quality of his 'self' in the ecstatic moment of release as a bridge (*dharma*) between those poles when he acts out the 'dance' and 'trance' through which he is transformed from one form into another. (513)

He emphasizes that the worshipper moves through this role of unification of realms in solidarity with the devotees gathered, merging his identity with theirs as their representative worshipper. He who approaches the heart and body of *Mariamman* gets close to her for the sake of the people, signifying oneness in his/her hurting body and *Mariamman's* history as a vulnerable being.

---

[28] Marudai, personal interview, 1 June 2014.

Younger presents stories that make up *Mariamman's* earthly life as suscep-
tible to pain and rejection. He relates:

> While at a deeper level Māriyamman's "power" is associated
> with fertility problems, the most frequent appeals to her have to
> do with sickness, and older books often called her the goddess
> of smallpox. Smallpox plagues were a regular occurrence in the
> hot season just after the time of this festival, and it is still
> commonly said that the purpose of the festival was once to in-
> duce the goddess to take the plague away. One of the stories
> associating her with smallpox says that she was once the wife
> of a Brāhmana and that she had won a reputation as being very
> beautiful and very virtuous. The three Brāhmanical deities,
> Brahma, Sivan, and Visnu, were intrigued by this reputation
> and arrived one afternoon to have a look for themselves. Of-
> fended by the intrusion into the quiet of her home, she cursed
> them to become like little children and then began to mother
> them. When her husband arrived, he was upset to see the gods
> treated in this way and cursed her with smallpox and sent her
> out to beg and spread the disease from house to house. While
> in this story she is the spreader of smallpox and, therefore,
> much to be feared, it is also she alone, who, if propitiated, can
> keep smallpox from one's door. (506)

This story places *Mariamman* in the caring lap of a Dalit woman as one who is
rejected, cursed, and polluted. Later in this chapter, I discuss the significance of
this aspect of *Mariamman's* association with smallpox in the section interpret-
ing the presence of this goddess in the life of a Dalit woman—Viramma.

I draw on Viramma's oral narrative published as *Viramma, Life of an Untouchable* to delineate the significance of *Mariamman* in the lives of Dalits,
especially Dalit women in whom her humanness resides through her indwelling
among her people. Viramma is a Dalit woman from Puducherry, a union territory adjacent to Tamil Nadu, who narrated her life story to ethnologists Josi-
anne Racine and Jean-Luc Racine in the 1980s. Based on Viramma's relationship with her local goddess *Mariamman,* I suggest a merging of humanness and
divinity in *Mariamman* and in her devotees wherein a shared mutual transference happens seamlessly. I will point to an interdependence in the closeness of
a relationship between this goddess and her devotees who nurture, preserve,
and serve each other.

In essence, Dalit spirituality is rooted in animism and hence different from
mainstream dominant sects of Hinduism. The worship of ancestors and the
worship of nature are fundamental to Dalit spirituality and symbolism. Their

spirituality is based on relationships, and sickness or death is associated with estrangement from the dead or nature; thus, offerings are made to resolve these relationships (Raj 82-83). Dalits' gods and goddesses protect the community from harm, and in turn, need to be pleased and satisfied with offerings of food and animals. There is an element of interdependency between the goddesses and the people. They do not exercise power over their people but only react with anger to unfulfilled promises or relationships with people (Raj 82-83). Younger notes that people seek *Mariamman's* help to answer prayers related to fertility, famine, drought, sickness, marriages, and other social problems that would make them targets of abuse. It is within this context of a spirituality that is deeply rooted in a collective action of protection and preservation from which Viramma speaks (501).

The collective identity of the *Paraiyar* is derived from gods and goddesses who not only protect them, but reveal their physical vulnerability to create and recreate within their devotees a sense of resilience. Viramma's narration affirms gods and rituals as integral to the *Paraiyar* community that shapes her self-development. Throughout Viramma's story, several ambiguities surface in relation to the external reality of life and the inner determination to live. These ambiguities are sustained by the internal power provided by the human nature of gods, and *Mariamman* is one such goddess who is one with the ambiguous character of Dalit life. Viramma specially narrates the story of *Mariamman*:

> *Mariamman* came to earth one day when her husband Isvaran was furious and drove her out, covering her with twenty-one types of spot. He cursed her and said, "Peuh! You're not worthy of my household! Get out of here! Sow the spots all around you and live on what people will give you to be cured!" Poor people like us saw this woman arriving all naked and covered in spots, and wondered who she was. (105)

According to the Racines, *Mariamman*—who was originally *Parvathi*—is cursed by her husband *Siva* for admiring a divine messenger, while she was in human form. Her son is ordered to cut her head off, but he regains his father's favor to bring her back to life. The son, in confusion, places the head of an untouchable—whom Parvathi takes refuge with—on Parvathi's body, and places her head on the body of the untouchable. Infuriated by this "ambiguous being," Siva condemns her to the earth, covered with spots and diseased, to wander around seeking refuge among people (286).

In this state of a spotted, vulnerable goddess, she is the embodiment of an unclean *Parachi* thrown out of the panorama of dominant Hindu gods. *Mariamman*'s divine powers remain in her as she wanders helplessly in the streets—she still has the power to curse those who fail to satisfy her needs. The divine and the human aspects merge in the figure of *Mariamman,* who reveals the divine in the human aspects of her devotees. Viramma's life constantly reflects this ambiguity as she is abused externally, but within her the tension between her internalization of her oppression and an internal sense of power derived from her community, gods, and goddesses merge.

Mariamman wanders the streets as a vulnerable naked woman, infected with disease and dependent on the *kuj,* clothing, and footwear provided by the *Paraiyar.* She empowers the *Paraiyar* who, as her providers, subvert their role from that of a dependent community to that of a community capable and worthy of providing for a goddess. Viramma informs:

> Some launderers at the wash house quickly soaked a white cloth in turmeric water and gave it to her to cover herself and treat her spots. Then she saw some cobblers. They prostrated themselves at her feet and gave her a pair of sandals so she could go around the world without hurting her feet. A bit further on, people from our caste were harvesting rice. They quickly picked a few ears, made flour out of them, offered that to the Mother in an unpolluted coconut shell and gave her *kuj* to drink. And the Mother carried on her way, granting favor to everyone who offered her underskirts, saris, *kuj* and balls of flour. (105-106)

The rituals involved in *Mariamman's* worship include providing her with gruel, as reflected in feeding the whole community that day, and bathing her idol with turmeric water that will heal her wounds and purify her. The villagers satisfy *Mariamman* because if she is not satisfied, she will inflict disease and other physical suffering upon them. Viramma prays to *Mariamman* to increase production in the fields: "If my aubergines and chillis don't take, I pray to *Mariamman,* 'Mother *Mariamman,* if my aubergines and my chillis grow well this year, I'll make you an offering of the first harvest'" (246). As a spotted goddess, *Mariamman* is sought, feared, and loved—all at once.

In comparison with caste goddesses such as *Lakshmi,* the goddess of wealth, *Saraswathi,* the goddess of learning, and *Kalaiselvi,* the goddess of art, *Mariamman* is the goddess of the people; she dwells in and is one with the *Paraiyar,* who are considered cursed and dependent on the mercy of the landlords. She is the incarnation of the people, as much as she is the incarnation of a goddess. She embodies their physical struggles, along with their inner spiritual strength as a community of people who suffer, but are resilient; who are forced to accept their state as unclean, but resist; and who formulate strategies of survival against all odds. The confidence of Dalit women leaders stands as imposingly as *Mariamman,* in an inner power that is uncompromising in its desire for change. They are both the inflicted and the ones who defer infliction constitutive of a natural impetus for transgression.

Mariamman offers blessings to those who show her favor in her association with smallpox. She could dwell in a person spotted by smallpox, who is treated as divine because of the descent of *Mariamman,* but is diseased nevertheless: divine ambiguity. The local priest will send her out of the person's body because of the disease she brings with her by alluring her out with offerings. If *Mariamman* is pleased, she will leave the person's body and bring about healing. Viramma says:

> You know what *mariatta* is, its chickenpox or smallpox. In the country we call it *mariatta* because it's *Mariamman,* the Mother, who comes in this form to make people give her a jar of gruel. She goes from person to person, from house to house, from *ceri* to *ceri* and everywhere she goes she takes one or two people. And when everybody has made her an offering, when everybody has given her what she wants, she leaves this world (105).

Mariamman embodies the divine and human ambiguity as both the inflictor and the healer. Her devotees experience her power by bearing her in their body as a disease that leads to an experiencing of her divine healing power when infliction leaves. As a disciplining mother, she reminds them of their dependence on her chastising love that inflicts pain to make her power of love more real. As much as the inflicted and healed are relieved that she has left their body, they are grateful for her blessing to choose their body to dwell in before moving on to another.

Viramma speaks of few other gods: *Murugan, Perumal,* and *Periyandavan.* Her understanding of the role of gods in her *Paraiyar* community suggests two important facets of spirituality: the inherent nature of Dalit spirituality as consistent with the reality of life and Dalit spirituality as a source of reliable knowledge of oneself. The gods are both healers and destroyers, those who provide and at the same time demand, and those who are loyal and demand loyalty. Viramma narrates a story about a boy who tried to escape into another village to avoid *Mariamman. Mariamman* meets him on the way and says, "You wanted to run away from me but I can be in front of you wherever you go! I am everywhere and I see everything!" (108). This story illustrates that Dalit spirituality is not about striving to run beyond this world of dilemmas but about making the dilemma of life an experiential reality to be embraced. Dalits will struggle with ambiguities but emerge resilient, for Dalit spirituality is not about metaphysical realities that exist separate from experience. The transcendence that Viramma elucidates in her narrative is not one where the human is transported into a separate divine space, but rather the mystery of the de-humanized becoming divine in their derisive state, and deformation is considered whole in itself. This happens as a collective experience provided by the spiritual beings. The gods and goddesses move, speak, create, and destroy within the physical realm of Dalits; there is no otherworldliness outside of one's physical realm. Dalits encounter those powers on a day-to-day basis; they constantly create and recreate spiritual consciousness as an individual consciousness that is an indistinguishable part of collective consciousness.

The community builds a temple in the *ceri* for such an endearing goddess as *Mariamman,* who is the sufferer and liberator. She bridges the human reality of suffering and the divine possibilities of change, healing, and transformation. Viramma describes the process when the whole *ceri* gathers together to pool money and labors to build the temple to honor this goddess. Viramma recounts their singing in unison during the building process:

> In this house good fortune will be born!
> Give what you should to Mariatta!
> We are going to make the gruel for Mariatta
> The measures of grain hidden away,
> You should give them to us!
> Kudukkudukkudukudukka…. (117)

This song describes *Mariamman* as the one who needs the grace of the *Paraiyar* because they make gruel to feed her. *Mariamman* draws her people closer to her in this reality of physical survival—this is the basis of the religious belief of the *Paraiyar*. They gather together to feed the goddess who will reciprocally provide for them and protect them.

As the song reverberates, Viramma's celebration of *Mariamman* is an affirmation of her *Parachi* identity as the spotted goddess helps her claim divinity in an untouchable state finding power in her role as provider. Comparing these festivities with other festivities, Viramma says, "Anyway, none of these temples has big festivals every year. Only *Mariamman* is entitled to that!" (116). Viramma gains an understanding of her potency as a Dalit woman who can transform traditions of punishment—*Mariamman* is regenerative power, life-giving power, and life-taking (for a creative purpose) power.

The festival to honor *Mariamman* becomes a symbol of proactive participation, providing the awareness that Viramma gains about herself in relation to her community. Younger states that "as a 'non-Brāhmana' ... she gives the oppressed a sense of cosmic importance, dignity, and strength" (509). While *Mariamman* is dependent on the community for the nurturing of her identity, she is the one who activates the spiritual energies of the people as well, especially the women in subverting her own punishment as a wanderer carrying pus. She demands the destruction of the old order of things and establishes a new order within which Viramma participates in the supreme being of *Mariamman* because she is a *Parachi.* Viramma's devotion to *Mariamman* transforms the unclean identity that socially marginalizes her among other castes and births her into an affirmative realization of her significance to her community who loves her. Through *Mariamman,* Viramma gains the power to rise above self-pity and above social relations of oppression that she otherwise cannot change. She is now able to speak boldly about her *Parachi* identity as she is endowed with female power and blessed with characteristics of *earthy humanness* in a freedom and sharing that she lives into from her childhood onwards (described more in chapter eight). Social punishment on Dalit women's bodies continues, but *Mariamman* incarnates endlessly in Dalit women who live their daily lives desiring and making change. Locally, nationally, and globally, organizations and individuals represent her many arms adorned with tools for change, subversively healing a social disease.

CHAPTER FOUR

Human Dignity and Social Justice: Locating Agency in Dalit Women in Pudukkottai District of Tamil Nadu, India

Dalit communities today continue to experience violence rooted in cultural stigmatizations promulgated by caste-based communities. In the first documentation of violence against Dalit communities published by Human Rights Watch (1999), researcher Smita Narula declares: "As this report demonstrates more than 160 million people in the world's largest democracy remain at the risk of systematic human rights violations on the basis of the caste into which they are born" (205). Dalit women, specifically, experience the most violence among the Dalit community because their identities are affected by additional variables of oppression, including those due to social views of their gender and sexuality that render them especially vulnerable to all strains of domination. As evidenced in several publications and news reports internationally, Dalit women are firmly establishing and grounding their own claims to human dignity and social justice within the global cry for human rights for every human being.

This chapter[29] explores violence against Dalit women in Pudukkottai District of Tamil Nadu in South India as expressed in their own words. I started listening to these narratives in August 2006 and have since maintained my relationship with the women. Through that continuous listening process, I seek to understand the voices of Dalit women as self-located, authoritative voices that claim human dignity and social justice in their immediate contexts, and to explain how their claims establish a separate niche in humanist activism. I adapt the word 'humanist' here to acknowledge that Dalit women's agency is a deep-seated characteristic of all human beings that desires, seeks, and demands dignity.

Caste, Human Rights, and the United Nations

It is essential to contextualize Dalit women's claims to human dignity and social justice in the framework of the universally accepted mandate of the Uni-

[29] Initially, this study was funded by the Summer Faculty Research Program of the College of Humanities and Social Sciences of the William Paterson University, New Jersey. An original version of this essay was published in: Om Prakash Dwivedi, V. G. Julie Rajan, eds. *Human Rights in Postcolonial India* (2016).

versal Declaration of Human Rights (UDHR), which was first adopted by the United Nations (UN) in 1948. A few articles from the UDHR that concern Dalit rights broadly include:

> Article 3: Everyone has the right to life, liberty and security of person.
> Article 4: No one shall be held in slavery or servitude; slavery and the slave trade shall be prohibited in all their forms.
> Article 5: No one shall be subjected to torture or to cruel, inhuman or degrading treatment or punishment. (Universal Declaration of Human Rights)[30]

By and large, historically, this chapter speaks to how Dalits have been unable to access these specific and basic human rights.

The UN has intervened in many situations where the human rights of peoples have been violated, including caste-based violence. The most notable achievement today for national and international Dalit movements has been securing the intervention of the UN through its various treaty bodies to monitor caste-based violence in Bangladesh, India, Japan, Nepal, Mauritania, Nigeria, Pakistan, Senegal, and Yemen. Dalit movements globally have been able to lobby for their human rights by uniting under the International Dalit Solidarity Network (IDSN)—established in 2000 and based in Copenhagen, Denmark—and in partnership with the National Campaign for Dalit Human Rights (NCDHR) in New Delhi, India, the first and only national body of such a nature.

Dalits first, however, gained international visibility in the human rights community at the World Conference against Racism (WCAR) in Durban, South Africa in 2001. A large number of Dalit women and men attended this international UN conference. Dalit organizational leaders from urban and rural India and Nepal, representatives from Human Rights Watch in New York, and several members of Dalit organizations participated as well. Dalit leaders and their supporting bodies at WCAR demanded the inclusion of caste discrimination as a human rights violation in the agenda of the Human Rights Commission (HRC) of the UN. The Dalit contingent at Durban, however, faced strong opposition from those Indian government representatives who were not in favor of identifying caste-based violence even as a form of discrimination, much less as a human rights violation (Prince Singh).[31] Despite such objections, the inclusion of caste on the HRC agenda in WCAR was a critical step towards the peti-

---

[30] For the full document, refer to "Universal Declaration of Human Rights." United Nations. un.org.

[31] Prince Singh conducted field-based research among Safai Karmachari communities in the state of Andhra Pradesh in the years 2001-2002.

tion for human rights from Dalit communities. Dalit leaders globally united towards the inclusion of a paragraph (para 109) in the proposed agenda for WCAR concerning caste discrimination. According to Paul Divakar from the NCDHR, UN representatives from the Indian government tried to keep this paragraph from being incorporated into the final agenda. This paragraph reads: "To ensure that all necessary constitutional, legislative and administrative measures including appropriate form of affirmative action are in place to prohibit and redress discrimination on the basis of work and descent and that such measures are respective and implemented by all states authorities at all levels" (NCDHR).[32] After it was announced that this paragraph would be retained in the final agenda of WCAR, Divakar expressed the following in a press release on August 8, 2001:

> The much disputed Para No.109, is on the agenda of the WCAR. The Chair also ruled that this Para goes un-bracketed to the WCAR at Durban. This is the only Para pertaining to Caste discrimination which had been lobbied for intensely by many Dalit groups from Asia as well as other Human Rights organizations all over the world. Indian Government campaigned hard to keep this Para out of the agenda of WCAR and also the declaration and program of Action. This is a historic moment for the Dalit activists and other HR organizations in solidarity with the Dalit cause as for the first time this issue has been raised at this level in the government discussion and held a global debate. (Divakar)[33]

The UN has released additional statements since WCAR concerning human rights and caste, and taken concrete measures to monitor and end caste-based discrimination globally. These measures have been tracked by the web-based narrative of the IDSN, tracing the development of the UN intervention in the violation of the human rights of Dalit peoples (IDSN).[34] The first UN-based study on the issue of caste discrimination was carried out by the UN Sub-Commission on the Promotion and Protection of Human Rights using the lens and the later codified terminology of discrimination based on work and descent (DWD). The phrase "work and descent" has become a part of UN terminology to reference caste-based discrimination affected by social identities based on birth, hierarchy, and occupation. Therefore, caste-based discrimination is interpreted by the UN to be a form of racism. This is defined in paragraph one of

---

[32]For more information refer to the National Campaign for Dalit Human Rights. ncdhr.org.

[33] Paul Divakar. National Campaign for Dalit Human Rights. ncdhr.org.

[34] For more information refer to idsn.org.

the draft "UN Principles and Guidelines," which is a legal framework used to eliminate discrimination based on identities of work and descent, as follows:

> Any distinction, exclusion, restriction, or preference based on inherited status such as caste, including present or ancestral occupation, family, community or social origin, name, birth place, place of residence, dialect and accent that has the purpose or effect of nullifying or impairing the recognition, enjoyment, or exercise, on an equal footing, of human rights and fundamental freedoms in the political, economic, social, cultural, or any other field of public life. This type of discrimination is typically associated with the notion of purity and pollution and practices of untouchability, and is deeply rooted in societies and cultures where this discrimination is practiced. (IDSN)[35]

Several UN bodies—including the UN Sub-Commission, the HRC, the Committee on the Elimination of All Forms of Racial Discrimination (CERD), and those monitoring mechanisms of the Human Rights Council—the UN Special Procedures and the Universal Periodic Review (UPR)—have carefully studied and formulated concluding observations and recommendations to the UN. Notably, in its Seventieth Session in 2007, the CERD published its concluding observations in its document "Consideration of Reports Submitted by States Parties Under Article 9 of the Convention (Human Rights)" in the specific section entitled "Concerns and Recommendations" (IDSN).[36] That section highlights the absence of India's report on caste-based discrimination: "The Committee regrets the lack of information in the State party's report on concrete measures taken to implement existing anti-discrimination and affirmative action legislation [...]" (Report of CERD).[37] The state could not provide any evidence to prove the changes it claimed to have brought about through its anti-discrimination and affirmative action legislations.

IDSN reports that at the thirteenth UPR session in 2012, the 19-member delegation led by the Attorney General of India boasted of the laws and policies that India put in place to protect its disenfranchised populations. In contrast, the IDSN highlights that despite those measures,

> The Indian delegation did not, however, respond to the immediate challenges, critical observations, and strong recommenda-

---

[35] For complete document refer to *UN Principles and Guidelines.* idsn.org.
[36] Refer to idsn.org.
[37] For the complete document refer to the report, "Report of the Committee on the Elimination of Racial Discrimination" Committee on the Elimination of Racial Discrimination. Seventieth Session, Seventy First Session. United Nations, 2007.

tions on caste discrimination made by states during the interactive dialogue by UN human rights bodies as reflected in the compilation of UN information and by civil society as compiled in the summary of Stakeholder's information-India for the review of India. (IDSN)[38]

Responding to questions raised at this UPR session about the increase of violence against Dalits in India, the Indian delegation stated that there were sporadic incidents of violence against Dalits and that those incidents were being dealt with effectively. Again, in contrast to those statements, the IDSN noted that the report of the Special Rapporteur in 2009 concerning violence against Dalits stated otherwise. In a press release by NCDHR in May 2012, several Dalit human rights organizations expressed their deep concern about this misrepresentation by the Indian delegation of the enormity of caste-based violence in India (NCDR).[39]

As these events reveal, the UN's intervention into caste biases in India reveals a historic moment in the human rights movement for the community of 260 million Dalits globally.[40] Additional efforts to eliminate caste practices continue at the international level, as evidenced in the September 2013 gathering of Dalit leaders and organizations in New York, USA, to strategize action plans moving beyond the Millennium Development Goals of 2015.

India and Caste-Based Discrimination

The 97th Amendment to the Indian Constitution (1950) was added in 2011. Article 15 of that Amendment speaks against the "prohibition of discrimination on grounds of religion, race, caste, sex or place of birth." Article 17 concerning the abolition of untouchability rejects the practice "in any form [...]. The enforcement of any disability arising out of "Untouchability" shall be an offence punishable in accordance with law."[41] The Indian government executed several comparable laws relevant to Dalit rights in the following decades, including: the Bonded Labor (System) Abolition Act (1976), where relief could be brought to those serving indefinite time in labor in order to pay off a debt to land owners; the Employment of Manual Scavengers and Construction of Dry

---

[38] The full document is titled, "Dalit Rights Activists Enraged at the Failure of Indian Delegations to Address Questions Raised at the UN," International Dalit Solidarity Network.

[39] Refer to India's Second Review, 13th Session. National Campaign for Dalit Human Rights.

[40] IDSN estimation

[41] The entire text of the *Constitution of India* can be found in india.gov.in. As mentioned earlier, the constitution was written by Ambedkar.

Latrines (Prohibition) Act (1993), meant to abolish the government's employment of Dalits to clean public dry latrines without proper amenities; and the Scheduled Castes and Scheduled Tribes (Prevention of Atrocities) Act of 1989, which would ensure the reduction of violence meted out against Dalits and those in tribal communities.

Yet, despite the existence of these laws, they have not been implemented. Human Rights Watch observes that "even as these Acts are in place, they have been executed [...] without a serious and sustained commitment to implementing constitutional safeguards and other national and international legal protections, [so] human rights abuses in their most degrading forms will continue against scheduled caste community members" (205). In a press release on 2 March 2007, the UN Committee for the Elimination of All Forms of Racial Discrimination (UNCERD) addressed the urgent need for the implementation at every level of governance in India of the following recommendations:

> Prevalent discrimination of Dalits, particularly in rural areas, with regard to access to places of worship, housing, hospitals, education, water sources, markets and other public places, needs to be checked by strictly enforcing the Protection of Civil Rights Act (1955).
>
> Mandatory training on the appliance of the Scheduled Castes and Scheduled Tribes (Prevention of Atrocities) Act (1989) for concerned officials, as there has been an alarming increase in the number of arbitrary arrests, torture and extrajudicial killings of members of scheduled castes and scheduled tribes by the police.
>
> With regard to the surmountable increase in cases of sexual violence against Dalit women by upper caste men, there needs to be immediate remedial and legal actions to ensure effective delivery of Justice to the victim. ("Concluding Observations on CERD")[42]

The legal documents noted, and the concluding observations of various UN bodies reveal the inner paradox and the superficiality of the outer structures called into place.

---

[42] The *United Nations Office of the High Commissioner for Human Rights* has posted the "Concluding Observations of the Committee on the Elimination of Racial Discrimination" of the Seventieth Session in un.org.

Dalit Women in the International Discourse of Human Rights

A critical dimension to this discussion is the unique nature of violence experienced by Dalit women. According to the national census in 2001, about 80 million Dalit women live in India. Over a period of three years (1999–2004), the Institute of Development, Education, Action and Studies in Madurai, Tamil Nadu, conducted a national level survey and study on the nature of violence against Dalit women.. Led by a three-member team (Aloysious Irudayam, Jayashree P. Mangubai, and Joel G. Lee), the results of this study were published in three volumes as *Dalit Women Speak Out*, in 2006.[43] According to this study, the violence that Dalit women experience—physical, emotional, verbal, domestic, and sexual abuse—goes unreported, unfiled, and unrecognized by local police stations. The over-500 case studies carefully presented, testify to the immensity of violence that these women are subject to repeatedly, and to the fact that if not for this probing study, the types of violence surfaced in most of these cases would continue and remain undocumented. This negligence and ignoring of violence against Dalit women make it difficult to gather and record statistical information on violence against Dalit women. Only one percent of the reported cases of violence against Dalit women results in convictions. The UN, however, with the aid of a Special Rapporteur on Violence against Women, has made significant observations in May 2013 regarding the nature of violence against Dalit women. The Special Rapporteur reports:

> In follow-up to the case [gang rape case in New Delhi in 2012 that received public outcry], the report by the Verma Committee (established as a direct consequence of the Delhi gang rape) and the subsequent anti-rape legislation ignored the vulnerability of Dalit, Adivasi and minority community women, and failed to include a section on aggravated sexual assault based on caste and religious identity. ("Dalit Women – Facing Multiple Forms of Discrimination")[44]

Such human rights segregation is a serious problem that demands urgent attention. Dalit women's cries for justice are being pushed aside when the rape of Dalit women goes unnoticed. To address this immense issue, a "National Tribunal–Violence against Dalit Women in India" was held 30 September to 1

---

[43] This voluminous work is a pioneering effort in listening to Dalit women's voices so that those voices will be heard and will count as testimonies to the violence they are subject to.

[44] "Dalit Women – Facing Multiple Forms of discrimination" is a report compiled by the UN Special Rapporteur on Violence against Women in connection with their visit to India during April 22–May 1, 2013.

October 2013, at the Constitution Club in New Delhi. Several reputed Dalit rights organizations in India organized this event to bring their otherwise silenced voices and their stories of violence to the forefront. Negotiations are under way with state governments to file reports on violence against Dalit women and to ensure that justice is provided in the cases presented.

The *All India Dalit Mahila Adhikar Manch* (AIDMAM) is a national forum of Dalit Women committed to issues concerning violence against Dalit women. It reports that on an average, 27,000 incidents of serious atrocities and human rights violations are registered under the SC/ST (Prevention of Atrocities) Act, annually. Despite the lack of disaggregated data on the extent of violence against Dalit women, there is no doubt that women are affected disproportionately in these incidents (All India Dalit Mahila Adhikar Manch).[45] The AIDMAM has brought cases of violence against Dalit women to the attention of the Indian government through forums where Dalit women publicly testify to incidents of violence. *Navsarjan* is a similar organization working side by side with Dalit women in Gujarat to eradicate manual scavenging and to gain access to safety, security, and human dignity through economic independence. It is to be noted that these initiatives are led by Dalit women leaders lobbying internationally for the protection of Dalit women: Ruth Manorama, Fara Naqvi, Manjula Pradeep, Palanimuthu Sivagami, Bama Susairaj, and Vimal Thorat (to name a few).

On March 9, 2007, the UNCERD observed that the "[...] de-facto segregation of Dalits persists" and expressed concern at the "alarming rate of sexual violence against Dalit women."[46] In an opinion piece released on 8 August 2009, Navi Pillay, the United Nations High Commissioner for Human Rights, stated:

> Caste is the very negation of the human rights principles of equality and non-discrimination. It condemns individuals from birth and their communities to a life of exploitation, violence, social exclusion and segregation. Caste-discrimination is not only a human rights violation, but also exposes those affected to other abuses of their civil, political, economic, social and cultural rights. (Pillay)[47]

---

[45] All India Dalit Mahila Adhikar Manch is a national body of Dalit women advocating for Dalit rights organizationally as a program of the NCDHR.

[46] Committee on the Elimination of Racial Discrimination, "Concluding Observations of the Committee on the Elimination of Racial Discrimination, India, Seventieth Session, March 2007.

[47] Navi Pillay in "Tearing Down the Wall of Caste." Prior to delivering this speech, Pillay was presented with a brick from a destroyed public latrine where Dalits worked.

Pillay, a South African of Indian origin, initiated and continues to support all UN-based efforts that address human rights violations based on caste discrimination. Most recently, she has brought global visibility to the plight of Dalit women and girls. At the side event of the twenty-third session of the UN Human Rights Council in Geneva in June 2013, Pillay proclaimed:

> Dalit women and girls are exposed to multiple forms of discrimination based on gender and caste and, therefore, vulnerable to several layers of marginalization and violence. The specific human rights violations that originate from the intersection of discrimination based on caste and gender include sexual violence, sexual exploitation, trafficking, other forms of gender-based violence, bonded labor, lack of or limited access to food, water and sanitation, healthcare, education, adequate housing, and unequal participation in political, economic and social life. A first key step required is to address and combat caste-based discrimination and untouchability is of course the adoption of legislation that criminalizes this practice and ensures accountability of perpetrators and access to justice for victims. (Pillay)[48]

During that session, Dalit women expressed their experiences of violence, and for the first time, a UN session was devoted to exploring issues that affected Dalit women alone.

Dalit Women of Pudukkottai

My interest in learning of Dalit women's experiences in Pudukkottai, Tamil Nadu started in 2005 during conversations with Deepthi Sukumar serving with the *Safai Karmachari Andolan Movement* (SKA) which is a national organization dedicated to eradicating manual scavenging, the demeaning work of cleaning dry latrines reserved for Dalits and assumed mainly by Dalit women.[49] SKA announces on its website that a major focus is "to organize and mobilize Dalit communities around the issues of dignity and human rights with regard to

---

[48]Navi Pillay, "Dalit Women Working Together towards the Elimination of Multiple and Intersecting Forms of Discrimination and Violence Based on Gender and Caste." At a side event on June 4, 2013, where this speech was delivered at the UN Human Rights Council, Dalit women and men participated with the strong presence of international advocacy bodies: IMADR, Human Rights Watch, Minority Rights Group International, and the International Dalit Solidarity Network. This was the first time that a UN event focused exclusively on the situation of Dalit women.

[49] Safai Karmachari Andolan Mission Statement can be found in Safai KarmachariAndolan.org.

manual scavenging accompanied by strategic advocacy and legal interventions."[50] The SKA reports that there are over 256 districts in India that practice manual scavenging. As of 2009, the SKA has successfully abolished this practice in over 139 of these districts. She identified Pudukkottai as one of the most caste-power-based places in Tamil Nadu. She suggested I contact the Dr. AWARD (DA) organization to explore this issue in Pudukkottai. DA primarily works with Dalit women and Dalit communities involved in the work of manual scavenging.

Sukumar spoke of Kalaimagal (referred to as Kalai), the Director of DA, as a dynamic individual who had gained the respect and confidence of both Dalit and non-Dalit communities in Pudukkottai District. Kalaimagal founded DA in 1995 with specific goals, including encouraginmg Dalit women to claim their rights in society and to seek justice boldly; to eradicate the practice of manual scavenging, and hence, to alleviate their lives; and to enable Dalit communities to be self-sustaining (DA).[51] DA is a member of the national movement of SKA. When DA started its work, there were over 3,000 Dalits involved in manual scavenging; now, there are less than 200 doing this work (DA).[52] The organization serves as an advocate for both Dalit women and men by emphasizing solidarity among Dalit peoples as the most effective strategy towards creating changes. They raise voices against child labor and helps with adult education programs and self-help initiatives geared to rehabilitate affected Dalit women.

Thai (Tamil=mother) is a hostel program of the DA where, at any given time, about thirty to thirty-five Dalit girls, ranging in age from those attending kindergarten to the twelfth standard, live in a healthy and caring environment.[53] Upon completing the twelfth standard, DA places these children in colleges where they will learn nursing, engineering, and liberal arts (the possibility of medical studies is being explored as well). DA negotiates with the state government to offer free land and housing for Dalits, and currently handles over forty-seven cases of atrocities against Dalits. Such organizations allow women to view prevailing caste-based conditions as changeable and to take an active role in that change.

Given the DA's effective praxis of creating changes, I contacted Kalaimagal and visited Annavasal in August 2006. It is a small town in Pudukkottai District of Tamil Nadu where the DA office is located. I hoped to have conversa-

---

[50] Content found in Safai Karmachari Andolan Mission Statement, *SafaiKarmachari-Andolan.org.*
[51] Trustees' statement in the *Dr. AWARD Profile.*
[52] Trustees' report in the *Dr. AWARD Annual Report.*
[53] I am proud to serve on this Board.

tions with Kalaimagal and her staff as part of my initial exploration into understanding how Dalit women in partnership with human rights initiatives express their desire to address the violence they face as outcaste women. Since then, I have had the privilege to listen to numerous testimonials by Dalit women on their courage and hope in addressing caste violence. Some of those conversations took place in the DA office and some in the homes of women affected by caste violence. The research I present herein explores three visits I took to Pudukkottai over a period of five years. In Pudukkottai, I travelled to about ten Dalit villages and two stone quarries, where I talked with young Dalit girls. During those visits, I spent time with Kalaimagal while travelling with her, observing her work, and strengthening relationships I had made during my previous visits.

Situating Caste in Pudukkottai

According to the 2011 census carried out by Pudukkottai District and recorded by DA, the total population of Pudukkottai is 11,618,725, and of that, there are 249,471 Dalits. DA reports that 71 percent of the Dalit population is educated to some extent,[54] and 61.72 percent are at least able to sign their name. Pudukkottai District is composed of about thirteen blocks or villages. As throughout much of the agricultural spaces of India, Pudukkottai is split into territories allocated to the Hindus and the outcaste Dalits. The higher castes that live in this region comprise the Mudaliar community, who are made up of sub-castes including the Vellalar, Chettiar, Kallar (comprised of Agamudiar and Maravar), Achaari, and Konar Ambalagarar, among others. According to Kalaimagal, these caste Hindu communities take great pride in their caste identity to the point of executing violence against outcaste Dalit communities living near them to maintain their caste honor. This separation is upheld in certain traditions, for example, wherein even if the shadow of a Dalit were to fall upon a caste Hindu's body, the caste Hindus must purify their bodies through a ritual ceremony of cleansing themselves either by attending temple to ask God for forgiveness or by monetary offerings to deities.[55]

Dalits in Pudukkottai are made up of numerous communities: the Pallar, agricultural laborers who comprise 7.41 percent; the Paraiyar, the drum-beaters mainly for funeral processions who comprise 6.66 percent; the Putharaivannar, are the launderers serving only other Dalits and comprise 0.27 percent; the Vannar are those who wash clothes for the caste Hindus communities and make up 0.13 percent of the population; the Panrikuravar, who are relegated to clean-

---

[54] Trustees, *Dr. AWARD Annual Report.*
[55] Conversations with Kalaimagal Arumugam in November 2012.

ing toilets comprise 2.49 percent; the Kuravar, who clean toilets comprise 0.52 percent; the Chakkiliyar, who process leather are about 0.2 percent; the Kaladi, whose work includes street cleaning are about 0.19 percent; the Valluvar, who perform religious rites among Dalits comprise 0.22 percent; and the Ottar, who clean toilets are 13 percent of the population. All these communities belong to the lowest rung even among Dalits depending on the specific task they perform.

Dalit communities have performed their traditionally delegated work for several generations. For example, Pallar remain agricultural laborers as bonded laborers due to the high debts that they owe their landlords. The Paraiyar men are the drum-beaters who announce deaths to the communities, and dance and beat drums while leading funeral processions into burial or cremation grounds (Arumugam). The Panrikuravar (pig-rearing nomads) are considered to be the lowest community of Dalits, who traditionally rear pigs for consumption and to clean up the streets as the pigs eat human waste (Arumugam). The women in this community are the ones who work in the dry toilets, scooping human excreta into baskets and discarding them in allocated dumps (Thekaekara 1-3).[56] The constant social linkage of excrement to Panrikuravar women concretizes social stigmatization as the waste of society.

Pudukkottai, like many other regions in Tamil Nadu, presents traditions wherein landlords maintain caste hierarchy to sustain the economic and sociopolitical agency of their communities in the region. The Kallar community, who own most of the property in Pudukkottai including the stone quarries, negotiate most of the building contracts in this region. They are vested with the political power to function as autonomous authoritative bodies in the region due to their wealth. According to Kalaimagal, the region has witnessed violent clashes between the Kallar and Dalit communities due to disputes over land, wages, and temple entry issues. Discrimination continues against Dalits in local tea shops, as Dalits are served tea in separate cups outside the tea shops normally owned by dominant caste members (Arumugam).

---

[56] Thekaekara's work is ethnographic in nature.

Dalit woman cleaning public dry latrines, Annavasal, Pudukkottai District, 2003.

A recent incident in the town Keezhakurichi, about twenty-five kilometers away from Pudukkottai, reflects these restrictions on the human rights of Dalits. This town comprises the Pallar and Paraiyar Dalit communities as well as the caste Hindus of the Kallar, Agumudi, Thevar, and Chettiar communities. Keezhakurichi is the site of the *Veeramma Kali* Temple, built by the dominant caste communities about seventy years ago, and hence, serves as a reminder of the religious fervor, power, and wealth of those caste communities. Dalits are not allowed to worship in the temple, to take part in any of the festivities, or to enter onto the temple premises. On April 30, 2013, a few young Dalits in the area attempted to take part in the temple festivities and were severely punished for it. As punishment, the caste Hindus cut the limbs of four young Dalit men with sickles and sexually harassed young Dalit girls. With Kalai's leadership, DA decided to seek justice in this matter; she immediately informed the press, and over six newspaper reporters including *The Hindu* published the news story. As a result, two television channels travelled to Keezhakurichi to telecast the story. A First Investigation Report (FIR) was booked, and reports were sent to the Makkal Thanipprivu (Tamil based organization of the 'People's Committee') in the office of the chief minister of Tamil Nadu. A court case is progressing as DA awaits the announcement of the trial date. The leader of the *panchayat* (local village council) was identified as the prime instigator and offender in this case (*Thina Mani,* May 1, 2013).[57] This particular incident was breaking news in Tamil Nadu, where the issue of denying Dalits entry into Hindu temples has been questioned and condemned openly by the press.

This temple entry incident testifies to the horrifying effect of politicizing religion and of maintaining caste hierarchy, as reiterated by the historian David Gilmartin's claim: "As an identity category conceptualized as ascribed and primordial, caste seemed to challenge not only equality, but also the very image of the free, rational, individual voter that underlay the concept of the people's sovereignty" (19). In this case, ironically, the Dalit communities who were attacked under the *panchayat* leader's orders were the very same members who elected the *panchayat* leader to power—not by choice, but out of fear. The *panchayat* leader considers the boundary transgression of Dalit voters as a serious offence because they broke the traditionally established legacy of obedience to the sovereignty of his position in the community.

Sri Veeramma Kali Amman temple, Keezhakurichi: a site of violence.

The *Panrikuravar*

During my visits to Pudukkottai in 2006 and 2007, I visited several Panrikuravar communities settled on lands allotted for them by the Tamil Nadu government. Three of these communities live on the banks of a sewer that has be-

---

[57] *Thina Mani* is a major Tamil newspaper.

come a stagnant pond.[58] Stray pigs and dogs congregate on those banks for their nightly rest, and children from these communities play along the sewer banks while taking a brief moment now and then to complete their school work. Such living conditions render them vulnerable to many diseases.

Traditionally, the Panrikuravar were known as the Kaatunayakkar (Tamil=forest dwellers) because they had lived by hunting for food, and were therefore nomadic. As such, the state government continues to document and recognize the Panrikuravar as "nomads" and not as "permanent dwellers," which would otherwise allow them to claim a stable home space. Hence, even as the Tamil Nadu government employs them to clean latrines, the Panrikuravar still do not qualify to receive benefits from the government. Categorized as "nomads," they cannot own land or claim the government's free rationing of rice, *dhal,* and kerosene, and furthermore, they are not able to secure admission for their children in school because they lack a residential address, which is required of children for them to be registered into a school. The DA has successfully negotiated with the Tamil Nadu government on the status of the Panrikuravar with the aid of district collectors and has gained residency status for most of these communities with the primary aim of making it possible for Panrikuravar children to attend school.

Dalit Women and Girl Children

The gender identity of Dalit women and girl-children render them more vulnerable to certain forms of violence, regardless of their labor. In Pudukkottai, Dalit women and girls work as laborers in fields, stone quarries, building sites, and farms by taking care of cattle or collecting cow dung to make cow dung patties for use as fuel. Kalai states that a young Dalit girl could start working in the quarry at the age of eight. The quarries that I visited in 2006 and 2007 are owned by the Kallar communities. In those quarries, Dalit women and girls work for a pay of between fifty cents and a dollar a day. All female Dalit workers carry heavy loads of stone on their heads and are constantly exposed to the dust and rock particles throughout their work at the quarry. Such work places them at risk for contracting tuberculosis because they are constantly being ex-

---

[58] Panrikuravar communities currently live in these specific areas in Pudukkottai District: Pudukkottai Municipality (Machuvadi, Santhaipettai, Thiruvalluvar Nagar, Ayanavaram and Mullainagar); Aranthangi Municipality (Santhaipettai),Thirumayam, Annavasal (Golden Nagar), Keeranoor (Pazha Kallukadai Theru), Illuppur (Irunthirapatti Road), Viralimalai, Karambakudi, Arimalam, Keeramanagalam, Alangudi, Manalmelgudi, Ponnamara vathi, Virachilai, Gandharvakottai, Kaverinagar, Mucknnamalaipatty, Eam pal, Kothamangalam, Jagathapattinam.

posed to fine dust particles. Dalit women workers face physical dangers because they must carry heavy loads of rock up and down the quarries, which range anywhere from 200 to 300 meters deep, and they work in exceptionally hot conditions.

Dalit women's gender renders them even more vulnerable to specific forms of caste domination. The literacy rate among Dalit men is 4 percent, and among Dalit women, it is only 2 percent.[59] Illiteracy, combined with severe poverty, yields them easy targets for violence perpetrated mostly by men from the Kallar community and by men from their own community. As a result, women face economic and sexual exploitation, along with physical and domestic abuse, and permanent psychological damages; furthermore, they are forced to live in the margins of the town in unhygienic conditions. Children who are able to attend school are discriminated against by the teachers and are subject to threats, teasing, and harassment from members of the caste communities. According to a DA report, on July 5th, 2013 in the village of Mathur, two young Dalit girls studying in the Swami Vivekananda Vidyalaya Matriculation School in the seventh and ninth standards were sexually harassed by young men belonging to the dominant caste. When the girls' parents made inquiries into this incident, the entire Dalit community in Mathur was attacked. Kalai is currently mobilizing legal help for this community to seek justice in this case, which she builds into the frame of the punishable offence of sexual harassment of women. As of September 2016, the DA was not able to secure the case due to the local politicians supporting the accused men, which is a human rights violation.

Young girls are considered a liability to their families because their sexual vulnerability might lead to events that would compromise their family's honor. To prevent potential dishonor to the family, girl-children in Pudukkottai District are traditionally married off at an early age to ensure their safety. DA reports that over twenty-five such marriages take place in a given village in one year. In her work, Kalai strongly addresses this issue, for example, by working with young Dalit girls to see that they remain in school even as their parents want to see them married. In reference to one of these tensions, in a phone conversation in October 2013, Kalai informed me that one of the girls from the hostel she had been working with did not come back after a weekend visit to her home in May 2013. Her parents had married her off to what seemed like a good prospect; regardless, Kalai intervened and made sure the girl enrolled in a school in the town in which she was married so that she could continue her studies after marriage. The Prohibition of Child Marriage Act of 2006—to some extent—has reduced the immensity of the problem of child marriage throughout India, but child marriage is still a major issue in rural Tamil Nadu

---

[59]Trustees, *Dr. AWARD Fact Sheet.*

("Child Marriage—Fact Sheet Nov 2011").[60] The International Planned Parenthood Federation in its September 2013 publication, *Ending Child Marriages*, states that child marriage is a widely ignored violation of the health and development of the girl-child and is one of the most persistent forms of sexual abuse against the girl-child that is socially sanctioned ("Ending Child Marriage – A Guide for Global Policy Action").[61]

Many international and local organizations, along with the Tamil Nadu government, address the issue of child labor and child marriage through combined efforts to create awareness, form self-help groups, and emphasize education. The organizations and Dalit communities see education as crucial to eliminating child labor and child marriage in these communities. However, attaining good quality education for Dalit children is yet another major issue for several reasons. In some cases, villages where Dalits live often lack schools; in other cases, the schools that are in existence are mostly dilapidated or may prohibit Dalit children from entering them. In situations where children can gain entrance into a school, the teachers force them to sit in the back of the classroom and treat them differently because they consider the children dirty. DA reports that in Pudukkottai District, Dalit children in schools are made to sit apart from other caste children, and furthermore, they are sent on errands and are told to clean school toilets. DA works with school systems to create awareness among teachers and officials of the cruelty and inhuman nature of this kind of treatment of children.

Narratives of Violence

In the few villages and quarries that I visited, Dalit women were willing to share their stories with me. When the women narrated their experiences, I handed a tape recorder to Kalai and sat down as a listener. It is in Kalai, their leader, that the Dalit women have a deep trust, and it was she who initiated the conversations. Dalit women spoke passionately about the desperation of their situations, their personal stories of victimization, and the ways in which they have survived both as individuals and as members of their communities. Each of these narratives bears testimony to a humanist concern for each other, a desire for justice, a strong nervous determination to resist in the midst of fear, and an audacious hope to see changes happen at least toward their children. They

---

[60] More information can be found in "Child Marriage – Fact Sheet Nov 2011." UNICEF. un.org.
[61] This document is part of the International Planned Parenthood Federation and the Forum on Marriage and the Rights of Women and Girls under the United Nations Population Fund.

shared these stories with the eagerness that I—a Dalit woman living in the United States, who represented a world outside of Pudukkottai—should hear them and transmit them to the broader world. A few of them wanted me to take their stories to the television stations! In this next section, I share some of their narratives, replete with laughter, tears, moments of long silences, emphatic gestures, and cursing as well.

Following is a personal narrative by Janaki, an eighteen-year-old Dalit woman, who faced repeated sexual abuse by Dalit men[62]:

> As a child, I lived in Thirunallur village with my parents. They worked in the homes and fields owned by Kallar—planting, weeding, and sweeping on their properties. They were not paid in cash for the work that they did, but came home with only rice and dhal. For money, they collected dung from cows, made patties, dried them, and sold them to be used for fuel and other cleaning purposes.[63] I did my share of the work along with my parents during the day and slept along the streets on sidewalks at night. My mother and father found it very hard to feed all their four children.
>
> As soon as I came of age at thirteen [years], they decided to find a husband for me and send me away. I was a [an economic] burden. One of my father's relatives, his name is Rangan, [a Dalit] son of Palaniyandy, offered to marry me in the year 2000. My father and mother said "yes" to him. Rangan took me away to his village, [about ten kilometers away and without having married her at the time]. When I went there I was treated very badly. Many men came to use me. I was terrified. I was beaten if I refused them, and I was threatened not to tell anyone. After about a year, I conceived but I was forced into an abortion after my stomach started showing. This made me very sick. I could not move, eat, or talk properly. In this condition, I conceived again and had a very difficult time. I almost died at childbirth and became very ill again. I was neglected and left to die. News reached my father and mother, and they came and took me home. Then I told them all that happened to me. Even

---

[62] Janaki Periasamy shared more details which she requested not to publish.

[63] Dry cow dung is used as fuel for cooking in rural India. The ashes of the burnt dung are used for cleaning pots. Cow dung is believed to have antibacterial property, and therefore, is used to coat the mud walls and the immediate grounds of a hut. According to Sainath, in a speech delivered on the event of his photo exhibition, *Invisible Women, Invisible work*, at the Asia Society, New York, 2001, Dalit women who collect this dung are contributors to the economy of the country.

after several months of my childbirth, I was still bleeding. My body had bruises [Janaki showed some of the bruises on her stomach, and arms as she was talking].

I was like a mad person, blabbering, and could not even go to the bathroom on my own. My father and mother took great care of me. They fed me rice gruel every day to get my strength back.

At this point in her narrative, Janaki turned to look at her father, Periasamy, who was seated beside her and who had been staring at the floor the entire time that Janaki had been speaking. He held Janaki's one-and-a-half-year-old daughter on his lap. Periasamy started sharing:

For two years we fed her, and then she started getting better. We took care of the baby. We could not even keep clothes on her because she would rip them in her madness. That was when the scoundrel came. Afraid of strangers, she would hide in her hut for days together. But somehow the scoundrel came to her. He was known to our family, said he wanted to help. We believed him. Curse us! Rangan came to visit and promised medical treatment for her. We allowed him to visit Janamma [Janaki]. *She was bedridden. Every time, when we were at work he came and raped her. We didn't know. Janaki was almost like a lifeless body, not knowing anything. Her stomach started showing. Then she showed gestures pointing towards Rangan. We are very, very angry. We are cursed! It must be him only* [curses]. *Who else came to our home? I called for a panchayat.* [64] *But* [waving his arms] *he* [Rangan] *was a panchayat council member, so they listened to his* [curses] *words and passed the judgment that he had nothing to do with Janaki and we were telling this to get money.*

Kalaimagal intervened at this point to state why and how DA was involved in this case:

Janaki's parents came to me. Rani [a DA staff member] *and me took up the case to fight for justice with Janaki. By now, Janaki recovered enough to be able to recall what Rangan had been doing to her. She gave a bold statement to the police of-*

---

[64] A local village council normally only headed by men. Now, however, Dalit women are heading these unions in many parts of India. For further details on a panchayat read Sarita Brara, "Dalit Woman Makes History in Rajasthan." *The Hindu*, September 18, 2012. thehindu.com.

ficer in charge at Pudukkottai. The entire people of Thirunal-
lur, especially the women, are supportive of Janaki. When Ja-
naki narrated her story to the police, she was bold in her
statements about identifying her victimizers as those who de-
served punishment. That fellow, Rangan, went into hiding and
his parents accused me and Rani of kidnapping him. I marched
directly to the police and said: "I will hold a dharna [silent
protest of fasting] *in front of the police station if you take any*
action against us." All the women from the Thirunallur village
thronged in front of the police station and shouted protest slo-
gans. The police then decided to search for Rangan and found
him hiding in a nearby village. When called for a semen test,
Rangan filled the container with phlegm instead! Can you im-
agine! This was a clear indication to the police that this man
had to be the rapist. The DNA test results are not here yet.

When I went back to Pudukkottai in 2007, Janaki came to see me at the DA office; she beamed with a big smile and gave me a kiss. Kalaimagal informed me that Rangan's DNA had tested positive in the rape case concerning Janaki and that he is now in jail without bail. Janaki stated that she boldly makes speeches to people about her experiences in the hope that what had happened to her should not happen to any other Dalit girl in Thirunallur. She said that all she wanted was for people to know who the father of her child was and for Rangan to be punished. During my visit, Janaki had been working closely with Kalaimagal while she was undergoing treatment for depression. Unfortunately, upon my return to the US, Kalai phoned me on August 6th, 2010 to say that Janaki had drowned herself in the local river the previous evening. The day before the incident, Janaki had brought her daughter to the girl's hostel and had asked Kalai to take care of her. Kalai notified me that the entire DA community was distraught. DA is now taking extra care to provide better psychological treatment for young girls who are as severely traumatized as Janaki.

Janaki's story reveals how the power dynamics oppressing Dalit women within broader society are replicated within Dalit communities, wherein Dalit women are prone to violence by Dalit men. While narrating her story, Janaki kept repeating that she felt duped by the men, especially Rangasamy, and referred to him as a '*candalla*' (traitor). She added that it hurt more when one of your own took advantage of you. Waving her finger, she had said that if only she had been economically on par with her rapists, they would not have dared to lay a hand on her. Even though Janaki's story had a tragic end, her legacy continues to surface in the lives of the girls she impacted before her death. This is evidenced, for example, in how she, in her own expressions of a humanist activism, was deeply concerned about other young Dalit girls. She created awareness among them that they should not agree to child marriage and emphasized in them the need to be educated and to hold jobs to avoid victimization.

Personal Narration by Chitra, a Staff Member of DA Who Worked as a Laborer in the Stone Quarries[65]

In July 2007, with Kalai's help, I visited with women at a stone quarry in Pudukkottai District owned by the Kalaimaan Company of the Kallar community. The quarry employs Dalits to break blasted rocks into smaller pieces and then load them onto trucks for delivery. Due to the nature of the work, most of the women laborers are wounded, infected, or maimed on the job. Women may eventually die or remain permanently disabled from work-related incidents. The laborers are not protected by any paperwork or medical insurance, and the companies will sanction a loan for necessary medical treatment.

Young girls and women are often required to travel in trucks to different bases where the rocks are loaded and unloaded from trucks. The girls are loaded onto the trucks along with the rocks, and are made to sit on top of the rock piles during travel for several miles. Often, the trucks are overloaded, making them unstable, and the vehicles meet with frequent accidents in which the girls are injured badly or even killed under heavy piles of rocks. In addition, the truck journeys often require an overnight drive, which places these young girls' lives at risk.

Chitra, who is now a staff member with DA, worked at this quarry since the age of five. She described the challenges she faced while on the job:

> *Akka* [older sister], *we are small girls. We are not protected by anyone while we travel on the truck. We travel in groups of about five or six. The truck driver is there and usually another boy. Most often we leave very early in the morning while it is still dark. Akka, at times like that, often, we are made to leave the truck and forced into bushes. The first time I saw this happen, I was eleven. I was terrified. These young girls were forced into doing that with these awful guys. Sometimes there are other men waiting in the bushes.*

At this point, Kalai added: *"The tragedy is that some of the truck drivers are frequent brothel customers and carriers of the HIV virus, which they pass onto these innocent young victims."* Chitra continued:

---

[65] These conversations with Chitra Kanniah in 2006 was the beginning of a friendship.

Once, one girl was singled out asked to get off in the middle of nowhere, and was raped by the roadside, while we all cried and screamed in the truck. We were threatened that if we were to speak about these things, we would all lose our jobs. Out of fear for our lives and our livelihoods, we girls keep silent about these abuses. But because of Kalai Akka, and her staff, we were told that we do not have to continue with this situation. Some of the truck drivers have been arrested, but many are protected by their bosses. There are so many girls there, Akka, still suffering in these situations [Chitra sobbed]. *When I told my father and mother that I was scared to work there, they beat me and said that I was only imagining things. For them money was important.*

Young girls such as Chitra need to leave their homes to work under such dangerous conditions to support themselves and their families as well. Even as they were forced to work under such precarious conditions to further the economic situation of their families, the young girls' work outside of the home, ironically, was interpreted by society as an attempt to further themselves and to gain independence as Dalit girls. For their seemingly "transgressive" activities, they were punished with sexual exploitation. Such exploitative situations are created to let the girls know that if they choose to live and to better their lives, for whatever reason, they are allowing risks and are responsible for the sexual violence to which they are subjected. Such attacks harm the girls' confidence, so that even as they struggle against one form of oppression— here, economic—they are faced with another that will ensure their continued exploitation in some way.

Chitra is now part of the DA staff working with Dalit girls and providing awareness-raising training sessions for them. Chitra stated that many girls who are afraid of getting onto the trucks often return to the manual scavenging jobs, which are at least less risky, even if the pay is much less and the work more demeaning. Kalai is now in the process of setting up tailoring units for girls involved in manual scavenging so that they could be self-sufficient. The employment of and sexual exploitation of these young girls is, no doubt, a violation of their human rights as defined by the UN and as addressed by the Indian Constitution. As stated in the 86th Amendment of the Indian Constitution passed in 2002, the Constitution declares clear statements with regard to children below the age of fourteen to prohibit them from working in hazardous conditions, protect them from exploitation of any kind and from performing work beyond their strength, and reinforce that all children have the right to access free education (India Tribune).[66] Those statements are backed further by The Child Labor (Prohibition and Regulation) Act of 1986 and The Juvenile Justice Act 2000 (Amendment 2006), which stress that children below the age of fourteen years should not be employed (Government of India, Labor Department).[67]

Dalit women working in the Kalaimaan stone quarry, Pudukkottai District.

Regardless of the existence of such laws in India, 60 million children still comprise the work force, as revealed by the International Confederation of Free Trade Union. Children below fourteen years of age constituted 31.2 percent of the total work force from 2009 to 2010, and among those, 67.4 percent were girls. Child labor results from a variety of but mainly due to reasons of poverty, a lack of awareness on the importance of education, poor educational facilities, as well as the lack of resourceful access to those facilities (Stephen).[68] Additionally, whereas children are paid a nominal amount of 20 rupees per day, the actual daily wage rate for adult workers for the same labor is 80 to 100 rupees

[66] The National Human Rights Commission in India records several articles on child labor in India. nhrc.nic.in/documents/LibDoc/Child_Labour_F.pdf
[67] More information can be accessed at labor.gov.in
[68] Hannah Stephen, worked with UNICEF, on education projects among Dalit children in the Chennai slum districts.

(Venkateswarlu).[69] That remarkable discrepancy drives employers to prefer to hire child workers. Child laborers work seven-hour days, which is far greater than the time they spend in school. That imbalance has serious implications on their school performance to the point that some are pressured to drop out of school and to join the work force full-time (Venkateswarlu).[70]

Personal Narration by Rani and Karuppaiah,[71] on the Abduction of their Daughter

The two-tumbler (cup/glass) system is a commonly accepted practice of discrimination against Dalits in rural India. Dalits are not allowed to drink from the same tea cups as the caste communities, and hence, tea stall owners keep one set of tumblers for their caste clients and another for Dalit clients. Additionally, Dalits should sit in separate spaces inside or remain outside the tea stalls to drink tea that they purchase. The tea stall owner will pour tea into a tumbler held out by a Dalit, which is reserved specifically for Dalits (Narula 2). The following narrative considers the case of Rani and Karuppaiah, who spoke out against this two-tumbler system, and the repercussions on their family resulting from it. Karuppaiah's narrative:

> *About thirteen years ago, we* [Karuppaiah and his wife, Rani] *took legal action against a tea shop owner, Gandhimati, who refused to serve me tea along with others. Like other places, in Thachampatty, they served me tea in a separate cup outside the shop because I am a Dalit. Gandhimati is from the Kallar community. She was arrested and made to pay a compensation amount to us. Infuriated that my wife had taken action against her, Gandhimati furiously stated that one day Rani would have to pay for her actions. Our daughter, Vijaya, was about five-years-old then; now, twelve years later, she* [Gandhimati] *wanted revenge. By now, some boys who come to the tea shop started disturbing my daughter. Gandhimati, with the help of her husband and two other boys who were causing trouble for my daughter, abducted Vijaya on her way home from school. We notified the police. Gandhimati's daughter was a police-*

---

[69] Venkateswarlu's extensive research reporting for the India Committee of the Netherlands provides accurate documentation on both the employment and rehabilitation of children in the cottonseed production in India.

[70] Kalaimagal reported the same situation among Dalit children in Pudukkottai district who face tremendous pressure from their own families to bring home wages to live on.

[71] When I met Rani Karuppaiah she was contemplating opening her own tea stall.

woman in the same district and begged the higher officers not to take action against her family. But Vijaya's schoolmates testified to the fact that they saw Rangasamy, Gandhimati's husband, along with two other boys take Vijaya away. Gandhimati, however, using her caste and class power, managed to publish a story in the newspaper, which stated that my daughter seduced two boys and had eloped with them. But the police, in co-operation with Kalai, filed a First Investigation Report on September 24, 2005. In this, they found that Vijaya was taken to a tsunami camp in Nagapatinam, further South, where she was repeatedly sexually abused. After about two weeks she was taken to Bombay where her abductors were waiting for a good offer on her to sell her to a brothel. After long investigations, Vijaya was brought back to us.

Kalai inserted:

On January 20, 2006 at around 2:00 am, we [DA] received a phone call from Vijaya.[72] She was sobbing, saying that she was at the Tiruchy bus station. We rushed and found her in a traumatized state and incoherent. She could not stop crying for several days, and had violent outbursts and fainting spells. Now through DA, she receives medical attention.

Rani, Vijaya's mother, added: *"Why must this happen to our child? We asked for justice, we did what was the right thing to do, we wanted dignity."*[73] I met Vijaya when I went back to Annavasal in 2007 as she was not in a condition to receive visitors in 2006; she was in a much better state when I saw her again. She was strikingly beautiful and spoke in a mild voice. She kept saying that she wanted to get back to school and become a teacher.

Although Rani was contesting caste-based discrimination executed only against her husband, her resistance became the platform upon which to build a broader collective resistance against the discrimination of Dalits in her community. The symbolic value of Rani's struggle is illustrated in several demonstrations that took place against caste discrimination by other Dalits. This included, for example, a demonstration in which several women from DA gathered in front of the police station and broke the tea glasses reserved for Dalits; in support of Rani's fight, they protested the traditional social practice that mediated their community's collective social agency. Rani's act of resistance called for a radical paradigmatic shift of Dalit agency from exclusion

---

[72]Kalai stated that all DA members are required to have the DA office phone number. Vijaya had written it in one of the school notebooks in the school bag she was carrying.
[73] Rani Karuppaiah shared these details in a personal conversation on August 3, 2006.

to inclusion within the broader community. Such bold expressions of collective agency are political moves that consciously place resistance at the heart of social change for Dalits.

As such stories reveal, the message from dominant caste members commands that if Dalits were to rise to claim justice, fight for their rights, and be recognized as human beings, they would be punished as a direct consequence for their actions. Rani chose to speak out against Gandhimati's humiliation and the injustice against her husband; Gandhimati, in turn, wanted to punish Rani, her family, and the broader Dalit community. Vijaya's body became the site through which Gandhimati chose to enact violence against Rani and her husband to ensure that all Dalits in Thachampatty would not dare to speak against the cultural practice of the two-tumbler system that insures the sovereignty of the Kallar community. Most disturbingly, but not surprisingly, Gandhimati waited for the twelve years it took for Vijaya's body to fully develop to maximize the dishonor that Gandhimati could bring to Vijaya's family.

Vijaya's story brings to light the experiences of many Dalit women and girl-children in India's sex trafficking industry. The Dalit Freedom Network notes: "Of the 3 million prostitutes in India, 1.2 million are children. Most of them are Dalits, trafficked into brothels" ("Sex Trafficking").[74] In its May 2009 issue, *Outlook India* reported that over 3,700 arrests were made in Tamil Nadu and Karnataka alone in 2007 for illegal human trafficking ("Tamil Nadu Tops in Immoral Trafficking").[75] The Self-Help Society of Pudukkottai District identifies Viralimalai, a town near Pudukkottai, as a significant sex-trading activity center serving clients and engaging sex victims from the Trichy and Pudukkottai Districts. The Society further reports that about 26 male brokers and 15 female brokers operate in these areas ("Justification for the Intervention").[76]

Young Dalit women and girl-children are at the highest risk for sex trafficking in India. In September 2008, Christine Joffres along with his research team published a study about the nature and intensity of sexual slavery in India. The study reveals that girls are more prone to sexual trafficking due to factors such as poverty and false allurements to join the Indian movie industry. According to their study, Dalit girls in Tamil Nadu are trafficked through all of these categorizations: "The most common form of sex work involves young women and

---

[74] This report comes from the Dalit Freedom Network, a church-based global organization advocating for Dalit Rights and focusing on educating Dalit children.

[75] This essay, "Tamil Nadu Tops in Immoral Trafficking" can be accessed through OutlookIndia.com. It debunks the myth that Tamil Nadu is the safest state in India.

[76] "Justification for the Intervention" is published by *Weaker Section Welfare Association*, founded in 1995 by social workers from Viralimalai, Pudukkottai District of Tamil Nadu. Their activities include rehabilitation of Dalit communities through legal intervention, healthcare and education.

girls from economically deprived and marginalized groups (i.e., Dalits) who have been "recruited" by brokers, sold to pimps or brothel owners (most of whom are ex-prostitutes), and forced into prostitution" (Joffres et al. 2008).[77] Most cases involving impoverished groups, such as Dalits, involve the abduction of young girls for sale into larger brothel operations. Despite national and regional laws in place to protect the girl-child (mentioned earlier) and to specifically address trafficking (Integrated Anti-Human Trafficking Units, Anti-Trafficking Nodal Cell State Program), the market for sexual commercialization and the rate at which girls are sold into this market is on the rise.

The United Nations Refugee Agency (UNRA) has commended India for endorsing the 2000 UN Protocol to Prevent, Control and Punish Trafficking of Women and Children (Trafficking in Persons Report).[78] The UNRA recognizes India's new Anti-Human Trafficking Units (AHTUs) instated by the Indian government's Home Affairs Department in 2009. Yet, despite these efforts and the move to imprison offenders related to the sex trade in India, Dalit women and girl-children remain vulnerable to sex trafficking. The United States Department of State's 2011 Trafficking in Persons Report on India states: "Overall law enforcement efforts against bonded labor, however, remained inadequate, and the complicity of public officials in human trafficking remained a serious problem."[79] International human rights bodies, such as UNCERD and the International Dalit Solidarity Network (IDSN), continue to urge India to implement laws to protect Dalit women and children, but the national government is falling below its potential efforts in this area (Hameed et al. 2010).[80]

Personal Narrative of Renuka from the Village of Keeranur

I met with Renuka in August 2006 in Keeranur, a Dalit village in Pudukkottai District. Just a few months earlier, Renuka's family and her entire village were punished because her son aspired to seek admission into an engineering college in Tiruchy. Renuka's narrative testifies to the consequences that a Dalit individual, family, and community will face if they dare to seek an education and a better economic status. As Renuka explains, the Kallar attacked their village,

---

[77] Joffres and her colleagues conducted a pioneering study that has made valuable contribution both as quantitative and qualitative resource on sexual slavery and trafficking for commercial sexual exploitation.

[78] Trafficking in Persons Report, 2011 from the United States Department of State provides a thorough analysis of human trafficking as a global crisis.

[79] Trafficking in Persons Report focuses on highlighting efforts towards the protection of victims trafficked for labor as well. It addresses the urgent needs of victims leading to sustainable changes in their lives and finding avenues of reintegration.

[80] See Kevin Bales, *Disposable People: New Slavery in the Global Economy* (2004).

reacting to the possibility that a Dalit could become an engineer, which is a prestigious position that should be accessed only by the dominant. About thirty-five homes in the village of Keeranur were destroyed in the raid that took place that night. Renuka recalls:

> *They* [the Kallar community] *came to us in the middle of the night, madam. Split open his head* [pointing to her husband]. *My husband and I work as daily wage laborers. They did this to us. We carry sacks of rice and vegetables on our backs to educate our children. I also work as a servant in Kallar homes, and sometimes I work in the fields. We know that our children have to study to make it big. Here,* [pointing to her son] *this is my son, Vijay. I have two girls also. This boy has to become a successful guy and help us. He is good in studies. Vijay completed his twelfth grade with very high grades, and we applied to an engineering college, and he was promised a seat based on his merit. We were really overjoyed by the hope that our family could soon have money and a good life when our son becomes an engineer. Selvam, a Thevar* [dominant caste] *lawyer in the same community, couldn't stand this. For him, it was, "How can this Pallar Dalit boy become an engineer?" When Vijay was returning home from school, two men beat him up. They threatened Vijay that if he did not stop studying, he would be killed. We were all terrified. We all went to bed that night. My husband and son slept on the thinnai* [a small cement, cot-like construction in rural homes] *in the verandah. We women slept inside. We woke up to a big cry from my husband. We heard attacking and banging and hitting noises. We were too afraid to get out to see. O God! I saw my husband on the floor bleeding and my son's neck bleeding from a cut. These guys then went into every home in our village, broke stuff, pulled women out. Some women had their hips and arms broken. The guys behaved in a very dirty way with our women. During the assault, they screamed: "Don't you dare dream of becoming better than Thevars!" Some of us in the village ran out and phoned DA. Immediately we got help. Those who could pick up some strength, pulled themselves to the main road, and blocked the traffic to get* [the] *attention of the police. Police arrested the twenty-three men that we identified. The government offered six thousand, two-hundred-and-fifty rupees to each of the sixty-three* [Dalit] *families as restitution and helped rebuild*

their homes. This is nothing to rebuild our damages. Look at
my son, Madam. He still cries thinking about that day. What
would I have done if both my men had died? What would I
have done with my girls? Now he is afraid to study.

Women from the village gathered in Renuka's home to speak out. They all
shared their stories of horror from that night with me. I could see that as they
continued to be haunted by the events of that night, the women were nevertheless determined not to allow that incident to maim their spirits. They showed
me the homes that were destroyed by the raid. I met two physically disabled
and mentally challenged girls who were pulled out onto the street and raped
that night and with women whose arms were broken. Pothumponnu[81] recalled
the night of the attack with a lot of emotion:

I knew that there was no use telling our local police. They will
never help us. I went to the sub-collector to get help. I dragged
my sister who still had the blood stains from her husband and
son. I said, "Do something. Look at her." I was not going to let
these guys go without doing something for us. Then they took
action and arrested over twenty-three men.

Alagamma, another young mother, proclaimed: *"We are scared to send the*
kids to school, but now we send them with an adult. We are still afraid, but we
will not give up on education. We give specific instructions to our children. The
police also give them protection." Upon my return to the village in 2007, I saw
that the Dalit homes and the spirit of the community were slowly rebuilt. In
2007, the women once again sat down to converse with me while stringing
together jasmine flowers with which they would adorn their hair. They claimed
peace through their assurance that they had the strength to overcome adversity.

In 2007, Renuka enclosed her open verandah with strong iron bars for protection. Even as the children from the village had returned to school, the adults
were even more cautious and watchful than before. Vijay studied in the Government Arts College. He lost his opportunity with the engineering college
because the merit seats were all filled. He had no money to pay the capitation
fee to enter the program. He has since joined the police force and now serves as
a policeman in Pudukkottai District.

The women in Keeranur understand that the entire community was punished
because one of them dared to overstep the cultural laws prohibiting Dalits from
education and economic progress. They are further aware that they were targeted specifically because they are Dalit, and through rape the dominant caste
instills fear into the entire community. When I asked the women about how

---

[81] The exact translation of Pothumponnu is "Enough of daughters." Here the name is a
pseudonym.

afraid they were of being attacked again, they raised their hands in unison and ululated. Pothumponnu said: *"They thought we could be scared away, but nothing can scare us, because we live for our children."*[82] The fear of being raped does not stop these women from educating their children and hoping for a good future for them. As this example reveals, Dalit women can overcome their sense of victimization when they partner with one another and with their communities. Renuka's insistence on keeping her son in school exhibits transgressive social agency, not only for her, but her entire community. And the positive effect of the courage of Renuka and her community is attested to in the rise in education among Dalit children in Keeranur. According to a DA survey in 2011, 21.32 percent of Dalit children in Pudukkottai District were enrolled in the school system as compared to 11 percent in 2007.

Deciphering Meanings of Victimization and Resistance

In each of these narratives, it is evident that a Dalit woman's transgression of the social space that is allowed by dominant society is unacceptable. For Dalit women, remaining socio-economically marginalized, passive, and silent is crucial to proving one's obedience to and acceptance of caste- and gender-based social norms. The history of Dalit women's passive submission to Kallar domination is difficult to challenge.

Most often, they challenge those norms by risking their lives in fighting for their human rights. Dalit women demonstrate their voice and visibility by aligning with and forging more unified social identities with other Dalit women. It becomes necessary for Dalit women to physically remove themselves from the social spaces that define them as vulnerable in order to form democratized, collective movements with one another. The DA works with women in the safe space it secures in its office in Annavasal. There, Dalit women gather to assert their agency collectively and work to strengthen solidarity among other comparable agencies. In that space, Dalit women move into framing their personal experiences of violence into broader humanist terms to bring about changes in their lives and demand human rights. Janaki, Chitra, Rani, Renuka, and several other women who are abused by various coercive forces meet regularly (at least once a month) at the DA office to share their experiences and to forge relationships with one another by singing together. They strategize activities of awareness and assess cases of abuse reported to the DA, through which they strengthen the power of their social agency collectively as Dalit women. In recognizing their strengths, they call upon other Dalit women to join and

---

[82] Pothumponnu shared these details in a personal conversation on August 3, 2007.

form alliances with them to actively resist and change institutions that sanction violence against them and their communities.

As of 2016, Rani and Renuka (along with many other women from Keeranur) remain members of DA by taking part in rallies and public protests. They recognize themselves as activists in the assertion of their collective identity and propel themselves toward social and political visibility. Renuka's determination and the support of other women from Keeranur helped Vijay to seek alternative ways to manifest his agency, which placed him on the path to becoming a respected policeman in Tiruchy. The people of Keeranur are educating each of their children despite their fears of caste-based violence against them. Vijay proudly displays himself as a figure of authority who looks out for any and every opportunity to stand up for justice under any circumstance. His sister, Vijaya Rani, has completed her B.Sc. college degree and teacher's training; she tutors several young Dalit children to perform well in their school examinations. Vijaya takes great care to ensure her son's education and make certain that he will not have to face the socio-economic pressures of being poor and the social restrictions accorded to Dalits in Indian society. Vijaya herself is gainfully employed as a tailor and is proud to be economically independent as a contributing member to the Dalit society and society at large. According to Janaki's wish, her daughter is staying in the *Thai* hostel where, through her education, she will secure a safe and respectable social and economic position.

With Kalaimagal's leadership and the solidarity provided by DA, Dalit women in Pudukkottai District claim agency and are involved in a humanist activism that surfaces a strong intersection between their individual and communal experiences of violence. That intersection, in turn, strengthens their collective desires as both women and Dalits in moving to transform the traditional dynamics of their social space. Most importantly, DA has gained the support of caste communities as well. Kalai mentioned that several caste state officials have been helpful in the Dalit fight for human rights, including a human rights lawyer based in Pudukkottai from the Kallar community; a Muslim lawyer from the Kallar community; a prominent businessman from the Kallar community; a collector from the Shudra community; and members of the CPM and CPI communist political parties comprising dominant caste peoples. With these social support systems in place, Dalit women here are motivated to be involved in strategic actions towards change. They continue to question and negotiate on their own terms the meanings mapped on their gendered bodies and minds, and on their communities. In gathering together as women and as Dalits, they continue to claim and manifest social justice and human dignity despite remaining vulnerable to repeated caste-based violence.

CHAPTER FIVE

Breaking Cultural Norms: Transformative Transgressions in Dalit Women Leaders

In the previous chapters, I began weaving a colorful thread into this book about the beginnings of my friendship with Kalaimagal (Kalai) in 2006. Here and in the next chapter, I present my conversations with Kalai and Rani: Kalai is the founder and chairwoman of Dr. Ambedkar Women and Children Regeneration and Development Organization (Dr. AWARD or DA), a non-profit organization for Dalits, and the *Thai* Education Trust, a residential program to foster a standard education for Dalit girls; and Rani is a disciple of Kalai and a staff member of DA.[83] As mentioned in earlier chapters, DA is the only non-profit organization with a Dalit focus in this part of Tamil Nadu involving Pudukkottai District. It proves to be a space of refuge, vocational training, leadership development, advocacy, and education, especially for Dalit girls and women since they are the most affected by caste-based violence. Learning about Kalai in the past eight years, about her childhood, her commitment to her people, and the story of the development of DA is awe-inspiring. Since my relationship with Kalai and Rani is personal and sisterly, it is not easy to step into an analytical discussion of their lives. I have, nevertheless, attempted to present their life stories interwoven with my observations on their leadership styles and strategies leading to social change.

It was during my visits with DA that I met Rani, and I have included my conversations with her because she works together with Kalai in all initiatives of the organization. They are examples of activism characterized by an *earthy humanness* where an ethics of caring leads to demands for justice and human dignity. It was not until the mid-year in 2014 that I decided to gather together my various conversations with Kalai and Rani which I had recorded on electronic devices and on paper over the past nine years. In May of 2014, I had the privilege to sit with Kalai along with Rani—on the two-acre grounds of a residential educational program for Dalit girls and a site for organic farming—to clarify and fill in the gaps in my knowledge about Kalai's life. It was there that I engaged in a long conversation with Rani, who detailed her life journey as a Dalit woman leader in her community. I will first lay out an introduction to each of their lives and follow with providing an opportunity to gain a deeper

---

[83] These conversations took place in Pudukkottai.

understanding of the characteristics and strategies of their leadership as active agents of social change. Storytelling is an integral part of this process of learning from these narrative testimonies of lived experiences. The life stories of Kalai and Rani continue to inspire me to act upon deeply ingrained desires for change without waiting for collaboration of supportive allies, but to create those allies and propel collective action groups through efforts geared by faith that are grounded in *earthy humanness* and a daring risk-taking.

Formations and Stages of Human Agency

Kalai spoke of her childhood with much pain, recollecting a rejected social space in which she grew up. Her voice, usually bold, softened into a thoughtful whisper whenever she shared details from her childhood. Her beginnings matter a lot to Kalai because of the struggles that have shaped her life and that continue to mold and fuel her determination to change a religiously-sanctioned and socially-circumscribed caste and gender-based dehumanizing life. Kalai was born in 1971 in Annavasal, a small town in Pudukkottai District of Tamil Nadu, India, where she continues to live and serve her community. She lost her father when she was three and her mother when she was twelve. Both worked as laborers in the fields, cleaned streets, and drainage places between the nearby villages of Karambakkudi and Maangudi. Her maternal grandmother converted to Christianity in her village Thiruvathangur near Thenkaasi, close to the state of Kerala. Her mother grew up Christian, and her father was a Hindu who followed Christian practices; and Kalai grew up as a Christian. Both her parents died in Annavasal, and she fears that their deaths were probably caused by unhygienic work conditions and pesticides. Her oldest brother, Subramani, took care of her four sisters and her three brothers, working as a domestic servant for a dominant caste landlord and later as a driver with the Tamil Nadu Transportation. Kalai explained that due to extreme poverty, she started working at a young age:

> I started working when I was about five or six years old. I cleaned streets, cleaned toilets, did work on farms, drainage gutters, assisted with dead body removal and cremation, and all kinds of that work. Then later on when I was about seven or eight, I started work in the stone quarry—Kazhugumalai, Sengulathupaarai, Karuvattupaarai, Paanangudimalai—all these stone quarries. Some days I attended school. I went to the Annavasal Aarambapalli (primary school). It was a Panchayat Union school. First to twelfth grade, I studied in Annavasal.

They gave me food in school. This was good, and I made sure I
went to school.

Kalai recalled the horrific incident when a thirteen-year-old girl was raped
in the same quarry where she worked. After this incident, her brother did not
allow her to work in the quarry, and instead, kept her with him to work in the
landlord's house. She recalls that he was "a nice Chettiar man" (a dominant
caste community) who helped her with her school and college education.

The beginnings of agency and desire for change start with Kalai's persever-
ance to educate herself. Kalai has prioritized education and is an outstanding
student. She holds a bachelor's degree in zoology (B.Sc.), a degree in education
(B.Ed.), a master's degree in zoology (M.Sc.), and recently gained an M.Phil.
degree in zoology as well. Kalai is proud of her accomplishments in education;
her face lights up when she speaks of them: "I studied very well. In tenth grade,
I scored 93% in math. But [school officials] told me to join the science group
for my higher secondary. I studied in that group and passed my twelfth standard, and I got admission into teachers' training." Kalai was able to gain a sports
scholarship due to her excellence in *kabaddi,* a local sport normally only
played by boys and men (Mazumdar 2016, 114-115).[84] She fondly and grateful-
ly honors her professor Chellammal Subramaniam who helped her with books.
During college, the landlord Chettiar allowed her to study in his own typewrit-
ing institute where she passed the higher grade in A level. She furthered her
skills in the Sanmugam Technical Institute and returned to the Chettiar's institute as an instructor. Kalai supported herself to whatever extent she could:
"Early morning, around 6 a.m., I started work and went to college around 8
a.m. My friends would give me lunch. I stayed with my brother and other sib-
lings. I studied under the streetlights and sometimes had to walk about one
kilometer to find a streetlight." Kalai was convinced that education was the
only way to prove herself of social worth and demand the respect of those who
scorned her Dalit identity. It is in that frenzy of challenging and reversing her
inscribed social identity that she has persevered in educating herself and, in her
forties, she has secured an MPhil degree, a penultimate stage to gaining a Ph.D.
What I admire most about Kalai is her determination to make things happen
whether for herself or for her community; against any restrictive force Kalai
always finds a way.

---

[84] *Kabaddi* is a game popular among Dalit men and played in villages in India that is
recognized as a national sport. Now played by women as well, two teams of twelve
compete to keep their players untouched by the other team as each player is sent to the
other team's zone. They enter the opponent's zone chanting *kabaddi* and before they
take a breath, they should return without being touched—an interestingly popular game
of touching among those called "untouchables." Described by Indu Mazumdar in *Com-*
prehensive Physical Education Class XII, New Delhi, Laxmi Publications.

In Kalai's life, she places marriage as a point of major decision-making because she had committed herself to work for Dalit causes, and she did not want
marriage to be a deterrent. She lovingly recalls that Rajendran [her husband
since] was working in Thamizharasan People's Rights Organization. He knew
about Kalai since she was an outspoken college student in the community:

> *He was carefully watching me, and I did not know that [Kalai*
> *laughs]. Then he came to the typewriting institute where I was*
> *working, and he asked me to type something. He just was try-*
> *ing to make contact with me! Then he cornered me in church*
> *one Sunday and asked about my interest in community work. I*
> *told him that I am committed to work for the rights of Dalit*
> *people. He asked if I was planning on getting married. I got*
> *mad and yelled at him saying, "How dare you ask me that*
> *question?" I accused him of following me and causing me*
> *trouble with this kind of an intention. He was calm. I said that I*
> *did not want to get married and be a slave to someone. I said*
> *that the guy I marry will not allow this kind of interest; I have*
> *to work for rights of Dalits. He asked if I would marry someone*
> *like him who will also do this work with her. I got very upset,*
> *and I went and told my brother. My brother came to church*
> *and met him, and I did not know that they became friends. First*
> *my brother hesitated because Rajendran—he is from Pallar*
> *group of Dalits [in an earlier conversation Kalai had men-*
> *tioned that Rajendran was Hindu]—and we are from the Pallar*
> *community doing the work of grave digging. We are one of the*
> *lowest groups even among Dalits. But Rajendran had no prob-*
> *lem. Then he came to my house often, and we got to know each*
> *other better; and we got married in June 1992. We do all our*
> *Dalit work together.*

In my observations of Rajendran, he is a great partner in fully immersing himself in the Dalit battle for justice. He is a calm and strong presence in taking
care of all the managerial and administrative aspects of the organization.

The first sign I see in Kalai of affecting social change in her community is
the bold step to speak up about the young girl who was raped in the stone quarry; she used the opportunity to speak to a higher authority whom she identified
as a potential ally:

> *During a college celebration, a highly ranked Government of-*
> *ficial, District Collector Sheila Rani Suganth, came and spoke*

to us about women's empowerment. So I walked up to her and told her about what had happened in the stone quarry. She came and met with the family of the girl who was raped—and also invited me to her house. We developed a good friendship, and she helped me start a non-formal education [a government-based education program] in Pudukkottai District. She encouraged me to start my own non-profit organization and guided me through the process. She provided me with all the training I needed; and I traveled with her, observing her work.

Kalai speaking at a public awareness event organized by Dr. AWARD, 2008.

Interactions with positive and influential authoritative figures continue through Kalai's journey with affecting social changes among her people. She worked with the state government's *Arivoli* programs which are education initiatives among those adversely affected by illiteracy. This involvement in 1992 led her to start her own *Arivoli* program and the forming of her registered non-profit organization in 1994.

In my conversations with Rani, she spoke less about her childhood and more about her involvement in demanding justice for Dalit communities. Her home village is Kalarpatti where she was born in 1981 and where she spent her childhood. Rani studied up to second grade because her parents had no means to send her to school. Besides agriculture work, she helped her father in the work of cleaning nose rings at the jewelers. Rani married her mother's brother,

Palanisamy, when she was thirteen and bore her first child at fifteen; she has two boys and one girl. Her daughter is in twelfth grade; one son completed a degree in civil engineering, and another son is in eighth grade. Rani sees the importance of providing education for her children to be able to break the mold of social stagnation and be skilled to claim a better economic condition for themselves. Rani continues with agricultural work in the one-hundred-day-work program where she is paid a hundred rupees per day for digging for government building projects; she does this work to educate her children.

Rani heard about the DA organization in 1998 through a friend and learned that the organization was recruiting capable Dalit women to work with Dalit rights. Recollecting her initial steps into active social change, she says "On hearing about the organization, I decided to go because I thought about why I should live here in this village and not know anything about the outside world. So, I decided to go and see *Akka* [Tamil=older sister]. I came with a daring courage" [The Tamil word that Rani used was *thunichal*]. Proving herself capable of boldly speaking up and acting for changes and claiming justice, Kalai employed Rani as one of her outreach staff. Rani proudly proclaims: "I went to the meeting as a capable person." This confidence in herself that one hears in her strong determined voice is a striking character in Rani. Since then, Rani has worked along with Kalai in aggressively claiming justice and human rights for Dalits in Pudukkottai District. Writing is inadequate to detail the effective partnership of these two women who not only embody and represent multiple nodes of intersectionality but who contain a thorough knowledge of the coalescence of multi-power structures and individuals. They verbally and collectively contend with hegemonic forces through their learned skills, inherited knowledge bases, persistence, and people power force.

Social Problems, Allies, and Assets

Kalai bears witness to all the different and unexpected ways in which individuals and organizations, combined with her skills for networking and building supportive communities, helped much in bringing her desires for active, positive changes as achievable reality. The previous official government Collector Sheila introduced her to the new Collector; her ongoing relationship with the National Campaign for Dalit Human Rights (NCDHR) helped her gain the skills she needed to question and change unjust social conditions; and her building of credibility among the police force and local politicians was crucial to sustainable changes. Her organization developed into a center that Dalits came to seeking justice, self-empowerment, tailoring, leather work and type-writing skills, training for economic self-sufficiency, and awareness building.

From thereon Kalai became the voice of her people, gaining more experience and training through several organizations to aid and represent Dalits in their legal battles for justice. In all her workings, Kalai has understood the significance of networking and has built supportive allies with both human rights organizations involved in various facets of social issues and state-based programs: PEAL [People's Education and Legal Awareness], THADCO (Tamil Nadu Adi Dravidar Housing and Development Corporation Limited), Bread for the World based in Germany, and Dalit Solidarity Forum in the USA, Inc.

Kalai describes the process by which she gained the knowledge and skills she needed to equip herself as an effective change agent. She met with Vincent Manoharan, a Dalit activist from Madurai who came to investigate and survey the situation of Dalits in the area in 1995. She met with him and told him about all the problems that Dalits had to live through every day, the worst of which was sexual harassment of women and girls. Kalai was invited to the town of Madurai to speak at a gathering of organizations and leaders working with the Dalit cause. Vincent, [whom Kalai refers to as 'Anna,' a brotherly term of endearment and respect in Tamil for an older male] came back to Pudukkottai District and spoke at several Dalit gatherings in all the three blocks—in Annavasal, in Viralimalai, and in Kundathoor Koil—all villages. Kalai said:

> He stayed for ten days and visited all the villages and stone quarries. The people also shared with him, without any inhibition, about all their struggles. They said how they were forced to receive food from the caste people and had to eat it, even if it was spoiled. They did not have a choice. This was their payment for a long day's work. They talked about how the teachers did not allow Dalit children, especially those from the manual scavenging community, to sit with other children. They were commanded to clean toilets. Even when I went to school, the same things happened. Vincent Anna visited these schools and observed all these issues.

Manohar persuaded Kalai to attend training on government laws and strategies to be able to question the government. He convinced her that without proper training, the work she was trying to do would be difficult and that she would either end up being killed or jailed and the problems would just continue. Kalai realized that she had some education and awareness and she should take the next step to build specific skills to be able to address discriminations and violence on Dalits. Kalai described:

> Our people did not even have a place to cremate or bury their dead. They had to just burn the bodies by the roadside. It was a

big problem and challenge just to cremate or bury our dead. This was our state. I thought about all of this and what Vincent Anna said, and I went to the training for twenty days in Sak-kiliyappatti, near Madurai. In that training, they taught me all I needed to know about preparing petitions, approaching gov-ernment officers, and submissions of petitions to police sta-tions. I was made aware of how the police will treat and react to these petitions; and so, I was taught how to ask for a receipt for such petitions, or else police will deny their existence. After this they told us when and how to contact the lawyer. I also learned how and when to visit the sites where unjust events had happened. They told me about what details I need to get and how people need to cooperate. They said I have to investigate if this is a true case. All these important things I got training in.

I learned how to organize people, form allies with other or-ganizations, how to publicize these issues, and call on media attention. I learned very important details about how to make the police write FIR [First Investigation Report]. I learned how to carefully follow up on an issue—after that filing of FIR, how to approach the police officers. All this was taught to us. We were also told of how the police would try to divert these is-sues. So how do we legally handle this? Well-renowned law-yers gave us the training. In 1997, PEAL helped us to form sangam [women's organizations], and they helped us to pay rent which was about five hundred rupees for our office.

In these and more current efforts to better equip herself to be able to under-stand, address, and attack a corrupt and power-driven system, Kalai excels as a formidable leader who confidently and willfully marks her expertise. Kalai is a major force in the Pudukkottai area who continues to make positive changes happen among Dalit communities challenging dominant individuals, institu-tions, and structures.

Kalai speaks of an inter-caste marriage conflict that she had to battle in the beginning stages of her active social participation in the village of Thirunallur. Three Dalit men from that village married girls from the dominant caste in a local temple, and when they came back to the village, the caste people attacked and captured the three men. The villagers made them into a spectacle of public humiliation by shaving their heads, stripping them naked, parading them on donkeys from their village to the temple where they were married, and brutally beating them. Kalai continued:

While this was happening, one of the organization members came to my office and reported the incident. So, I went to Thirunallur with my husband and two men who were also staff members. When we reached the area, they were dunking them into water tanks with their hands tied with the intent of drowning them to death. This was at about 1:30 a.m. When they saw our vehicle approaching, they came towards us with heavy sticks and knives. We went to the local police station about seven kilometers away in Illuppoor. The police station was locked. We screamed and banged on the door, and after hearing who we were, one police constable came with us to the site where they were trying to kill the three men. After seeing us come with the police, they [dominant caste] *released the three men. Then we brought all three to Annavasal, and we admitted them into the General Hospital. We were able to save their lives even though they had lost a lot of blood.*

Kalai demanded the police to file the First Information Report (FIR), and they denied the event and refused to come to the hospital to see the three men who were beaten up. She organized the Thirunallur villagers to stage a *dharna* (a mass silent protest strategy). Kalai narrated:

All the Dalit people and several organizations came and took part. After seventeen hours of Dharna, they finally agreed to file the FIR. However, the police said we had to take the case to the SP [Superintendent of Police]—*only they should file the FIR. After we got there, we saw that about two-hundred and fifty people or more were already gathered to oppose us in the name of a Peace Committee. They all forced us to say that this incident had never happened. We did not give in.*

The District Collector accused Kalai of instigating caste violence and threatened to arrest her. Kalai recalls, "I was not afraid. I said, 'Let me see how you will arrest me.' I sent information to twenty-seven Dalit organizations, and the next day, almost all the organizations came to Pudukkottai and then again, more than one hundred of us went on a *dharna*." Eventually, the senior police officer was convinced of the actual happenings and filed a FIR on all the hundred and twenty-seven people who were involved. Kalai continued:

The leader of the three higher castes [Kallar, Maravar, Agamudiar] *came to attack me, and the CPI* [Communist Party of India] *secretary rescued me. He covered me with his shawl and quickly put me in his jeep and made sure I was driven home*

safely. After this, they arrested all those on whom the FIR was
filed. We made sure the affected families were protected and
kept them in our Annavasal office.

Kalai recalls this event as a major breakthrough for her organization in establishing themselves as capable and in building trust among Dalit communities. It
was impossible for the local political forces to comprehend the magnitude of
the issue and the active, result-oriented, productive aggression among Dalits
led by women.

Another remarkable achievement for the organization was drawing attention
to the horrific happenings in the Ilupakkudipatti village. Twenty-two Dalit
families lived there as bonded laborers and were treated as slaves locked within
thorn fences so that they could not leave. These families had to take orders
from the Kallar caste and were severely punished if they disobeyed. Kalai
spoke of a cultural practice there that when there was a Dalit wedding, the girl
could not sleep with her husband on the first night but had to spend it with a
Kallar man. The Dalit new husband was sent out of the house, and the Kallar
man would go in to deflower her. In Kalai's words:

> *This was set as a normal cultural practice of the place a long,*
> *long time ago—a traditional way. The women in the Kallar*
> *community were proud of this practice. They would proudly*
> *say that their husband has gone to this particular house that*
> *night. It was like an entertainment for them but also an im-*
> *portant practice. Like this they were slaves and had to do eve-*
> *rything that they were ordered to do. They cannot disobey and*
> *could not leave the village at all.*

Kalai learned of this practice when one of the victims, Karupayee, who was
newly married and came in from another village, ran away pretending to go to
the bathroom in the fields and came to the DA office. Kalai said, *"I could not*
believe this. I told her, 'This sounds like a cinema story. What are you saying
ma?' So I decided to go to that village myself. I stayed in a Dalit home; they
told the Kallar that I was a niece visiting from out of town. I was amazed at
Krupayee's courage knowing well what the consequence would be." Kalai told
me that when they came to know the truth, the caste villagers wanted to punish
Karupayee and raped her in the fields. With tears, Kalai recalled that this incident horrified her, causing more anger along with frustration. She could not
give up.

I admired Kalai's carefully but quickly thought out plans to gather enough
details and witnesses to this cultural practice of sexually victimizing young
Dalit brides. Kalai continued her stay in the Ilupakkudipatti village under the

pretense of solely remaining there to launch the State government's program on self-help through savings. Kalai brought Dalit women together and gathered testimonies against Dalit bride abduction and other cultural practices that kept Dalits enslaved. Kalai said:

> *This took me a long time. I had to build trust among the Dalit women for almost a year. Only then did they stop being afraid to talk with me. I actually then started a sangam as an AWARD women's group but they* [the Kallar] *still thought it was a self-help group. We made Karupayee and another woman, Sivapayee, as the sangam leaders. After the Kallar came to know about what Karupayee had done and about the sangam, they did not let me back in, and they beat up both the women and their families. They stripped Karupayee in the fields when she was at work and sexually molested her there.*

At this point, Kalai took Karupayee (who was raped) to the police station to submit a petition and then admitted her in the General Hospital in Annavasal. Karupayee was punished for exposing an accepted cultural norm as an unacceptable practice that degraded Dalit women. To the dominant caste community in that village, her act was a disobedience to a submission to this local cultural practice of sexual abuse. Since Kalai was a member of the District Vigilant Committee (for Dalits) and the Welfare Committee (who monitored policy implementation), she could gain press attention for the atrocities in Ilupakkudipatti village. Kalai said, *"Because of this, I was able to provide visibility to the issue. The police arrested about twenty-three Kallar men because of our efforts. All the women spoke up to the police and the press about what happened to them."* It was important that Dalit women speak about and testify to the injustices they were subject to. The caste communities threatened to kill Kalai. She said, *"They threatened to kill me, and they tried to bribe me with a lot of money, but I was not afraid. I said, 'All I want is justice for my people. If you offer all that the affected are asking for, then we will consider withdrawing the case.'"* The demands were specific: the Kallar men will not come into the Dalit homes and sleep with their women; Dalits should be able to leave and enter their village whenever they wanted; Dalit children should receive education; and Dalits will not be slaves to Kallar anymore. With police as witness, the Kallar agreed to these demands and Kalai decided to withdraw the police case. Kalai reported that the UN filmed a documentary on this case and since the pact was made, says Kalai, there has not been too much trouble here for Dalits. Kalai informed of a similar practice in the Village of Mathur, and DA intervened to bring justice there as well.

Kalai has demanded that the state government should implement its programs to benefit Dalit communities. With the use of THADCO, she has addressed the issue of landlessness and insufficient living amenities for Dalits. Kalai said:

> *Akka, remember I told you that Dalits did not have cremation or burial grounds? We secured grounds for that as well. This is by the main road closer to Tiruchy. Also Akka, we got three cents of land for each family* [100sq ft=1 cent]. *We got them free patta and all. We demanded this from the government based on the Adi Dravida* [Adi Dravidar is a term used to refer to Dalits as those belonging to the early Dravidian race] *Welfare Program.*

They acquired the burial ground in Mathur after great struggle with the government securing funds from the Tamil Nadu Housing for Adi Dravidar Development Corporation. The government provided the basic needs such as water and electricity to Mathur. She was happy that now Dalits in Mathur are able to work and are educating their children. She persuaded the government to build fifteen houses in that village for Dalits. She said that since 1995, she has ensured that this village would receive benefits from the government.

When I asked about other issues she addressed, Kalai spoke about the two-tumbler system. She explained:

> *A Dalit could only drink tea out of a glass reserved for them in a corner and had to sit outside the tea shop where the tea will be poured out into the glass. Then they had to wash the glass and place it where they took it from. This practice is prevalent in several parts in Tamil Nadu.*

DA reported several of these cases, and arrests were made when Dalits were discriminated against in tea shops. To answer my question of what other incidents stood out for her as major battles, Kalai replied, "There have been many. Oh, did I tell you about Mani in Irunthirapatti?" She narrated an event that happened in 1999 when Mani's arm was cut off because as a Dalit he dared to take part in the bull festival. Traditionally, rich Kallar families bring their bull and after processing them down the streets, the bulls are let loose and the Kallar men will run after them, and the one who catches a bull and ties up the bull will receive a reward of either gold or clothing. (Now the Supreme Court has banned this practice due to animal cruelty). Mani was angered that Dalits were not allowed into this sport, and he let loose a bull belonging to a Dalit on the day of the festival. The Kallar were furious and cut off his right hand that let the bull loose. DA took up this case and secured a compensation of five lakhs rupees for Mani. The Kallar involved were all arrested but came out on bail; and Kalai states that this case is still pending because the Kallar are using money to bribe the police. In an exhibition of class, caste, and patriarchy through the bull sport, the Kallar further pressed their dominance in the exclusion of Dalits from this sport. The Kallar saw Mani's act of anger and rebellion in setting the bull loose as an act of defiance and sought to teach him and his people a lesson of the consequences of transgressing boundaries. Mani knew he would be punished and still wanted to make his strong statement as well. In letting the "Dalit" bull loose, he unleashed his refusal to be tethered to and by caste dictates. Kalai endorses this anger and demand for equal treatment of Dalits.

Cremation ground for Dalits, Thachampatti Village that Kalai secured
February 18, 1999.

Other issues that Kalai spoke about included protest about unpaid labor: "Dalits are forced to beat the *Dappu* drum for any occasion, but mostly deaths. They must beat the drum and dance in front of the dead body carried to the cremation ground. They do not even get paid for this work." She mentioned temple entry issues where Dalits are not allowed to enter certain Hindu temples. Most importantly, DA has been working towards the eradication of manual scavenging as member of the National Safai Karmachari movement. Manual scavenging is the work that Dalits do in cleaning dry public latrines. Kalai informed that since 1992 they have been fighting for the eradication of the practice of manual scavenging. In 1996, she mobilized a protest where around twenty-seven manual scavengers—who were women—went on *dharna* in front of the Union office in Annavasal carrying baskets on their heads at the *dharna;* the baskets were not just symbolic, but tangible and visual texts of their dehumanizing work. They protested for an entire week until the Collector responded, and the government followed issuing orders to destroy some of the dry toilets. Even though in 2014 the Supreme Court ensured implementation of this banned practice, it continues in India. However, Kalai takes great pride in DA's success with significantly reducing this practice in Pudukkottai District.

Kalai stated that the first and foremost issue facing Dalit women today is the fear and the reality of rape:

> First of all, the raping of Dalit women—very easily they do it [Kalai said, "easyaa"]. When caste girls are teased they make big deal of it, but Dalit girls are stripped [raped], even at a very tender age. I have been affected by that at a very young age when I had no knowledge about sex at all. It is that age, and at that age itself, they sexually harass. The little girls don't know anything about that; this is sex or this is how one gets affected, even that the girls don't know. To be affected at that age and to use Dalit girls is such a normal matter here. We fought and raised our voice against this problem. This is what we did first because one of the worst kodoooram [tortures] upon women is the sexual kodooram. We first fought against this vankodumai [horrific torture] of forcing a Dalit girl into sexual activity.

DA has been involved in rescuing young Dalit girls made victims of sex trafficking. Kalai reminded me of Vijaya, whose story appears in chapter four, and narrated two similar cases where Dalit girls were abducted:

> Another incident like that happened in 2007 when Thayalna-yagi from Vaiyalogam village was taken to Kualalumpur, promising her a domestic servant job. She was duped. Poor thing. She was sold as a prostitute. She called me and we booked a case, and the Government got involved and rescued her. This was in the newspapers. The one who sold her was a man called Dharman from Tambaram. He was a hotel manager. After all this, the woman withdrew the case when he gave her five lakhs rupees as a bribe. Money is so big for our people, and she did this. What to do, Akka? For this case, we nearly died when Dharman planned to cause an accident on us as

we [Kalai and her husband] *were travelling on our two-wheeler. Luckily, we were taken to the hospital, and our lives were saved. Then in 2009, Jothi from Thirunallur went to work in a company in Erode as a laborer. That company sold her to a man from Orissa for prostitution for 10,000 rupees. The fellow from Orissa further sold her for 50,000 rupees. With the help of Vincent Manoharan from NCDHR, we booked the case, got a lawyer. We went with the lawyer to Orissa and rescued the girl who was in a Naxalite area. So many cases like this Akka.*

As mentioned earlier, sex trafficking is a major force of victimization that Dalit girls are subject to, and DA rescues girls placing the lives of their staff at risk.

Speaking of her challenges and capacity to build financial support for Dalit activist initiatives, Kalai stated that, *"PEAL gave funding for us through Bread for the World, based in Germany. Then Jan Vikas helped us; the Saraboji Trust helped us. We availed [of] local Government funds. I got the Indira Ratna Award in 2008. They gave 50,000 rupees for that."*

When I asked her who awarded the Indira Ratna Award, she explained:

HEKS from Switzerland. They are a human rights organization. Suddenly, one day I got a phone call. I had to tell them I can only speak Tamil. They said they heard about me, and one of their people from Chennai came to see me and all that. WPP from Germany—I think they are the World Women's Day Prayer Group, and they also helped us. The People's Progress for India based in USA gave us funding for the manual scavenger rehabilitation programs. The D. deVoe Foundation in [the] *US, the churches you contacted for us in New York* [The Episcopal Diocese of Rochester] *all help now with our Thai education project. We received checks from the MDG* [Millennium Development Goals] *funding of your church as well. A lot of individuals contributed as well. You are helping us a lot.*

Kalai explains the importance of social and organizational ties in accomplishing recruitment for collective power and group mobilization. She invests in institutional relationship building and provides an affirmation of the benefits of supportive networking among Dalit individuals and communities. Kalai's micro entrepreneurial structural changes in the life styles of Dalit communities leads into recruiting the support she needs from Dalit communities to effect larger structural changes that need the cooperation of the Government who will respond to numbers and methods involved in making demands. The life-changing stories of determined Dalit girls who attend school and receive the training they need to be economically self-sufficient and placed in jobs by Kalai, testify to defying a culture of rejection and punishment. These children are the history makers who instigate and move onto a different social cycle grooved by Kalai's efforts through building organizational relationships. This is how she describes the *Thai* Education Trust she co-founded with friends:

> *In 2005, I started this with you because it is very hard for Dalit girls to be educated. I wanted to do this. Because of my own life story, I decided to do this. Only education can help us, Akka. Now, through this focus, about one hundred Dalit girls are earning now without having to go clean toilets and the streets. They are nurses, teachers, mechanics, tailors, leather workers, and so on. I secured forty-seven post-metric scholarships for Dalit girls and boys. This government program came out in 1992. No one implemented it. The first one was Christudoss Gandhi, who fought for this along with all other Dalit organizations; finally now this is implemented.*

Rani is a beneficiary of DA's focus on Dalit women actualizing potential to change oppressive situations. She, in turn, is able to move into larger areas of social problems that Dalit women should tackle. In my conversations with Rani, she identified *saaraayam* (locally brewed alcohol mentioned in the Prologue) as one of the major problems in Dalit villages and proudly spoke of her accomplishments in addressing alcoholism. She said, [mentioned in the Prologue] *"Such a big problem that you can write a movie story based on this. Me and that Akka* [pointing to Kalai standing close by], *if we are sitting here alive—I mean there was no guarantee for our lives. We gave importance to this problem."* Rani pointed to the enormity of this issue because of the intersecting of various dominant powers to keep *arrack* in the Dalit villages. The rich caste people provide the Palmyra trees, Dalit men are used to climb the trees and tap the arrack, and politicians build arrack shops that Dalits can easily access. The police are bribed to turn a blind eye, and the caste men make a profit out of poor Dalits who become dependent on and addicted to arrack as their only means of escape from an oppressive reality. Those who brewed the *arrack*, who drank the *saaraayam*, and those who were affected by it and died were all poor and Dalit. Those who made money and business out of it were those from the Kallar (dominant) caste.

Kalai being awarded the Indra Ratna Award by HEKS to honor her brave leadership among Dalit women, 2008[85]

Rani described the various ways in which they attacked this problem and eradicated the brewing and selling of *saaraayam* in their villages. Rani, along with Kalai, organized a protest with several Dalit women whose lives were affected by arrack. The Police officers decided to respond and raided the villages where arrack was brewed. Those who were at a loss in their business and were arrested were furious with Rani and Kalai. They threatened to kill them and scorned them saying, "'That Rani in Thinallur and Kalai from Annavasal should wear a *vetti* [a loin cloth that men wear] and the men in the villages should wear *saris* [women's clothing].'" Rani and other Dalit women were falsely accused of diverting the police from their own crime of hiding arrack in their homes and selling it for huge profits. Rani boldly argued with the police and called for a meeting in Annavasal with all the local police officers and the senior police officer. I hear a call for consciousness and conscientiousness when she states:

---

[85] The Indra Ratna Award was instituted in memory of the two courageous women, Indra and Ratna, who were ruthlessly murdered when Dalit women protested the sale of illicit liquor at Bheemanthope village, Tirvallur District.

We asked, "Did we hide arrack in our bathrooms? Who saw this? Why are you talking about us in such a dehumanizing way? Did we entrust a matter to you as something that never happens in our villages? You are an officer; if you do this, our district will develop and we women can go to the forest and fields. When we don't have firewood for our stoves, we have to come this far; we women have to go to the forest to get firewood, and we cannot come courageously into these areas because one guy will be drunk and lying down in the forest and some guy will be drunk under the tamarind tree. So, he can do anything in that state in that afternoon time as well. We came to tell you about this, but you did not take any action, so through our organization we will take care of this." This is what I told them.

Thai Children with Kalai, staff Chitra and Lata, 2015.

Further, Rani said:

I boldly questioned the police officer, "We came to you and said that they are doing all this but you did not accept our concerns. But you are saying that we are the ones who are brewing the arrack. Touch your heart, and tell us there is such a thing as a moral consciousness [Tamil=*manasaatchi*]. *We are all human. Please tell us." This is what we said in the meeting in Annavasal, and we said all this over the mike.*

After the meeting, Rani went to the Collector Sheila Rani Sungath demanding justice, and she took legal action on the negligent police officers and the arrack owners.

Rani declared that they eradicated arrack brewing and selling problems with the help of the District Collector. This is when Rani courageously stated that she did not fear death and wanted to accomplish something that her people would remember her by. When I asked Rani about all of this, she said:

We battled through 2005, 2006, 2007, till 2009. After this, we fully eradicated this. We confiscated barrels and barrels of it.... All the politicians from all parties opposed us; even when they opposed us, we didn't let go. Lots of people were cut up. There was a boy Palanisamy from Thinnallur. They cut him. His head was cut and he was struggling for his life, and we took him to hospital in midnight, took him to GH [General Hospital] *and admitted him there. The next day, they broke the hand of his grandmother.*

It took courage and determination to secure a safer life at the cost of violent retaliations to accomplish this eradication of arrack. When I asked Rani how her personal life was affected by arrack, she said [quoted in Prologue]:

My husband would come home drunk.... I suffered a lot. After suffering so much, the day I came to DA, from then on I became courageous. I thought that either the arrack should be destroyed or my husband should rectify his ways. I was determined to do both. Now my family is doing well. Otherwise, anytime this was my only big problem.

The eradication of arrack meant a personal redemption for her as well as for her community. The following dialogue ensued when I asked whether there was any arrack brewing now in Pudukkottai District. Rani and Kalai vehemently responded:

Rani: *No, now there is not.*

Kalai: *No, not at all.*

Rani: *Out of the sixty-three houses, only two houses did not even touch the arrack. Sixty-five houses were into the saar-*

aayam, full and full totally into that. Both men and women drank. We broke and destroyed everything. We ourselves went on a raid. All over ourselves, we were covered with that syrupy solution.

Roja: *You broke everything?*

Rani: *We broke and took all the barrels out. In the middle of the house, they would brew the arrack. To that extent our village was a despicable village.*

Kalai: *The police would come and misuse the women. They would come into the house and take women and misbehave. All these things happened. Too much injustice went on. Coming into homes and humiliating the women. They abducted young girls* [Dalit] *and raped them.*

Roja: *If the police behaved like this, who did you go to?*

Kalai: *We have no respect for the police.*

Rani: *We do not respect them.*

Kalai: *We went to the higher authorities. If even they did not take any action, we would do the dharna. We would sit on the roads as protest. We can never say that the police have been helpful in any way with any of our battles. The first enemy was the policeman. They will not file a report on anything, Akka. After procedurally and repeatedly filing petitions and approaching higher authorities in the District, Thaaluka, State, and those levels—and after a huge dharna—only then they even took legal action on the plea.*

Enraged as spotted goddesses, Kalai and Rani destroy every real threat to dignity in their daily life. It is clear that both women led the agitation against arrack brewing and selling without any support from the local authorities, not even the police. Vested in their own collective power, these women proved themselves capable of disrupting normal life for the caste communities through *dharna* and several other protest rallies. Stumping the police and other local caste people in mustering people power is a major accomplishment. Activism is their way of life in which they attack targetable power structures, locating and thwarting them in a real way. Such direct activism stands far above volumes of writing and theorizing in confronting their own humanity and breaking through the illusion of existence; they demand a real human life of dignity. Restless leaders move into more dangerous and prospective zones seeking to destroy through creative energy.

Dalit women in Pudukkottai District protest manual scavenging.

Rani was elected leader of the Women's Dignity Forum in her district in 2004, when she was only twenty-three years old. In 2005, Rani won the public council elections (tamil=*podhu thogidhi*) in a difference of 267 votes and became a *panchayat* (local governing body) member. I asked Rani about what she thinks could have led to her victory in the elections. She said that the arrack eradication was a major victory, and that people saw that she was bold and capable of getting things done. She said that she acquired fifty-three ration cards (a card that would allow people to receive rice, kerosene, and sugar as welfare benefits from the government) to provide for families who suffered from hunger without basic provisions. She recounts:

> *They said that they had to complete five years after the first one was issued; they tell lies, and expect bribes. So, I tried very hard. I was not a member* [of panchayat] *at that time. I was with this organization* [DA]. *There was a very good man who was the town chief at that time. I spoke with him and said, "So many people are affected. People are suffering without a ration card, without the twenty kilos of the society rice that they should get. You and I know what has to be done. Let's make them aware of this, and let's get it for them." Saying this, I secured fifty-three ration cards to be distributed to Dalit families.*

Kalai leads protest rally against *saaraayam*, Pudukkottai, December 16, 2003.

Acquisition of ration cards for Dalit families was another major success as a leader. Rani kept building upon her list of accomplishments as examples of an ongoing construction of trust-building among her people. In the *sangam* initiatives, Rani launched a small-scale savings investment for Dalit women in her village and in the neighboring villages. In her words, "I introduced the people to the small-scale savings scheme and took them into the ways of the outside world." Rani fondly recalls comments such as, "'For her activities, if she stands again for election, she is the one who will win.'" The support and trust of her people become crucial assets to negotiate with strong social and political bodies who have remained opposed to Dalit empowerment as a cultural norm and have historically ignored Dalits as human beings who have a right to live with dignity.

In her proud narration of how Rani brought into effect the suspension of a police officer, she points to the specific forces she had to call into accountability and those major influential allies with whom she worked. Rani identifies the police who are instigated by local politicians and religious leaders, as the main collective adversarial force against Dalits. All of them target Dalits who speak up or who show promises of economic viability, or simply because of their courage. The politicians do not approve of Dalit leadership or Dalits gaining power and popularity even among their own people, and they will adapt any means to terrorize rising Dalit leaders. Religious leaders repulse at the thought of Dalits crossing over into forbidden sacred spaces engraved by the historic power that religion has vested in them. The police are not willing to lose any opportunity to make more money through bribes offered by the politicians and religious leaders to terrorize Dalits. Rani understands very well the monetarily driven negotiations where justice is bartered for inhuman violence and Dalit bodies and lives are consumed.

One of the primary roles of Kalai and Rani—as of *Kali*—is to motivate communities, especially Dalit women in this case, to actively and courageously fight their battles. I asked Rani whether her courageous acts inspire and encourage other women in her village. To this she replied:

> *Yes, they are encouraged and excited. Not all of them. I will say, "I will follow you, you go ahead," and then they will go and take the initiative. If a pipe breaks or tube light does not work, even if it is a small matter, they will come to me only. They will say, "You are the one who will talk to them boldly," and send me. I realized, "Even after I clearly explain things to you, you are pushing only me. I am always hitting against all hurdles and moving forward. You all should gain courage within yourselves and move ahead boldly." Even after I say this, they will say, "You come with us."*

While people-power is one of the major resources for their human rights battle, it takes a lot of effort and time in building trust and the confidence they need to mobilize and gather individuals and communities. People look for changes to their living conditions and environment, as well as for accessible resources, viable recourse, and financial self-sufficiency before even considering making a commitment to be part of sustainable solutions.

First and foremost, in and through the changes in their own lives, Kalai and Rani are living examples of changed social conditions for Dalit communities to learn from. Both have gained the attention and respect of influential individuals and forces that normally have not viewed Dalit individuals as those with any social power or self-worth. Just as their spotted goddess demands respect by being and doing, so do they. Second, they prove through successes that major changes can be accomplished in their communities. Third, when victimized communities see the interventions of positive external forces, they are strengthened to know that all external forces are not power-ridden, grinding pestles. Animations of intersectionality come alive in this kind of direct activism that is about doing and not just assessing.

Kalai and Rani have toiled to provide alternatives for Dalit individuals and communities. The Annavasal office of DA has been that space of providing the following:

Roja: *Can you specifically talk about the alternate work provided for those who refuse manual scavenging work or the stone quarry work?*

Kalai: *Akka, 2006 onwards, we are trying to provide all kinds of training for Dalit peoples—tailoring, weaving, thatching, broom making, shoe making, and bag making.*

Roja: *Where do you provide these trainings?*

Kalai: *Right here in our Annavasal office.*

Roja: *For how long?*

Kalai: *For six months.*

Roja: *Who provides the training?*

Kalai: *For the shoe making and all that, the National Leather Institute came and did the training in the Award office. We got local teachers to teach tailoring and weaving. The Adi Dravida Nalathurai* [Adi Dravida Welfare Program] *did the other mechanical-related training like motor repairs, wiring, driving, mechanics in car shops, scooter shops, and that kind of work. We also helped set up wholesale business for wastage iron and steel waste products. Through THADCO, we have provided cattle—like cows, goat, and sheep. Our people are able to use that as a means of income. We have purchased sowing machines for our girls with the help of THADCO, DRD, the District Rural Development Office, and NAVAD which is a bank that gives loans. Through Women's Development Program of the Tamil Nadu Government, we have provided loans for small businesses.*

One hundred houses have been built in Pudukkottai District as apartments. In 2012-14, group houses were built through DAWDO, the District Adi Dravida Welfare Office. All these battles with the Tamil Nadu State Government started in 1995, and until now, we are fighting with them to make these benefits available for us. This has been a long and hard struggle with the authorities to make these things happen. All good schemes [programs] *are there but not being properly implemented to benefit those who deserve it.*

Roja: *Do you experience resistance from caste communities when Dalits receive all these benefits from the Government?*

Kalai: *Yes, a lot. They try to stop the actual building process itself, they have destroyed newly built homes, they steal building supplies—all kinds of these things they do. We try to keep mov-*

ing on in the midst of all this with the help of police; sometimes they co-operate.

Through specific, result-driven initiatives, DA has been the provider of consistent sustainable alternatives for Dalit communities in Pudukkottai District. Such alternatives have been key in gaining positive people power that DA turnkeys into the communities.

Dalit Female Activism

Women's labor rights proponent Mary Fonow recommends a discursive framework to view human rights in the feminist interpretations of social change (222). The collective action she points to as major people-power and woman-power is the solution to practically attack and dislocate conniving power structures. As a group, the centrality and marginality shuffling can be productive in expanding the truth in human rights that the "Campaign for Respect for Human Rights and Labor Rights" announces as that which encompasses "the right to be free of sexual harassment and domestic violence, the right to join union, the right to participate in politics and the right to work in a safe environment, and the right to a decent standard of living" (qtd. in Fonow 223). When women like Kalai and Rani gather around these specific demands, they gather the numbers needed to operate as an advocacy group that knows its right to demand justice. Collective action opens private spaces, narrows the diameter of a controlling centrality, and brings into focus marginalized invisible spaces.

Kalai and Rani practice intersectionality in their clear identification of a meshing of patriarchy, police force, political powers, religion, class, and caste in their lives, and the monstrous ways in which they insidiously manifest themselves in Dalit communities. In a frustrated effort to locate where the center lies, the police force in Kalai and Rani's testimonies fumble between local power structures and the higher government authorities with whom they have formed allies. It is rare that government officials are uncorrupt; Kalai and Rani just got lucky or perhaps the government officials recognize their capacity to approach media and other higher bodies in the power hierarchy. Through collective action powered by a *restlessness* and eagerness to cause changes and with their knowledge of hegemonic structural connivances, Dalit women blur the vision of power structures. The shuffle of movements between margin and center are powered by a combination of planned and spontaneous Dalit cultural strategies of resistance and protests.

In my observations on the careful steps that Kalai and Rani stride, I am struck by an unyielding battle between the inner strength of will that flows to the community from a resilient Dalit leader and the real fears that stem from dangers of daily life that are (at least) pretentiously dismissed to account for a fearless and selfless leader. These women leaders along with their people are surrounded by conflicting, alternating modes of physical and mental existence: submitting to humiliating hard work in bended gestural positions but proud of their hard work and earning for their family; looking for creative ways to survive even while fully aware of economic deprivation and exploitation; existing as "polluted other" and therefore "untouchable" but sought after for sexual exploitation; and flung into ambiguous spaces in a simultaneity of bodily and mental fragmentations as both invisible and selectively hyper-visible. Such ambiguous life situations leave people weakened in mind and body as they are tossed between anger and fear, rebellion and submission, untouchable and touchable, and helplessness and hope. They are in spaces separated from caste communities, but their existential ground is an exclusivity where "*selective touchability*" and "*selective visibility*" are conditions of the exhibition of brutality by the very same power quotients.

An *earthy humanness* moves Kalai and Rani into active spaces of resistance and change. In many ways, I revere them as incarnations of *Mariamman* in their ambiguous existence as "dirty," rejected women who are determined to harness a restless energy in that rejected state and mobilize a distillated collective energy for change. They care about their community and therefore employ "difference" as tools: they are out on the streets demanding with loud voices, they are out in the night guarding their people, they will lie about their identity to enter forbidden spaces, and they are not ashamed to own their *Parachi* identity. As spotted goddesses, they pierce the dominant forces by calling into being a power vested in them by their anger, which leads to strategies of protest and change and destroys the threatening forces. Kalai and Rani seek partnership between individual and collective inner strength of will along with efforts to form alliances between existent supportive structures and the new ones they create. This careful working of partnership is crucial for fortifying internal and external supportive systems to rise above a cultural actualization of a mere being in whom resides a collection of imposed properties of physical and ideological existence as Dalit. In this mission, Kalai and Rani live out the transgressive power of a collection of diverse expressions of rebellion and agency to contend their ambiguous existence.

CHAPTER SIX

"The rabbit *I* caught has three legs": Rebellion and Dalit Women's Activism

> *There is a rebel in me—the Shadow Beast. It is a part of me*
> *that refuses to take orders from outside authorities. It refuses*
> *to take orders from my conscious will, it threatens the sovereignty*
> *of my rulership. It is that part of me that hates constraints of*
> *any kind, even those self-imposed. At the least hint of limitations*
> *on my time or space by others, it kicks out both feet. Bolts.*
> —Gloria Anzaldúa, Chicana feminist scholar.

Inspired by the human social agency in Rani and Kalai and the communities they mobilize, I desire to dwell with Gloria Anzaldúa's claim: a rebel in any form should and will break free from both within and without cultural constraints despite threats to punishment (38). The complicit partnership of external authoritative structural manifestations and a coercive inner submission of the mind controls the lives of people who are broken and left to dissipate in body and mind. Such a horrific, manipulative power alliance ensures a complete possession of their lives where transgression of authority is read as disrupting cultural normalcy, and therefore, transgressors are labelled rebels and punished as seen in dominant narratives. The life stories of Kalai and Rani live out repetitive rebellious transgression as a main strategy of leadership to the point where transgression is entrenched as a way of life—as a Dalit cultural praxis boldly set in a tradition of punishing the social transgressor—and at the same time, this transgressive trait should be recognized as a product of a resilient rebellious character in Dalit communities. In this strategy of leadership, authoritative forces and internal psychological limitations are overcome, and this practice of overstepping boundaries spreads among neighboring Dalit communities as a ripple effect. Kalai's and Rani's narratives on leadership are gripping in their daring courage despite a conscious awareness of inherent dangers that they encounter to bring about rapid, radical, long-lasting, and sustainable changes. This is the conscious awareness, this "shadowy beast" which Anzaldúa identifies, that one should overcome and look beyond if the "bad" woman is to claim a fearless life of dignity (38).

I remind the reader here of my adaptation of the idea of *earthy humanness* (discussed in the Introduction) as an inherent characteristic of Dalit women in whom spontaneous activism is a way of life. Challenging traditional impositions of stigmatized "differences," Rani and Kalai adapt transfiguration of such "difference" into human agency leading to social change. In them is an unconditional ethic of ensuring the physical, spiritual, and economic wellbeing of their people. Their cultural practice of identification with another is the root to demanding social justice and claiming human dignity. This practice of activism is grounded in personal and communal experiences in daily lives where they are required by dominant forces to submit, but they choose to disobey.

Kalai and Rani speak to their conscious awareness of both the dangers involved and a determined strength mingled with a desire for change. Their agency is situated in their natural desire to change specific cultural normative practices that mangle Dalit lives, bodies, and minds. As Dalit women who are part of strong kinship structures, they are determined to use their collective voice to create visibility for their communities as dignified, strong, and secure with deep caring values and respectful kinship structures. In Kalai and Rani resides a natural spontaneous questioning that refuses to accept injustice in any form (as they admit in our conversations) and a subversive appropriation of the term "fierce," Doniger's English word choice in her translation of the *Manusmriti* for the Sanskrit term "*candalla*" (traitorous low being). Doniger uses the term "paradigmatic untouchable" to further explain "fierce untouchable" (317). A subversion of a "fierce"—filthy, traitorous, and low into a "fierce,"—fearless to lose anything that it has not already lost and to gain what it has lost, is pivotal to gaining just that. It is a natural rage that agitates an adamant demand for a transformative democratization where the human personality of a Dalit will be recognized. As angry women, they attack what is experienced as a threat to the peace and strength of their family and destroy what stands in the way of a strong sense of communal collectivity. Energized as spotted goddesses, such adaptive subversion establishes a new framework of self and cultural identities.

Spotted Goddesses and Spontaneous Activism

Dominant caste voices take hold of the very psyche of those they submerge where those affected begin to believe in external voices that internally manipulate the psyche of individual and collective consciousness. In a rebellious trope, Kalai and Rani reject authority and establish the right to live a life with dignity and pride. They daringly position themselves against dictatorial power structures claiming family and marital values, individual and communal morality, history, and spirituality—the very presence of which they have been denied within their culture. They are rebels who ragingly "turn tables" as they fearlessly tread into murderous zones, trusting in their own positive cultural strengths of resilience and rebellion, and breaking through restricted spaces.

Anzaldúa follows the powerful declaration quoted as an epigraph to this chapter with an analysis of a patriarchal and heteronormative culture that she points to as a specific trait of the spaces to which the women she knew and grew up with are confined. She names the roles and spaces within which the woman is expected to remain and perform her useful female role as a "good woman" (39). In the lives of Kalai and Rani, a cultural norm has been conditioned by religious thought and practice as well. This norm has inscribed the construction and realization of allocated social and mental spaces for Dalits where they dare not extend their imaginations outside those dictated realms. Kalai and Rani stretch and break through those dictated boundaries by applying methods derived from their very own cultural behavior that includes a Dalit adamancy in a refusal to accept their denigrated status.

Narula notes that attempting or desiring to cross over boundaries of servitude and poverty only results in terrorizing punishment. She reports: "Their [Dalit women] subordinate position is exploited by those in power who carry out their attacks with impunity" (Narula 166). Dominant communities consider it their prerogative to carry out violence upon those they consider their slaves. Narula provides evidence from various states in India in her report including the brutal massacre of Dalit men, women, and children in Bathe, Bihar in 1997 as punishment for demanding more wages of their landlord (Narula 166-178). They were shot while they were asleep by a mob attack by the dominant castes. Narula writes:

> In Laxmanpur-Bathe, Bihar, women were raped and mutilated before being massacred by members of the Ranvir Sena in 1997; in Bihar and Tamil Nadu women have been beaten, arrested, and sometimes tortured during violent search and raid operations on Dalit villages in recent years. (Narula 166)

She confirms that Dalit women are abused in police custody as punishment for male relatives hiding from caste communities. Nationwide, Dalit women are targets of rape and all kinds of sexual violence but mostly in poorer states such as Bihar, Haryana, and Orissa. Haryana has seen innumerable rapes that have driven families out of their villages to seek safety. Divya Trivedi reports:

> This is what a week in Haryana for a Dalit looks like—gang-rape of a Dalit woman at Luhari Ragho village in Hisar; gang-rape of Dalit girl at Gamra village in Hisar; attack on a Dalit basti at Talwandi village in Hisar where 10 people were in-

jured; suicide by Dalit minor girl at village Kalayat in Kaithal
district; caste-based atrocity with a Dalit boy in Hisar city; rape
of Dalit girl at Pillukhera village in Jind and attack on a Dalit
basti at Ballabhgarh in Faridabad district. (*The Hindu* Sept 21,
2013)

Such violence is an exhibition of power to terrorize vulnerable communities.
The acts of violence and rape are both punishment and entertainment, and now
these rapes and violence are video recorded on phones and widely distributed.
The victims and their families are threatened that it will be publicly viewed,
and this leads to their suicides.

In Tamil Nadu, the Southern regions have seen several cases of violence
against Dalit women. In fact, *The Hindu* headline reports, "Atrocities against
Dalit women occur more in South." The NGO Evidence based in Madurai,
Tamil Nadu recorded over 125 cases of sexual violence on Dalit women in a
span of four years between 2009-2013. They note that unreported crimes numbers are much higher and add: "The number of violations against Dalit women
is at its peak. Apart from male dominance in economic status and society, caste
serves as a catalyst for violations against Dalit women" (Evidence).[86]

In the years of 2012-2014, atrocities including rapes and killings were reported in all major newspapers in India. As reported in *The Hindu*, two young
Dalit girls were gang raped and hung on a tree in Uttar Pradesh in May 2014.
They were attacked while relieving themselves in the fields. The police were
reportedly compliant with this rape ("Abominable Crime" n.pag.). Remaining
within spaces and roles is a tragically necessary behavior sealed by authoritative bodies to which Dalits and specifically Dalit women must carefully adhere.
Kalai and Rani are always ready and armed with courage to cross boundaries
knowing the risks and the consequences they walk into.

As spelled out in the *Manusmriti,* a Dalit woman's role is not to be the
"good woman" (that Anzaldúa points to with respect to her cultural context),
but to remain the elemental "bad woman" living into forced figurations as quarrelsome, immoral, ugly, lazy, loose, and servant of the caste community (chapter three). Proving herself to be capable of social worth is not her expected
function; if she does that, she oversteps her natural state of being that has been
divinely ordained, and therefore, she should be punished. In referring to the
marginalization of gay and lesbian persons, Anzaldúa insists, "Deviance is
whatever is condemned by the community" (40). She further explains how in
her experience, the message of the condemning community is that a deviant
woman is to be feared and kept under control (39). Kalai and Rani live into the
"fierce untouchable," breaking free of remaining trapped within dominant nar-

---

[86] Evidence posts annual reports on their website. www.evidence.org

ratives as one to be feared and controlled. If she is submissive, quiet, rape-able, and forgiving of her caste-minded society and acquired kin in her dictated status as woman, Dalit, powerless, and poor, she can exist. She cannot desire to live her life as a self-fulfilled or socially-fulfilled individual who will seek her safety and that of her family and community of women and children. If she were to do so, she would not just be placing herself at risk, but Anzaldúa's "shadowy beast" would most certainly be physically, morally, and psychologically mutilated. Soorpanakha in *Ramayana* was not allowed into the physical nor into the emotional world of Rama; she was mocked and abused for desiring him. Valmiki details the consequences of thought and behavior that dares override dominant ideal expectations.

Similarly, rebellious transgressive Dalit women labeled as deviant "Other" are not permitted to be present and operative in claiming their rights to responsible, social action-seeking amelioration. In that case, why and how would "shadow beasts" emerge as non-frightening, shaking the weight off their backs and proceeding with a steady gait towards opponents who stride freely in open prerogative and entitled spaces? Dalit women—who wipe their face of the dripping caste excreta that they carry on their heads, or dodge flying debris from the stones they break in the quarries, or lean into the garbage on the streets, staring into and breathing the stench of cast-out social and human discharge mirroring their "dirty" image—have the compelling need to kick and scream.

The narratives on transgressive methods adapted by Kalai and Rani leading to social change serve as evidence of their adaptation to transgression as a natural spontaneity in their everyday work. Kalai's efforts to educate herself is a transgression of boundaries where traditionally for over several centuries Dalits have been denied access to education; she carries this into her children's lives and in her *Thai* initiative to educate Dalit girls in her community discussed in the previous chapters. Her son is trained in the shipping career as a naval third officer. Her daughter graduated from high school with high scores and is now in medical school. Rani places great importance on education as well and takes great effort to educate her children so that they may escape the vicious cycle of unreachable opportunities. In each of their efforts to build and enrich the lives of Dalit communities, both women adapt transgressive measures to thwart oppressive forces that keep them enslaved.

Kalai and Rani narrated several incidents that are examples of rebellious transgression of boundaries in the boundless space that the nature of *earthy humanness* in activism makes possible. Their activism draws upon the existent cultural strengths of Dalit women from within a specific culture where spontaneity of language and emotions is a cultural trait. Anzaldúa points to the aspect of wailing as indicative of the Indian (Native) woman's history of resistance where in the Aztec culture it was a means of protesting the lesser status of women (43). Bama points to such specific cultural behaviors of Dalit women—wailing; performing special rites for women in birth, coming of age, and death; a quarrelsome voice; spontaneous expressions of Dalit language, dances, songs, and storytelling; and many more—as signifiers of specific cultural strengths (*Sangati*). Bama confirms in *Sangati* that Dalit women are strong, conniving, and creative in ways that express their rage through transgressive tropes. For example, Bama writes about Rakkamma who runs out into the street and exposes her private parts to stop her husband from beating her (62). Sanmuga Kizhavi is another rebellious Dalit woman in *Sangati* who is enraged by the fact that a young Dalit girl was severely beaten for accidentally brushing against her master's pot of water. She urinates in the water bowl of her landlord as her spontaneous innovative method of revenge (Bama 118). There is no room for discouragement or processing of liberation when creative rage ascends naturally to establish courageous silent actions of rebellion measured by their own pride in the efficacy of such actions.

Kalai and Rani continue to speak with authority and ownership of their agency and activism which reveals spontaneity as a way of life and the only way by which rebellious activism can happen. In their war against arrack, they could not gain the support of the police or any other local authority. Rani claims, "We broke and destroyed everything. We ourselves went on a raid. All over ourselves, we were covered with that syrupy solution [arrack]." Just to picture Dalit women charging into arrack hiding places and breaking bottles and barrels is enough to suggest that spontaneous activism is the most effective counter force to spontaneous exercise of power. That spontaneity becomes the center of an outpouring of a positive destructive energy (embodied in the goddess *Kali*) that is fired by the desire to live a life of peace, security, and dignity. Rani spoke of how her husband and other Dalit men would physically abuse Dalit women due to the influence of arrack; they were a threat to their children's well-being and education. The anger on arrack is directed to an activism that will destroy any hindrances to accomplishing its goal. Angry Dalit women refuse to accept the negligence of those who should address the problem and take it upon themselves to raid the villages if the police will not do it. They will call for a *dharna* where Dalit women and children will come in large numbers to protest; they will stop the major highways and the functioning of police stations.

Voice is a major asset for Rani in whom argumentative speech proves to be a major weapon in the battle for justice. One of the major strengths that stands out in Rani is her ability to speak boldly for rights of Dalits; she claims voice as her major quintessential character trait from the time she was young. Married at the age of thirteen and bearing her first child at fifteen, Rani did not settle for a life of servitude to her family, her in-laws, and her masters. Poor, uneducated, and Dalit, there is very little that Rani can rely on to focus attention on her suffering self and her community; she pursues social responsibility as a human response to injustice. She holds on to voice as her major asset that she acknowledges and recovers, for it is in that tool of rebellion and protest that she locates, assesses, wrestles with, and demands justice for the struggles of her people. The urgency of her speech originates from spaces of ambiguities and complications in relation to her imposed identities and daily life experiences. Her methods of protest and change are varied extensions of her voice, which is personal and deeply ingrained in her as her birthmark and the effects of which she simply cannot deny to herself. It is that personal asset of voice that becomes her political, social, and cultural tool. Her testimonies lead her voice as a naturally gushing expression that breaks through people, institutions, boundaries, and oppressive structures in its becoming a collective voice for and with her people. The main targets of her voice are: personal struggles for herself and Dalit individuals, accountability of caste communities, responsibility of Dalit patriarchy, responsibility of the police force, poverty, alcoholism, and the physical dangers of Dalits.

From within her space of being shunned by society, Rani acts in order to create subversive modes of protest and rebellion. Recollecting her initial steps into active social change, she says that on hearing about the Dr. AWARD organization, "I decided to go because I thought why should I live here in this village and not know anything about the outside world? So, I decided to go and see Akka. I came with a daring courage" (The Tamil word that Rani used for courage was *thunichal* which means "daring courage"). Rani made the choice to transgress boundaries drawn for her by her husband, in-laws, caste communities, traditional narratives, patriarchal national discourses, and other dominant cultural forces of power. As a result of her disrupting the pedagogy of the nation, she stands between forces of domination and the dominated. She states that she has nothing to lose, except her life.

In declaring a liberating belief within her of not fearing for her life and developing this belief through her own unique frame of reference, she denies the power of threat to those she opposes by blowing out *their* point of target: her life. One of my favorite lines in my conversations with Rani is when she says, *"Whatever it is, I can talk fearlessly. I cannot do and will not do the kiyoo kiyoo talk [hesitant and submissive talk]. Whatever it is, I will talk about it openly."* Fueled by fearlessness and openness in her voice, she finds her liberation to act. Proudly acknowledging her accomplishments in using her voice she says, *"If there is no water or electricity on my street in my colony, I will act fast and go to the vice president or to the thalaivar [to say]: 'This is the deprivation in my village.' No one would say that; only I would do that."* Through the use of voice, Rani locates power in herself, activating cultural dissonances in the eyes of hegemonic power structures and subverting a denigrated character trait as the loud Dalit woman.

With the confidence in her voice, Rani's leadership develops into one that continues to disrupt cultural and national expectations. She fathoms ways in which interconnections between various incarnations of oppressions and dominant forces unsurprisingly and naturally converge on the bodies of specific groups. In assuming such narrative positions of self-location from which they speak, dance, or sing, Dalit women are inherently bold whether they are from spaces that they have crossed into or spaces in which they physically remain. This boldness is crucial to inviting the immediate community into a solidarity that strengthens their capacity to be subversive. They continue to embrace meanings not intended by the dominant traditional cultures that have imposed specific identities and meanings upon them.

Rani recalled her direct war with the police to free two of her relatives who were arrested with no cause or evidence but just because the upper caste had instigated a lie. While at a bus station, Rani heard about the arrest of her relatives, and she dropped everything and headed to the police station where she used her strong voice to wrestle with the police. In Rani's narration, looking at the police officer, she recalls,

> I said, *"So, YOU should have enquired properly and figured out who is the one who is being unfair and who is being unjustly affected by all this. Because the whole village came, you put these people in jail. What is justice is what you should enquire about."* He said, *"How can you say that the rabbit you caught has only three legs?"* [A common adage used in referring to adamant claims].

Rani commented that a surge of courage came over her that day when the police officer laughed at her claim. She proudly said:

> I responded to his ridicule claiming, *"Yes, the rabbit I caught has only three legs. The whole village thinks they are enemies. But I think of the whole village as the enemy. You have to release the boy and his mother. The other two—I am not sure if they killed them, not sure what they did to them. They have been missing since 2 a.m. People are searching for them. You have to account for them too."* He said, *"You are not talking properly. How can you talk to a police officer like this?"* I said,

"Sir, I am not falsely accusing you of anything. I am asking you to fully enquire the truth."

Rani continued:

I claimed justice, spoke the law; his name was Maran, the PC [Police Commissioner]. *I argued and claimed justice all night long. I decided to fight. I argued, I fought, and then he decided that this lady is not going to stop, and he said: "You can ask for yourself about what this boy has done that the whole village is against him?" I said, "You ask him. There is no fight with you and them and with me and them. Whoever filed the case against them, let them come and we'll enquire. But don't do things to this extreme extent." They had him sitting in his underwear. Then they brought them out and he* [the Police Commissioner] *said, "Ok ma, you finished this with your claim that the rabbit you caught has three legs! But ask him to repent and lead a better life." He said this and as I was watching, they hit him so hard that he flew from one end of the room to another. Terrifying anger came upon me. I put my life on the line every time I had to speak up. I said, "There is no justice in this. How much money did they pay? How much money did they pay this station that you are beating up this boy so badly. What did he say? He only answered your question. Did he say anything wrong? Or did he not answer the question? Why?" He yelled, "Why are you bringing money into this?" I replied, "Of course it is money that is asking you to do this. Without bribe, this work cannot be done." All the anger against me, they were showing on the boy and attacking him. Then I thought to myself that I shouldn't say anything more and let me bring the guy out and then discuss this. After this and that, it was about 6:30 p.m., and then he said, "Take him." I brought them out and asked them not to go anywhere else but to go to the Annavasal office.*

Rani leads *Women's Day Rally* in Thirunallur, Pudukkottai District, March 11, 2007.

After a while, Rani went back to the police station and enquired with the junior police officers about the Police Commissioner with whom she had battled. She asked, *"Is this how things happen in this station? Is this justice?"* Rani recalls one officer saying: *"Ever since this man took over, this has been happening. If more people like you spoke up, he will be transferred or made accountable in some way. Everybody is afraid to question him."* Rani emphasized his words: *"This same situation must not come upon anyone. Even if it does, as long as this station is concerned, a murder can happen. You are asking about what is right and not even about justice. This is not the time for justice and what is right* [Tamil=niyaayam]. *Only money is the ruling factor now in this station."* Rani is convinced that for the sake of money, such kind of "drama" goes on.

Speaking about bribes, Rani says:

> *If we had paid about ten rupees* [a figurative number that could mean ten thousand], *then he would have said, "What did he do that is so bad that the whole town is against him?" That's what he would have said. But we don't have to pay money to argue this case; we are capable of arguing for ourselves. Then we went directly to the Collector's office, we wrote the report and*

they asked me to narrate all that happened, and I stated every-
thing. He was suspended for one month.

While Rani described in detail this entire situation, what stood out for me was her adamant subversive grabbing of the adage, *"Yes, the rabbit I caught has three legs."* Rani was determined to prove innocence even if it took the entire day and night; she wrestled for justice. She placed her life at risk at the steps of the police station battling and arguing for justice. Rebellious spontaneity allows no room for careful thought towards self-protection. Adorned with the strength and force of determination, both Rani and Kalai erect themselves and rise as spotted goddesses wherever and whenever they should. They stand at the junction of power, vulnerability, and danger when they could have been arrested as well. In this specific situation, Rani had to take on this fight between authority and agency without much time to plan and follow implementation strategies. Any lapse of time meant increasing chances of more physical abuse that could lead to death which will be covered up by the police; she had to act then and there. Rani claimed,

> *I am not saying this for the sake of my pride. From that day*
> *till now if anyone says, "Kallarpatti Rani," immediately they*
> [police officers] *salute me.... Ah, yes. Immediately, they salute*
> *me ... in Viralimalai and here. Only if my parents had let me*
> *finish fifth grade, I would have gone far.*

Rani strongly believes that if she could accomplish this much with a second-grade education, she could do more if she had completed fifth grade! The natural clay-like kneading of a stubborn confidence, childlike innocence, and raging anger held together by an *earthy humanness* make Rani unique and lovable. For organic leaders like Kalai and Rani, activism is an urgent spontaneous response to human need for justice and dignity: a way of life.

Another illustration of rebellious spontaneity is leadership in Kalai's *dharna* to eradicate manual scavenging, a primary mission of DA. To protest this dehumanizing work, Dalit women involved in manual scavenging went on a *dharna* carrying the baskets used for carrying human feces on their heads. *Dharna,* as a method of social protest in visible public spaces, disrupts the normal day-to-day life of larger circles of social life—groups of people sit to block local streets, roads, and highways. If the police and other officials will not act to help them, they will take it upon their heads, even literally, to draw the attention of the public and higher government officials. In this protest, they stood as spotted goddesses armed with baskets filled with human excreta running down their face. Kalai publicly demonstrated such daring agency in those involved in manual scavenging as her major strategy for social activism. Kalai testified:

Since 1992, we have been fighting for the eradication of the practice of manual scavenging [the practice of employing only Dalits to clean unsanitary public toilets]. *In 1996, we requested the district Collector to implement the law against manual scavenging. He denied that this practice existed in our area, even after we took him to see the work that Dalits did. Around twenty-seven manual scavengers—who were women—went on dharna in front of the Union office in Annavasal. They all carried baskets on their heads at the dharna. For a whole week, the manual scavengers went on strike as dharna, and then the Collector responded, and the government issued orders to destroy some of the dry toilets. Slowly, we made changes happen year by year; about two to three dry latrines were destroyed, and proper public toilets were constructed. We are still fighting to totally eradicate this from our area. We would go to the Grievance Day set apart by the Collector's office which happens once a week. This was every Monday. We would go every Monday and give petitions to the Collector's office. Even now we do this.*

Such protest is a powerful illustration of the performativity of agency as change-seeking restlessness that stems from that locale of a culture of collectivity in a spontaneous juncture of modes of resistance to authority. Those working as manual scavengers went on a strike to further demonstrate their vested power in refusing to remove human feces which nobody else will remove. Their voices are oracles in the silent but loud visibility of the public spectacle of *dharna* and in the stench of an overload of feces in the dry bathrooms. Their spontaneous acting out of anger against *saaraayam*, manual scavenging, and other deterrents to their right to a life of dignity is a cultural ceremonial for survival just as their cultural aspects of wailing, singing, and dancing are ingrained in their daily lives.

Organic Intellectuals and Self-Givers

The two leaders— Kalai and Rani—embody Antonio Gramsci's concept of organic intellectuals who are from the earth and give abundantly to those with them (Forgas 302). They take charge of their destiny as those in control to defeat any impediments that would deter their productive life. Gramsci's intellectuals have a certain degree of active social productivity. He asserts:

The mode of being the new intellectual can no longer consist in eloquence, which is an exterior and momentary mover of feelings and passions, but in active participation in practical life, as constructor, organizer, "permanent persuader" and not just a simple orator (but superior at the same time to the abstract mathematical spirit); from technique-as-work one proceeds to techniques-as-science and to the historical humanist conception without which one remains a "specialist" and does not become a leader [dirigente] (specialist + politician). (Forgas 321-22)

In each of the examples provided by Kalai and Rani on their determined actions towards social change, there is a unique chain of practicality, creative methodological construction, organization, and consistent persuasion. They galvanize an activist methodology ingrained in a cultural science of collective identity. The momentum of working together in turn brings about changed situations and justice in personal lives affected by caste-based violence and discriminations. Kalai and Rani have created and established a culture of resistance and rebellion against injustice and denial of the basic human right to live fully with human dignity. They do so by first making people own a collective communal identity, "*kuzhu unarvu*" (Bama). [87]

Making their living space a safe, livable, and peaceful environment is the focus of major initiatives led by Kalai and Rani. They assess the lives of Dalits around them, continue to identify specific needs, and work towards transformation without waiting for or depending upon outside approval. Led by such independent autonomous leadership, families, children, wives, daughters, and mothers are all active participants in change-making initiatives. In redeeming the essential character of the space, culture, and people, they redeem its identity, culture, and history as well. *Arrack*-free spaces are free from domestic violence. The husbands, fathers, and brothers not only stop beating their women but they bring home the money that they would have spent on *arrack*, and the home becomes a safe and peaceful environment with more economic security; these homes become safe communal spaces as well. Creating and sustaining such spaces provides self-worth, productivity, and a positive identity.

Each incident and initiative that Kalai and Rani describe testify to their selfless giving. They place the needs of their people before any of their own immediate family needs. For two years, Kalai housed over twenty young Dalit girls in her seven hundred square-foot home in Annavasal because the dorm building project for the *Thai* educational program was not completed, and the owner of the rented building where the girls stayed asked them to leave since the value of his house was going down because he housed Dalit girls. Kalai decided to build a dorm on a two-acre plot of land that she had purchased about

[87] In a personal interview on July 17, 2002, Bama identified a collective identity among Dalit women as *kuzhu unarvu* (collective feeling).

twenty years before with the help of the organization Bread for the World, with a vision to build a school for Dalit children. Every time the girls in her care prepare for exams, Kalai provides them with all the necessary emotional and physical care they need to perform well. There were times when Kalai would call me prior to an exam and cry a lot on the phone saying that she hopes all the girls would do well in exams. In that example, the girls who graduate from high school, on pursuing higher education and securing jobs, continue to come back to the space of *Thai* to provide care, support, and mentorship to the younger girls.

In the case of the Ilupakkudipatti village where Dalit families were imprisoned and Dalit brides were forced to sleep with the upper caste male, Kalai acted in both a selfless and a carefully organized manner. The fact that she went into the village and lived there to investigate further was a great risk that she took. She says, *"So I decided to go to that village myself. I stayed in a Dalit home; they told the Kallar that I was a niece visiting from out of town."* In the case of the inter-caste marriage issue in Illupoor, she says,

> He [the District Collector] *accused me of instigating caste violence and threatened to arrest me. I was not afraid. I said, "Let me see how you will arrest me." I sent information to twenty-seven Dalit organizations, and the next day, almost all the organizations came to Pudukkottai and then again, more than one hundred of us went on a dharna. The SP supported me and asked me to narrate the incident. I narrated all that had happened, and seeing that the District Collector continued to accuse me, the SP decided to investigate further.*

Kalai added:

> The leader of the three higher castes [Kallar, Maravar, Agamudiar] *came to attack me, and the secretary of the CPI* [Communist Party of India] *rescued me. He covered me with his shawl and quickly put me in his jeep and made sure I was driven home safely. Then, after this, they arrested all those on whom the FIR was filed. We made sure the affected families were protected and kept them in our Annavasal office.*

The lives of Kalai, her family, and her staff are at a daily risk, but she continues in her fearless self-giving vocation.

Rani spoke of her daring fearlessness in an incident of battling with the police force:

> They [the government office] *suspended them* [corrupt police officers]. *They did this. After all this, what they did to us, is they hired men to finish us both. They said, "These two should*

be finished; we should not leave them. We lost our earnings."
They said these things, Akka, in Annavasal. I could not move
about there. I am not desirous [Tamil=*aasai*] *of my life. Even if*
I die—"She died and because of her death, our village is doing
well"—this is what so many people will say. I openly said, "I
am not desirous of my life. I am not desirous of my life even as
a thread measure" [Tamil=*oru nool kooda*]. M*y children are*
small, but I know that somehow they [village community] *will*
save them and bring them up. I said that and I dared.

For Kalai and Rani, their own lives do not matter; when they openly declare their fearlessness to die, they say it with pride. Every time Kalai travelled to rescue young girls, especially in her travel to Orissa to rescue a young Dalit girl from the Naxalites (branded by the Indian Government as an internal terrorist group), it epitomized the selflessness in her activism and the dissolution of segregated spaces as personal and communal, "me" and "them." Such leaders operate on the principle of a collective identity of solidarity where "we" is central to any justice-oriented and redemptive action. Kalai and Rani are not afraid to cross any kind of social or cultural barriers in which they could lose their lives. Their battles for justice necessitates a focus on *earthy humanness* in their response to human rights violations without much or any monetary reimbursement for the risky work they do.

Kalai has established a strong social justice base in Pudukkottai District where she has built trust and earned the respect of community leaders. She uses these human assets to bring attention to human rights violations against Dalits. The police officers and the local government officials have become her strong support and allies in all her efforts to bring justice to Dalits in Pudukkottai District. Her accomplishments as a Dalit woman transfer onto the lives of the Dalit communities she works with as they walk into the DA office space with hope, pride, and confidence. What grips me most about Kalai and Rani are the selfless ways in which they give of themselves without counting the cost. On several occasions, they have pawned their meagre belongings to help the distressed—to pay for a hospital visit, education, or funeral expenses. (I heard this from those who have benefitted from their help.) Kalai has built a boarding facility for young Dalit girls through her *Thai* program on a two-acre piece of land. What I learn from Kalai and Rani are ways in which a re-appropriation of selflessness extends to a continuum of humanness, where—as a human condition—claim to a selfish purpose cannot remain selfish but can only break free and find meaning in serving the larger community as a sustainable movement.

Selfless *Sangam*

When Rani speaks of the *sangam* in her village, it is evident that women have bank accounts; but the money is part of a shared pool from which they help a family in need. They spread a sustained culture of selflessness and invest in the longevity of such a culture as central to their humanness, thus demonstrating an assertion of their human dignity. Rani said:

> *Then after that, we started three sangam in my village itself. We work with those who do not know anything about the outside world; we take them outside and what they do not know, we make it known to them and create awareness [Tamil=vivagaaram]. If you look at the case of one woman, she remarried after her first husband died. She has four girls, no boys. I talked with her and made her realize, saying, "Come here. Why are you struggling like this living in this village? It's ok if you are living only with your husband; you have your husband and your sister-in-law living with you. You are [economically] suffering." I told her that and about joining the sangam. Just like this, I tell others one by one, just as how. I told this woman and showed her another village—she tells other people in that village; and lots [of sangam] have developed.*

Rani wants the women to benefit from the *sangam* in a way that they would be economically empowered and in turn have more confidence and control over their lives. In the sangam, the women help each other's families in times of dire need:

> Rani: *We have meetings, then, secondly, if they have taken lots of loans so they are in difficulty. Say, for instance, they want to educate their child. We save may be fifty rupees, whatever we can that is convenient for us; if we are daily wage laborers and if we give that money to the sangam, we can save here. According to our income, we save just among ourselves; we have one rupee as interest and instead of borrowing money from outside, we lend money to each other among ourselves. Say, for instance, for childbirth expenses, for child's education expenses, and all that—whoever asks, we give. Even if they are from the outside [our village], if they ask us for these specific reasons, we say, "Here, take."* [Notice use of collective terms: "our, we"].
>
> Roja: *That's a great system.*

Rani: [Rani nods] *Yes, we will just give. Same way for children's education—we say that we don't want any interest; they just pay back the primary—because this is just ten people's concern* [meaning, they are few in numbers]. *So, we do that. One time, one person needed money, but they were not sure if they could pay back. They wanted to give their gold amulet charm. I refused to take it, but I took it because they insisted. But they paid the money back, and I gave them back their amulet. Like this for each concern, we have done a lot to help. Secondly, the huge problem we have here is the illegal brewing of arrack. Just to address this itself, we started this organization.*

Rani has started three *sangam* that continue to benefit Dalit communities. She does not receive any monetary benefit from these *sangam,* but she acts out of a social consciousness to construct a culture of self-sufficiency and economic security for her people built on the foundation of a Dalit ethics of care. She assures them and convinces them of the monetary and emotional support they provide for each other, propelling them towards higher gains such as higher education and starting their own small businesses. She provides opportunities for her people to perceive themselves as agents of change within the concourse of their natural *earthy humanness.* They take full charge of their lives and are empowered in this actualization of human agency. Space, culture, social needs, and human attachments collude to respond to a specific situation—an urge to be an active social participant representing a space and cultural community filled with human dignity, strength, and confidence. Finding ways to claim such spaces is the priority for Rani and Kalai as they force meanings out in practical and productive spaces involving qualitative assessment that the two women initiate in this region.

I learn from these life stories an earthy activism that is human, where agency disturbs a Dalit's deep-seated, unarticulated, and unclaimed desire to be the "dirty" (unrestrained) woman she is said to be, to rise as the "shadow beast" who can courageously shake her body in the rising. The re-appropriation and the re-defining of the "Other" deviant woman happens in that process of disrupting and shaking off imposed restrictions and rising as both her own self and her communal self; the "Other" seeks to dissipate the "Othered" space in building altars where human dignity is uplifted, transforming the "Othered" state. There is more strength in that process of stripping than in claiming a status where power structures need to be duplicated in demanding ownership of education, land, and money.

Kalai and Rani tap into already existent cultural strengths; Rani's accomplishments of starting *sangam* in the neighboring villages is a concept that rests at home with a Dalit culture of looking for shared resources. In Rani's description of the operations of the *sangam* quoted in the section above, she used the word "we" when referring to the members, participants, beneficiaries, and operations of the *sangam*. They channel the benefits towards education, childbirth, or any kind of financial need a family might have. The pool of money created and sustained is a financial source for the community. The earthy, indigenous human characteristic of sharing from a pool of natural resources is an integral part of organic intellectualism where a system of communal collective security protects its people from any kind of danger. Collective response to need emboldens a community in its requisite solidarity and confidence-building measure—here, Dalit communities mirror this strategy where caste communities accomplish collective terrorizations. Rani convinces members into a commitment to pledge not just their money but to safeguard their concerted human concern for each other. As a group, she mobilizes them to invoke a coalition of forces to confute social powers that coagulate to endorse keeping Dalits in a deprived social and economic condition. The power gained through this coalition extends into the war against the social evil of arrack. There are built-in constructions of a social responsivity and personal trust amongst the *sangam* members. Such coalition fosters and affirms a sense of positive identity and self-worth that glues them amongst their reality of dependent receptacles of hegemonic competition for hierarchy, power, and control; their counter culture is validated in the *sangam*. New alliances between individuals, households, villages, and organizations are birthed in those traits of trust and responsivity producing political, legal, and economic rights for those otherwise victimized.

Disruptive *Dharna*

Dharna, discussed earlier in this chapter, is an example of effectively applying Dalit cultural scientific methodology of a self-giving collective identity. When Kalai spoke about the eradication of manual scavenging as one of the primary objectives of her organization and their relentless fight for the eradication of the practice of manual scavenging, she brags about *dharna* as an effective method of protest that they adopt. It is a visual and a moral confirmation for the participants and the onlookers of the self-giving collective strength in their gathering together. Another example that Kalai provided of *dharna* was when rebellious young Dalit men and women were attacked and sexually abused in December 2013 in the village of Keezhakurichi. They were punished by the upper caste communities for attending a temple festival and entering the holy premises traditionally forbidden for Dalits; they transgressed boundaries. She said:

Young Dalit boys were attacked with sickles and were severely cut in their arms. There were rape attempts made on young Dalit women who were shopping at the bangle shop at the temple fair. They were stripped and publicly exposed and humiliated. We took up this issue and went on dharna in the Annavasal bus stand and in front of the Collector's office...about more than one hundred of us, including children and babies. Then they pulled out the 144 law of curfew for one hundred days for those people. Still, this case is going on. One lakh and fifty-five thousand rupees was given as compensation to those who were cut. Initially, the police did not file an FIR on them but filed it on our boys. I went directly to the SP. One of the boys who was cut, it was his wedding the next day. They put him in jail. I fought very hard to bring him out. Still, this case is on trial.

This pattern of social transgression and violence that follows as punishment calls for social protest. Even in the absence of promise of positive responses to their protests, it was important for the community to make their presence known and provide visibility to the reasons for transgression of boundaries as their social right.

Kalai explained a similar situation in the village of Thirunallur (discussed earlier) where Dalit men who married out of caste were severely beaten, their heads shaved, and were subject to the public humiliation of being paraded naked on a donkey. Since the police did not co-operate to file an FIR, Dalit communities went on a *dharna*. Kalai recalled:

Due to this incident, we organized all the village folks, and we sat on the road in front of the police station, blocking the road as Dharna. All the Dalit people and several organizations came and took part. After seventeen hours of Dharna, they finally agreed to file the FIR... I sent information to twenty-seven Dalit organizations, and the next day, almost all the organizations came to Pudukkottai and then again, more than one hundred of us went on a dharna. The SP [Superintendent of Police, a Senior Police Officer] supported me and asked me to narrate the incident. I narrated all that had happened and, seeing that the District Collector continued to accuse me, the SP decided to investigate further. When he learned the truth, then he filed the FIR saying that a social injustice has happened. He said that even if hired authoritative bodies come, I will show them the FIR. He filed an FIR on 127 people—all those who were involved.

Dharna—as a collective performance—is a cultural ritual of protest that should happen to gain social visibility, social concern, *and* social justice. It is a concentration of positive energy where the sitting down on the ground is a statement of public proclamation of what they as a community rightfully deserve. It is a counter-performance to the public spectacle that they are made into in their raping, lynching, naked parading, public beatings, public harassments, and much more. On most occasions that Kalai spoke about, *dharna* yields an expected outcome of gaining the attention of those in jurisdictional power. A communal transformation happens in the realization of the power that *dharna* holds for the people; it reveals an inner strength of selfless giving as a determination for social change. It affirms a Dalit world view of caring and resilience; Kalai and Rani accomplish this affirmation among their people through their own self-giving and relentless social outreach, proving the power vested in a selfless collective identity safeguarded by spotted goddesses.

A sense of ownership of who they are is key to these leaders who not only propose but summon attention from people to the idea of common spaces, common struggles, and common purposes. Rightfully, they claim inspiration from the life of Ambedkar as their leader where a movement of resistance, rebellion, and agitation are crucial in the establishment of a cultural, political, and historical presence. Kalai and Rani rise above subjugation as an immediate social condition and subversively cull and become organic intellectual apparatuses propelling this cultural behavior of a refusal to coexist with polluted matter which they are forced to see, touch, and embody in the caste principle. This embodiment results in an internalization as a natural co-product of a religiography—a mapping and patented etching of their polluted being in religious discourses. In a culture of resistance, however, they reject ownership of their bodies and minds in a process of groveling but rather in a movement of an imminent demand and adaptation to an ownership of their positive resistant selves. I have to mention the powerful words of Caribbean-American poet June Jordan sung by Sweet Honey in the Rock, a black feminist a cappella group singing about responsivity: "We are the ones we've been waiting for" (Jordan).[88] Internal self-empowerment galvanizes the essential sense of ownership as a radical mass phenomenon among the peoples against despotic systems and structures. Kalai and Rani have planted and nurtured this germane shift in the mindset of their people.

---

[88] "We are the Ones We've Been Waiting for" are the words of poet June Jordan in "Poems for South African Women" presented to the UN on August 9, 1978.

Dharna demanding justice for Thirunallur, March 22, 1997.

In that same culture, Kalai and Rani intervene into the disruptions to their practical day-to-day life and establish stable living conditions. They awaken the consciousness of individuals in powerful political positions who can question and call into action the implementation of policies to the favor of Dalits who are subject to culturally normalized, inhuman treatment. Drawing upon those institutional arsenals, they restore and reconstruct socioeconomic, political, historical, and cultural identities that they fearlessly encounter as they negotiate with state machineries. The District Collectors, government officials to whom the police force and other local power bodies are accountable, prove to be of immense support to both these women. Through allies, they gain the respect and co-operation of the police force, bank officials, and government-based programs that should rightly benefit communities as well.

Dalit communities are able to learn and experience new support systems and modes of life where they could be free of encumbrances and focus on a quality of life lived with dignity, even with their meager income. They introduce and activate methods of countering overt expressions of hierarchy that lead into dehumanizing situations by drawing from existent strengths and urgent desires for a meaningful life. Clearly, they organize individuals, families, and larger community bodies around deterrent issues and enable them to subvert such situations; Kalai and Rani have consistently been infusers of energy and hope in the midst of hegemonic cultures of acquisitive greed and inhuman practices upon Dalit peoples. Most importantly, they have provided their communities with the courage to interact and negotiate with caste communities, and Dalit women are able to question their own men as well. The question of breaking free from within and without has lucid illustrations in these two organic lives. Rani and Kalai have capacitated their peoples in overcoming external and internal restraints: their people have come to believe in their own moral integrity and intellectual and physical capabilities to be the loud and the quarrelsome women they always have been to thwart unprecedented controlling forces. Kalai and Rani continue to live as beings of a higher organic kind, as courageous "dirty" women who will risk their lives and use their natural spontaneous cultural behavioral strengths to establish productive spaces both physically and conceptually.

Anzaldúa reminds us:

> Because, according to Christianity and most other major religions, woman is carnal, animal, and closer to the un-divine, she must be protected. Protected from herself. Woman is the stranger, the other. She is man's recognized nightmarish pieces, his Shadow-Beast (39).

What would be the nature of this beast that would dare to break the invisible chains that cause intense pain? Who will redefine this "shadow beast" that has been culturally identified as the "Other?" What will she lose if she dares to start imagining the other side of being the "Other?" Ceasing to be the "Other" will be her ultimate imagination, but going that far in her desires, she will have to seek equalizers in caste behavior and economic security, guaranteed moral and personal safety, the same quality of water to drink, the same space in the classroom for her child in the local school, and the same air of audacious confidence with which her child can walk. Velutha, the Dalit servant in Arundhathi Roy's *God of Small Things,* dares to love and touch a "touchable" woman from the high caste as he comes into the full awareness that he has "nothing" further to lose as an untouchable (316). What could be worse? Rani iterates, "I am not desirous of my life." Fear of losing life is of no concern here, but sustaining a "fierce" active *earthy humanness* that will pervade people's minds in transforming the ways in which they live their complex lives is imperative.

In their direct demands for the physical, spiritual, and economic wellbeing of their people, Kalai and Rani succeed in a transfiguration of their traditional figurations from passive negative beings to active positive leaders. Claiming their cultural norm of identification with another, they instate social justice and human dignity. Drawing from lived personal and communal experiences, they establish activism as a cultural practice—a way of life. *Change-seeking restlessness* is at the core of their being where deep desires for change are honored and are often transformed into direct action. They personify a subversion of stigmatized characteristics as "different" in their relentless battle where "difference" is a tool-like-armament. In both Kalai and Rani there is a strong presence of a conscious awareness (independent of imposed notions) of violation of human rights, since they are directly affected. They are the practical organic incarnations of an *earthy humanness* where legal rights and human rights fit into their Dalit ethics of simply caring for one another. In these life stories, we see rebellious transgression of dictated spaces if we as listeners and engaged onlookers would allow those indicators to surface. The inherent moral imagination in Dalit women recognizes their human limitations to achieving social freedom and invigorates them through their *earthy humanness* into new strategies of decisive and effective action.

CHAPTER SEVEN

Singing Bodies, Dancing Minds: Diverse Spaces in Songs by Dalit Women

In my prologue, I identified my time in Dalit communities surrounding the town of Karunguzhi in Tamil Nadu from 1991-92 as the beginning of my long-standing relationships I built in the years that followed. I soaked in the spontaneous singing by women at several occasions including birth, coming of age, wedding, worship, work, leisure, and mourning. Since my husband was the local priest with the Church of South India[89] (CSI), we were often invited to community gatherings. I was drawn to the strength in the voices of Dalit women, which are a combination of melodious and guttural singing that are calming and stirring at the same time. Later, when I turned to a focused research on oral narratives by Dalit women, I re-immersed myself in the simple *earthy humanness* of the songs as the singers drew me back into their embrace.

In the past twenty years, ethnographers and sociologists have increasingly turned their attention to gathering information on social, family, and extended kinship structures evident in the lives of Dalit communities. Songs by Dalit women that are central to a Dalit community, however, have not yet been widely recognized as valuable forms of representational earthy literature. Since these songs have not been commonly heard by nor presented to a larger audience, they have not been available much in written form to be included in literary or other socio-cultural discourses on resistance and activism.

To explore and gain an understanding of songs and to better engage with the singers, I traveled to over twenty-five Dalit villages in the Chengalpattu district of the state of Tamil Nadu (where I heard the songs presented in this chapter) during my visits in 2002, 2003, 2005, and 2006. In this chapter, I express my relationships with these lyrical narratives as they help me gain a deeper understanding of the singers' experiences, ethics of life, relationships, and affections by which I am deeply influenced. I attempt to explain how the songs sustain me

---

[89] Church of South India (CSI) is a mainstream Protestant denomination in South India. This exists as the body of the North India in the Northern parts of India. The CSI was formed in 1947 when the Presbyterian, Reformed, Congregational, Anglican, and some Methodist churches merged as one Protestant church body in India. As reported in the Wall Street Journal in "High Price for Religious Conversion?" (23 December 2009) about seventy percent of the CSI and CNI bodies are made up of Dalits.

daily in my self-understanding as I live out my being in my not so visible identity as a Dalit woman and my visible identity as a woman of color in the US.

I must admit that I embarked on this journey into songs with assumptions that I would mostly hear music expressing religious sentiments and daily struggles, but later knowing that my assumptions would melt. These powerful narratives challenged my own academic readings and ideas on resistance, rebellion, activism, social change, and moral and social agency. Within this oral narrative tradition, intricately interwoven themes splash in a diversity of assertive declarations. These lyrics include transgressive notions: a command over experiences of untouchability that only a person treated as "untouchable" can express; an honest response to Dalit female identities in both positive and negative descriptive circumstances; and actual physical spaces, elements of nature, and real people being called into their full transformational capacity. In imaginative realms of active resistance, these songs transcend social, cultural, and economic barriers and use a political language of resistance that simultaneously rages, coos, and laughs to cope with a brokenness. The resurgent transformative activities in these songs are numerous and touch on all aspects of life—social, political, spiritual, relational, familial, romantic, and erotic.

Songs are earthy expressions of Dalit culture, identity, subversive assertion, and affirmation of relationships. They are the thread, the color, the texture, the scent, and the movements that dwell within the seamless tapestry of the earthy lived experiences of Dalit women. These experiences are interwoven through these songs along with desires to transcend into freer realms. These tapestries are alive with symbols and images that both harbor and release various embodiments of Dalit women, drawing us into celebrative spaces of positive identities and into spaces of resistance to forces that break them. As I nestle into the soothing lyrical embrace of these songs, I shudder and awaken into their fierce power of closeness and tensions that holds the various threads of meanings that breathe, laugh, and sigh together. As viewers, readers, and listeners of various discourses that surround us today, we should be open to engage with the diversity of meanings that directly speak to the overt and covert propositions and desires for change in Dalit women. For this reason, I present here a few songs as an invitation to find personal meanings and connections in these lyrics to whatever living experiences that are a part of us and of which we are a part. I hope that these songs bring us closer to these communities of Dalit women who rise above a mental state of victimization to claim a mindset that transports them to diverse spaces of transgressive action.

Listening to these songs for the first time, I felt the power of the interweaving of aesthetics, politics, and protest. I feel this power moving in multiple surprising directions to create new tropes that intersect in a fusion of various

transgressive desires. While these voices carry experiences that are uncondi-
tionally attached to spaces where they find rest from day-to-day experiences of
hardship, they vocalize various expressions of women's resistance as well.
These expressions are unconditional in their nature of being without expectations from an entity of listeners. The spaces and times exist in their life forms
as willed and wished for by the singer where they invoke imagined and real
people, experiences, and events. Without a constraining framework, such a
spontaneous and ingrained praxis of resistance seems to outweigh normally
known modes and spaces of resistance such as vocal protest in stipulated visible public spaces, public rallying, or political writing. Songs in this section of
my book deeply problematize concepts of space, time, and mind in non-
adherence to limitations, while they de-problematize the same in such singing
of reflective consciousness that connects people, nature, and experiences even
in imagined transgressive spaces. Such lodging in and attachment to spaces of
freedom and self-determination valorizes female subjectivity rooted in *earthy
humanness* and sung in free and bold voices that open diversified meanings of
resistance.

Soaking in Cultural Generosity

Since the time I lived in Karunguzhi, and volunteered there as an education
counselor among young Dalit girls, I have continued to visit the villages in this
region once every two years. The Dalit villages that I visited in Tamil Nadu lie
within a radius of about twenty-five miles around Karunguzhi. One of my main
resources of information on these regions was Guna Dayalan, a member of Social Action Center which is a non-profit organization in Karunguzhi. Dayalan is
a social activist and consultant for Dalit groups and individuals who seek legal
help and guidance in initiatives leading towards economic self-sufficiency,
education, and jobs. Dayalan works in and around Karunguzhi, and during my
visits, he would take me into the remote villages on his little scooter.

I would take a two-hour bus ride from Tambaram, a suburb of Chennai
(where I stayed with extended family members), and Dayalan would meet me
at the bus station. There were days when I stayed in Dayalan's home in the
village of Pasumpur, a simple hut with two separate spaces, plus an outdoor
cooking space and an outdoor bathroom. I was pampered by his wife who
would provide me a feast of rice, *sambar* (spicy lentil soup with vegetables),
and the greens and pod of the *murugai* tree cooked with garlic, mustard seeds,
and cumin. These are some of the healthiest and tastiest foods that I have had—
organic and seasoned with affection. We would normally reach a village at
around ten in the morning and be greeted with snacks such as *rasku* (biscotti)

or *porai* (dry bun). Usually the *porai* or *rasku* is dunked in a glass of tea and relished as a midmorning snack. (Because I was not a tea drinker, I was offered a glass of milk instead.)

Normally, younger women would be out at work, and older women stayed home taking care of children. I would spend an entire day there talking with the older women and eagerly awaiting singing moments. I watched babies fall asleep on their grandmothers' laps in response to an afternoon lullaby, and many times the songs lulled me into an afternoon nap as well inside a cool hut smeared with cow dung. At around four in the afternoon, I would be offered a *rasku* or *porai* with some milk, and at about five in the evening, the younger women and children would return from work. They would arrive in groups, and almost everyone had a bundle of hay or firewood on their head. They would head to their homes and tend to their children; later, they would eat rice or *ragi* porridge (which they generously shared with me) and settle into small groups to chit chat; suckle babies; tell stories that involved kings, queens, and demons; or dramatically retell cinema stories. There would be a few kerosene chimney lamps flickering here and there, or a hue of light from a dying cooking flame flickering between three stones that had just held a mud or aluminum pot cooking a porridge. Moments like these were just so real, stripped of all pretensions.

Over time, I observed that despite the effects of external influences of popular mass media which have permeated Dalit colonies with modern songs and cinema music, Dalit singers have succeeded in preserving an oral lyrical tradition. Popular music is more attractive to the younger generation and, in fact, it is possible that in the next few generations the traditional folk songs may diminish in popularity and may not be passed on to future generations. The threat of extinction makes this listening and this documenting process more urgent as the songs speak. Women in the Dalit communities were eager to talk with me and had no inhibitions to my small tape recorder. In addition to these important recordings, since I already knew a few Dalit women in each of the villages, it was enjoyable to experience their loving hospitality. I basked in the unencumbered trust and pampering as I learned to love my Dalit identity more.

Most Dalit women I met were agricultural laborers subject to an enslaved situation working for dominant caste land owners who exploited them economically and sexually, or they worked in rice mills as laborers who processed paddy into rice that could be marketed. Their day started at about five every morning in order to complete their morning chores before heading out to the fields with some *pazhaidhu* (rice cooked the previous night and soaked in water overnight) or *koozh* (porridge made with broken rice) to physically sustain them through the day. They weeded or planted in the fields as laborers, returned home at dusk to cook a simple meal for their families, and ended their day at about eight in the evening. Working in rice mills involved hard manual labor as well in winnowing and carrying sacks of rice to be processed and sent to retailers. Dalit women are considered unskilled laborers in Indian society; they work for a low wage of an average of fifty rupees (about 85 cents) a day in this particular area. The women are paid less than the men and are forced into sexual servitude to their landlords and to the owners of rice mills. Having lived in Karunguzhi in a house opposite a rice mill, I witnessed Dalit women being brought into these places after dark for sexual use. Even after several years of interactions and relationships with communities of Dalit women who live within daily exploitative conditions, I continue to ask the question: "What is it that sustains Dalit women day after day?" Self and communal sustenance is a mode of survival rather than a strategy because it is their deep characteristic to live out their role as sustainers.

I recorded most songs in their natural occurrence as laments, lullabies, and work songs in the fields, while some songs were sung just for me to hear and record; some were along fields while at work and some leisure songs recorded while seated in groups after a long day's work. The women I met with practiced the tradition of singing, speaking, and dancing to their songs under shaded trees, by the side of fields when they rested a bit, inside their huts while suckling their babies or singing lullabies, or under a dim street lamp which served as a communal meeting place. The songs were not necessarily sung in a group but were often built into a group session as women chose to join in. These spaces were not performance spaces because there was no specific audience for these songs. Even if all the women did not sing, everyone participated by joining in the chorus or keeping rhythm with their swaying bodies.

Listeners and singers are both participants in this self-expression because individual women as lead singers are gradually joined by a chorus of others who raise their voices as they arrive or who keep time clapping. A community of women who gather around the lead singer (this lead singer is either self-elected or persuaded) become participants by dancing or singing with her and by using refrain and repetition. Most often, the women gather in circles and dance the *kummi*, a Dalit folkdance. They dance rhythmically, turning inward into the circle and clapping with their hands extended into the center of the circle as they reply to the main singer in a refrain, all moving in a circular continuity, most often led by the lead singer. The song harmonizes with circular motions of the bodies of women while repetitious refrains accompany these motions, and vice-versa. Dancers are in partnership with their language, breaking into multifarious rhythm and content depending on the region, individual, and communal experiences.

Songs and Meanings

Margaret Trawick, an American ethnographer who lived in Tamil Nadu for several years, writes on the nature of songs of Dalit women from the Chengalpattu district in "Spirits and Voices in Tamil Songs" (1993). She observes the close relationships that women cherish with each other and with nature as they work in the slushy fields. The sense of closeness with each other places the landlord at a distance as he dictates from the shade of an umbrella near the field where they toil. The songs that emanate from the bent bodies of Dalit women in the fields express their relationships with each other and with the soil and plant life around them as they work. In *Notes on Love in a Tamil Family* (1996), an ethnographic study of towns in Tamil Nadu, Margaret Trawick identifies the different forms of Dalit songs: "laments, work songs, songs of clandestine love, put-down songs, songs of social commentary and songs that mix these various themes" (196). The songs in this chapter, however, reveal an energy and a celebration of Dalit female identity in its intricacies of representations of the realities surrounding Dalit women in rural South India.

This chapter aims to provide an opportunity for the reading listener to indulge in the multifarious experiential meanings that these songs elicit. One question I ask myself is, "What informs my interpretation of these narratives?" Surely my academic background in disciplines of anthropology, comparative literature, sociology, and women and gender studies direct and foreground the ways in which these songs speak to me. My Dalit roots play a significant role in the closeness I feel with Dalit culture and, therefore, with the women and their lyrical expressions. When I would ask a singer about the meaning of a song or specific words or lines in a song, almost always the first response would be a gleeful giggle which spread among the others standing or sitting nearby. At times, these giggles meant a mock refusal to acknowledge my question on such explicit expressions. It was unusual for the singer to explain things, and this was the first time someone wanted to write down the meanings of the songs!

Such questioning was strange and comical for those whose songs were as natural and real a presence as the strong tamarind trees in their villages and as ambiguously mixed as the sweet, sour, and tangy taste of the tamarind pod that lingered on the tongue for several hours after one spit out the pit. I found myself needing to be sensitive not to disturb their normal, natural, and spontaneous relationships to the songs. The meanings that I draw from these songs are significantly dependent on the time, space, subject, and the singers' tones, facial expressions, gestures, and movements. The first song presented here was at the celebration of a girl coming of age.

Living in the vicinity of these villages and sharing a pastoral care role in Dalit communities because of the priestly presence of my husband, I developed affectionate relationships with the women in this region who helped me find meaning in the songs as I began to get to know to some extent the content of their daily lives. When we lived in Karunguzhi, by around six or six-thirty every morning without fail, we would have someone ringing our door bell for various reasons. Each person at the door that early in the morning had either walked a long way or ridden a bicycle for several miles to get to our home in the town. Some of the issues that I remember vividly include an older Dalit man who wanted to tell my husband that his son died the previous evening after being bitten by a snake while returning home after working in the fields; the mother of a young girl who was devastated that her daughter hung herself (but was luckily saved) because of a quarrel with her husband; a father needing money to send his son to college; an older man who was kicked by his master in the field while working because he could not repay his debt; and a father with his fifteen-year-old daughter who was raped. For these and many more reasons, Dalit communities sought our counsel. Our home was the office of the Social Action Center, a non-profit organization started by social justice-minded church leaders to seek support for and empower Dalit peoples. Such exposure to the lives of Dalit communities helped me frame my own questions and seek meanings in these songs. The following discussion and descriptions are a result of an immersion into the exuding colors, textures, and sounds.

Songs of the Soil

Thulukaanam from the village of Uzhuthamangalam sang the first song presented as a dialogue between a mother and her daughter. She used a dramatic gesture of raising her right hand above her head when she sang as the voice of the mother with an authoritative questioning of the daughter. She brought her hand down in a swishing motion whenever she sang the daughter's response to the mother's questions. Soon other women joined in the response of the daughter, giggling in the process as well. When I asked Thulukaanam when this song would normally be sung and why, she chuckled and said that this would be sung at any time but especially when a girl comes of age. When I listened to this song, it seemed a playful responsive song wherein the daughter counters her mother's questions regarding the appearance of her daughter's body and the loss of her bodily adornments. In the process of translating this song, apertures of connections with various possible meanings formed in my thoughts.

Surely, the playfulness of the mother-daughter relationship reverberates in the daughter's constant "talk-back" to the mother who is concerned about her young daughter. She quickly invents clever answers that are simple but lucid in a purposeful discreetness that teases the listener into wondering what the truth could be. The mother's questions are representational both of her wishes and fears for her daughter, and the daughter's questions speak to her desires and inherent fears as well. As a refrain, the mother refers to her daughter as the "multicolored parakeet," a common metaphor used in cinema music to refer to the beauty of fair-skinned women. The mother appropriates this forbidden status of beauty for her Dalit daughter who is traditionally considered unclean, fearsome, and ugly as explained earlier. The "multicolored parakeet" could refer to the beauty of a daughter in the eyes of a mother; the daughter, however, could be rejecting this image. She desires to embrace herself as she is, just as she experiences nature embracing her body and playing upon it. Into the mother's playful tone, the daughter injects a sense of reality as she rejects the popular metaphor of beauty. Could this rejection mean an awareness of the need to protect herself? She is already vulnerable in her stigmatized identity as "ugly" and could fear more danger in her mother's appropriation of her as the beautiful "multicolored parakeet."

The mother's use of the image of the parakeet brings out the pride in her bragging of her daughter's beauty. Thus, the mother transgresses into a space of definition that is normally not used on Dalit girls, and the daughter transgresses by wanting to embrace her own beauty as she is (normally rejected by society) and does not see the need to borrow an image from caste language. She claims this identity as her own, even if it is one that refers to her state of constant exposure to danger. She expresses a need to clutch those fleeting moments of simple joys that are interspersed within lurking danger. The daughter possesses a knowledge of the dangers that will occur almost as a necessary consequence of the label "multicolored parakeet," and therefore fears that this type of beauty in the eyes of the caste communities would render her even more desired, whether for revenge or pleasure. For every attempt that the mother makes to idealize her daughter's beauty and their relationship, the daughter interrupts with reminders of the existence of the continued challenges to their survival, especially her survival as a vulnerable Dalit girl who would be punished for considering herself beautiful. Within the caring aspect of the mother-daughter relationship, the daughter's functional roles of fetching water and selling buttermilk imply a sense of social, economic, and cultural responsibilities, which is complicated by her desire to break free of them. The listener is left to wonder: Is this a song that suggests that the young girl's beauty is being celebrated, or is it a warning that her beauty lures lurking dangers of punishment for her presumptuousness?

Song 1, Singer: Thulukaanam from the village of Uzhuthamangalam

You took a small pot and went to get water
What did you do for so long my daughter?
What did you do for so long?
I watched the way the water came up to my breasts and did the
kolam[90] on me, my mother, did the kolam on me.

I know the wonder of it, my multicolored parakeet, my daughter, my multicolored parakeet

Do not call me a multicolored parakeet, mishaps will occur, my mother, mishaps will occur.

What I put on the nose, how did it become deformed and broken?
My daughter, how did it become broken?
I walked with arms swinging wide with the buttermilk pot and the swinging hand from the back hit it down, my mother, the swinging hand from the back hit it down.

Oh I know the wonder of it, my multicolored parakeet, my daughter, my multicolored parakeet
Do not call me a multicolored parakeet, mishaps will occur, my mother, mishaps will occur.

What I put on the feet how did it become deformed and how did it get off, my daughter, how did it get off?
I saw a thief and I walked fast crying in fear and a stone hit my foot and it broke, my mother, it broke.

I know the wonder of it, my multicolored parakeet, my daughter, my multicolored parakeet
Do not call me a multicolored parakeet, mishaps will occur, my mother, mishaps will occur.

How did the redness of your lips that were beautiful like a red kovai fruit become less red, my daughter, become less red?

---

[90] *Kolam* is an artistic design with rice flour displayed on the ground just outside the front entry of a home. It is a mark of delight to please the eyes and soothe the senses as one enters. This practice originated as an act of kindness to feed ants and has now taken on larger proportions involving colored powders displayed at all celebrations.

I saw the temple and I bent down to pray and the temple pigeons devoured them, my mother, devoured them.

I know the wonder of it, my multicolored parakeet, my daughter, my multicolored parakeet,
Do not call me a multicolored parakeet, mishaps will occur, my mother, mishaps will occur.

The suggestive responses of the daughter lure us into imagining the daughter emerging as a free-spirited young Dalit girl, but at the same time we are surely made aware of her limitations. The description of her work of collecting water and selling buttermilk convey a sense of freedom—of wandering among the hills and the village boundaries—that allows the daughter to decide when and where she needs to be. Her self-excusive responses could suggest a resentment of the questioning and controlling voice of her mother. The daughter acknowledges the series of "mishaps" that might occur as a result of her wanderings, but she is willing to accept them as a consequence of her seeking self-fulfillment in the water. The water, she acknowledges, either cajoles her or embraces her to the extent that it could just consume her in a consummation—yet again she holds the listener wondering. The more she seeks independence in earning a living, the more vulnerable she is as her body becomes more visible and punishable despite establishing an independent identity. The ambiguous, opposing pairings of visibility and invisibility, touchability and untouchability, freedom and danger, and beauty and vulnerability are depicted as inevitable elements of the daughter's life. She calls herself to be prepared as both strong and vulnerable—relishing life while aware that she will encounter danger.

In the daughter's responses to the mother's questioning of being late from fetching water from the river, her explanations highlight the mother's sense of oneness with her daughter as the mother identifies with the delight of playing in the river. She says, "I know the wonder of it my multicolored parakeet, my daughter." Finding joy in nature seems to bond the mother and daughter in providing the common experience of sexual pleasure and a sense of freedom. The completion of the task of fetching water becomes secondary to participating in the sensuous experience of the free play of water caressing her body. The strict order of her mother to bring back a pot of water to her home has to wait while the daughter enjoys being a part of this play. In that choice, a deep union with nature becomes integral in affirming a sexual identity when the daughter proclaims that the water did the *kolam* on her. Her body, as she describes, is transformed into a passive space that nature herself claims as her own. The intimacy the daughter claims to have with nature validates her desire for freedom, self-sufficiency, and a positive Dalit female identity—her body is indeed beautiful and desirable in an earthy relationship of caring love.

On the one hand, the mother takes pride in the way she has adorned her daughter with bracelets and anklets (which could refer to an actual adornment or could represent a desire); but she is anxious when the daughter does not return home on time, fearing that her beauty enhanced by her adornments have rendered her vulnerable. The simultaneity of beauty and danger embodied in Dalit women is evident in the mother's alarmed questioning when the daughter comes back without the ornaments and with lips that have changed color. The daughter alleges that the nose ring fell off when she was walking with her arms swinging high as she carried the pot of buttermilk—a gesture that could suggest liberation or an act of defiance against restrictive authority. The act of losing her bracelets, nose rings, and anklets as well as the redness in her lips reveal the daughter's attempt to break free from the mold into which her mother places her. The daughter allows nature to free her from these adornments, which to her signify an imitation of the caste woman. Different from Soorpanakha, the young Dalit girl defies being coerced into this image and struggles to be liberated from such constraints. She strips herself of the identity imposed on her by her mother as she conceives herself as the new and free Dalit woman who embraces a playful independence in carelessly losing her adornments.

The daughter further explains that she has lost the redness in her lips because the temple pigeons devoured them near the temple. This image suggests a sexual encounter in the temple premises. She was probably raped, and in that act of violence, she could have lost her adornments and the redness on her lips. Alternatively, in line with the idea of her embracing her identity and freedom, it could be a consensual sexual act she experienced as a consummation that has been building within her ever since her bodily pleasures were aroused by the river's intimate play on her body.

The temple is no doubt that of *Yellamma*, an important local deity in this district as Sathi Clarke observes in *Dalits and Christianity* (1998).[91] According to Clarke, Dalits in this region claim:

> … the positioning of the image of the deity at the boundary of
> the colony suggests that the goddess presides over the colony
> and safeguards its perimeters. In this case, the image of Ellai-
> yamman [another name for *Yellamma*] is strategically situated

---

[91] Clarke was involved in field work for his research in the Chengalpattu district of Tamil Nadu among Dalit communities in 1991 and 1992. I was involved in translating some of the primary resources for his research from Tamil to English. He is a liberation theologian who situates organic cultural religious practices among Dalits in the framework of self-empowering subaltern discourses.

> on the boundary that is regularly used as crossing from the col-
> ony into the outside world. (101)

This reading suggests that the daughter has traveled to the boundary of the village and has been protected and guided by *Yellamma*. Boundary territories are feared by the people of the village and are normally avoided by women for fear of abduction; the daughter is defiant in venturing into such forbidden are-as. If she is speaking of rape, one wonders if she refers to it as punishment for her economic independence, and if not, the experience has further enhanced her sense of freedom.

The concept of the "*Amman*" as the deity who protects her people is a strong religious belief that Dalit communities here in the Chengalpattu district hold on to. One cannot miss the connections with *Amman* and "*Amma*," the Tamil word for mother in their functions as nurturer and protector. In the physical absence of *Amma*, it is *Amman* who should watch over young girls who should fend themselves in dangerous spaces, irrespective of a result of transgressive behav-ior, allurement, or abduction. The watchful eye of the mother who notices changes in her daughter's physical appearance plays the role of the *Amman* who will safeguard the daughter. The singer leaves the listener guessing wheth-er the young girl is fabricating excuses to hide a joyful sexual experience from her mother or to protect her mother from the pain of knowing her abduction and rape. All the three female figures in the song—the mother, daughter, and *Yellamma*—are placed in both protective and vulnerable roles as they rely on each other. *Yellamma* depends on the testimonies of both the mother and the daughter to assert her divinity in her role as the protector; the mother needs affirmation of her motherhood in the daughter's strength, beauty, and obedi-ence; and the daughter needs both the mother and *Yellamma* for continued care and protection, irrespective of whether she was forced or has willfully em-braced a sexual union.

The tone of the singer, however, is filled with sarcasm and humor, which privileges the interpretation that the daughter tries to hide a sexual experience from her mother. The mother, in turn, identifies herself with such lies to hide her own mischief as a young girl when she says, "I know the wonder of it my multicolored parakeet." The conversation between the two turns into a narra-tion of a sequence of events that the daughter seems to playfully devise as she goes along. The song is an example of the spontaneity and vibrancy in the songs of Dalit women. The incorporation of humor in the reactions to the pos-sibilities and realities of danger that balance the tragic reality of vulnerability is evident in this song. The singer uses humor as a narrative technique in order to highlight ambiguity's role as an integral part of Dalit women's lives; to affirm that, the women gathered around laughed as this song was sung.

The fact that the daughter blames the loss of her ornaments and innocence on her interactions with nature provides the humor in the song. Nature becomes her consort in the sexual mischief in which she has been involved. She may have removed her ornaments in the course of physical intimacy. The lack of luster on her lips is suggestive of her secret flirtations, and the loss of her ornaments suggests a loss of her virginity. The mother is aware of these possibilities and keeps prodding her daughter with questions, evoking the pleasures of youth. The daughter's sexual freedom in the face of the danger of physical harm is the mother's main fearful concern, camouflaged in her humorous and playful questioning to find the truth. The rhythmic song in its use of the pattern of questions and answers highlights a pulsating dynamism emphasized by suggestive colors, movement, and sounds: the multicolored parakeet; the red *kovai* fruit; the colorful *kolam;* the act of drawing the *kolam*; the daughter walking with her buttermilk pot; the swinging of the hands; the river dancing on her body; the daughter running away from a thief; the fluttering pigeons; the gurgling, enticing sound of the river; and the tinkling of the anklets.

The song is rich in its use of exquisite language and images drawn from the daily lives of Dalit women who fetch water from the river and those who are street vendors. The poignant nature of the song lies in the way these common images and occurrences interconnect to enhance the co-existence of both freedom and danger in the life of a young Dalit girl. The familiar picture of the Dalit woman walking the streets selling buttermilk with arms swinging wide is indeed a striking image of seductive prey that could invite the attention of prowlers. A common cultural image of a Dalit woman drawing water from a river (denoting the necessity to do so because of denial of easy access to water in Dalit communities) extends into an image of a young Dalit girl lingering on the river bank, wanting to move beyond her necessary task. She divulges a sexual desire in the sensuous feeling caused by the delicate caressing of the water in drawing a *kolam* on her body or by an actual secret lover. The image of a pigeon devouring her lips conveys a sense of the urgent, consuming nature of her lover as well. The juxtaposition of gentleness and aggression embedded in the lyrics bring out the ambiguous daily realities in the life of a young Dalit girl expressed in mundane images. In continuity with the theme of mother-daughter relationships, the following is a song that a daughter (singer) offers to honor her deceased mother.

Song 2, Singer: Saanthi from the village of Irusaamanallur

O mother who gave birth to me,
Deeply affectionate mother,
As I tied up the wooden cart,
I saw my mother who gave birth to me in front of my eyes,

You came in front of my eyes and I raise royal flowers to you
O mother, who gave birth to me will fill your eyes too.
I tied the bottle cart, and I saw you O mother in front of my
eyes,
I brought flowers of worship, O mother who gave birth to me
to worship you.

A deep sense of devotion of a daughter towards her mother manifests here as the young woman acknowledges that the mother has provided for her, and now the daughter fondly recalls her life with her mother. This constant dwelling of the mother in the thoughts of the daughter is reified as an appearance to her daughter. The mother's memories sustain the daughter in the strong Dalit spiritual tradition of the worship of ancestors. In awe, the singer worships her mother in her sagacious realization of deep respect and admiration as deity and as the archetype of omnipresent beauty, power, and wealth. This vision is possibly an act of self-recognition and recognition of the mother as a deified caring figure who continues to sustain the community through her spiritual presence and her daughter's physical presence, which suggests a cycle of loyalty of female provision of sustenance.

Hindu studies scholar W. T. Elmore points out, "Even when one god is found in many places, the people never think of it as a general god with world relations, but only as their local deity" (10). This observation leads me to hear in this song an appropriation and a localization of a deity in relation to her mother. As the singer offers her mother flowers and worships her, the deification becomes a personal claim to the power of love and relationships in the context of the larger community of women. Such recognition or creation of a local deity, as pointed out by Clarke, is common among Dalit communities and indicates a desire for protection (101). The mother figure continues to live in the memories of the daughter as part of her spiritual tradition and protector.

Song 3, Singer: Saanthi from the village of Irusaamanallur

O Mother who gave birth to me
You were seated, O Mother,
on the banks of the river,
You were seated like a Kueel (a black song bird),
Not knowing that you were a Kueel, O mother who gave birth
to me they came and shot you with a bomb.
On the banks of the Lake O Mother, you were seated like an
elephant,
Not knowing that you were an elephant the wicked traitor, O
mother,
Killed you with an arrow, O Mother who gave birth to me.

It is customary for Dalit women to gather in a circle in a home where there has been a death and they lament together. They sing of the dead person in particular and about all the dead family ancestors, many of whom they may not know personally. This lament is by Santhi as well, remembering her dead mother. These lines of mourning represent the mother figure as beautiful and tender as a *kueel,* a common black bird found in the rural parts of India known for its sleek body, its swiftness, and its delicate singing or cooing. The *kueel* is beloved for the ways in which it imitates any voice that calls for its response, suggesting to the listener that the daughter's song could be a way in which she longs for a response so that she could hear her mother's voice again. The elephant evokes the magnificence and strength of her mother, suggesting that she is not only slender and swift like the bird, but looming as a powerful presence as well. There could be intentional visual effects in the proximity of these images, which are a part of the singer's natural mode of speech and thought that establish the mother's tender beauty as well as her protective physical and spiritual strength.

The mother is deified as the one seated on the banks of rivers and lakes just as Dalit deities are part of the village. The tradition of the resilient presence of beauty and strength in the Dalit woman continues in the revelation of the mother to the singer/daughter. This aspect of the cycle of physical survival tied to spiritual revelation confirms the source of life of a Dalit woman to the singer—the omnipresence of the mother is real. The earthly death of the mother is overcome by the birth of a daughter, who now testifies to her splendor and to the continuity of a positive Dalit female presence.

Song 4, Singer: Anjalai from the village of Valarpirai
>What gain did he find in the place he went to cut grass?
>The mud probably appears like a peacock and the peacock's fledgling.
>If I have a spear, I will melt it
>If I have an arrow, I will make delight with it.
>
>O brother, O brother on the soft bed where I lay
>An arrow came and fell.
>O brother take that arrow
>And come running.
>
>O sister-in-law, affectionate sister-in-law
>On the soft bed where my older brother lay
>An arrow came and fell.
>I took the arrow and old rice and new rice

With dancing steps, Oh!
My brother asked me to run and come.

O brother-in-law, O foolish brother-in-law
Take some old rice and some new rice
Take some milk and your brother's new son
Climb up the top of the hill.

O sister-in-law, O sister-in-law, affectionate and loving sister-in-law,
The bed that I used my brother lies on, so I cannot lie on it.
I cannot eat the rice my brother ate
I cannot chew the beetle leaf my brother chewed.

If he asks, "What is the wound on your chest?"
What can I tell him O sister-in-law?
O brother-in-law, O brother-in-law, O children of the goatherd,
I measured and brought them grain, I brought them toothpowder.
The wall I could not reach, I used a ladder and I coated it with mud;
For the wall that was too big, I used ten loads of mud.
I took old rice, I took old rice
And as I come with fast running steps,
If my brother asks about the wound on my chest what answer will I give him?

As I came running with old rice,
As I came running with new rice,
A sharp rock went over my chest is what I will say.
....
O younger brother, O younger brother!
....
Past the Punga tree and past the tamarind tree and past the neem tree, and past the venkita tree,
Past the peacock, and the peacock fledgling,
Past the kueel, and the kueel's fledgling,
I stood near the Maavatti (mango) tree,
The fireworks that I sent with one hand, I am now sending with both hands.

This song declares the affections as well as the complications in kinship structures as the singer—identifying herself as a girl—addresses her brother, her sister-in-law, and other close relatives. She leads the listener to believe that she sings of sentiments in relationships as the singer calls upon people to witness certain changes in her life. The lyrics depict the loss of a relationship the singer had with her brother as they ate together, slept on the same bed, worked together, and shared the same food. She sings, "Take that arrow and come running … / With dancing steps my bother asked me to run and come … / The bed that I used my brother lies on, so I cannot lie on it. / I cannot eat the rice my brother ate / I cannot chew the betel leaf my brother chewed." The brother is a protective figure to the sister, while she in turn provides him with food as the nurturer. The sister cannot continue in her closeness with her brother because he is married now; it is the sister-in-law who now eats with him and lies on the soft bed that the singer had used. Now that bed is a marriage bed, signifying a relationship which she is not a part of; and she can no longer chew the same betel leaf her brother chewed on because her sister-in-law has the right to do that now.[92] Trawick records her keen observations on the brother-sister relationship in Tamil cultures wherein the bond is cherished as a very close one, and it is idolized in Tamil poetry, theatre, and cinema. When the brother gets married, the sister feels abandoned by her brother and finds it hard to accept the love that the brother will share with his new wife.

The sexual intimacy that is part of a marriage elicits the images of a spear and arrow, carrying sexual innuendos. The abundance of sexuality in the brother's marriage creates the woman's longing for a sexual partner evident in the allusions she makes. The girl continues to claim that there is a wound on her chest and worries about the brother questioning this wound. The claim might point to various possibilities: the aggression of a sexual encounter, a wound inflicted through a gesture of mourning for having to stay away from her brother, or a symbol of her broken heart. In all her sensual and sentimental hurts, she continues to seek fulfillment in her role as the nurturer of the family.

The girl tells her brother-in-law and children of a goatherd that she brought "them" food and toothpowder. The "them" could mean her brother and sister-in-law, or it could be a general reference to the people around her as she establishes her capacity to nurture and provide for all to strengthen relationships. Her actions and interactions provide an insight into how she perceives herself. Earlier, she mentions that she delights in the arrow, old rice, and new rice as she dances carrying them. Her vivacity could emanate from the sexual energy

---

[92] Betel Leaf is commonly used in both rural and urban parts of India as a chewable relish filled with Areca nut and sweetening substances used for digestive and sometimes intoxicating purposes as well.

and the physical sustenance she gains which she identifies as necessary ingredients in the strengthening of relationships.

The sister, in her own state of distress and desires, runs free asking the people along the way if they have seen her husband, her sexual mate. She runs past the *punga* (beech) tree, *puliyam* (tamarind) tree, *veppam* (neem) tree and *vengai* (Indian kino) tree; all these trees hold high medicinal value and are therefore considered sacred. She runs past *mayil* (peacock) and *kueel* families and reaches the foot of a mango tree. According to the girl, compared to all the other trees in the village, the mango tree is the one that bears the most luscious and delicious fruits. She paints a powerful image of herself running wildly towards her destination. It is under the mango tree that she perhaps experiences a sexual outburst when she says she lifts her hands to set off fireworks.

The song begins with the girl wielding the powers of the spear and arrow and ends with sending fireworks into the sky from under the *maavatti* (mango) tree. She seems to have transformed mere physical strength into a sexual energy through the delight in her body: "If I have a spear, I will melt it / If I have an arrow I will make delight with it." The girl urges her brothers to recognize the arrow that has fallen on their beds and run with it into the open space to create delight and send fireworks into the sky as well. She calls listeners into experiencing a sexual energy as she urges them to follow her lead in her wild run to the point of consummation under the mango tree. In Zora Neale Hurston's *Their Eyes Were Watching God,* Janie—lying under a pear tree and watching a bee impregnate a flower—experiences the "ecstatic shiver" of sexual union (11). Janie seeks love that would make her whole, and it is in her third lover, Teacake, where she finds respect, comfort, and pleasure. It is in belonging to a simple community that Teacake is a part of wherein Janie's true love finally blossoms for her in life's journey.

As the young Dalit girl in this song runs, looking for love and community, she establishes that community as the nurturer who provides food and shelter along the way. She provides "them" with rice, toothpowder, and milk. Using toothpowder is a luxury and a sign of prosperity in a Dalit village where people normally use the branches of the *veppam* tree to brush their teeth. She specifies that the toothpowder is for a child; she shares her bounty with the children of the goatherd, in anticipation that they will grow into productive members of the community who will provide food, material wealth, and sexual energy. The girl is further involved in the process of building a home for her community: if the wall is too tall, she will use a ladder to reach it to coat it with mud; and if the wall is too big, she will use ten loads of mud to coat it. Nothing will stop her from fulfilling her task; as the builder, provider, and nurturer of her community, she will overcome every situation rather than being stifled by it. The image of the home signifies the dwelling of a nurturing and productive sexual energy where children will abound. She will continue to build a home that will hold all her positive, productive energies together and where her roles as mother and lover will continue to merge. Productivity and fertility take root as she runs with food and mud to construct and sustain relationships—the expressive delight of her life.

Song 5, Lead singer: Ratinam from the village of Vallarpirai, joined by a chorus of women

> I took five plates of mud, *Yellamma* Yellam
> And I laid a road of gold, *Yellamma* Yellam
> O you little boy who walks down that road, *Yellamma* Yellam
> What is the reason for your snooty walk? *Yellamma* Yellam
> Why do you have your hand on your hip? *Yellamma* Yellam
>
> I took six plates of mud, *Yellamma* Yellam
> And I laid a road of gold, *Yellamma* Yellam
> O you little boy who walks down the road, *Yellamma* Yellam
> What is the reason for your snooty walk? *Yellamma* Yellam
> Why do you have your hand on your hip? *Yellamma* Yellam
> (The song continued naming a number of plates of mud until
> the singers started to disperse).

A group of about eleven Dalit women sang the *Yellamma* song as they danced the *kummi*. As a lead singer sang the first line, the women gathered around her repeated the line with the refrain, "*Yellamma* Yellam." The singer calls upon the deity *Yellamma*, the guardian of the territory of their colony, as her partner in the act of transformation and reversal. This song was sung under a *veppam* (neem) tree after a long day's work.

The *kummi* song suggests transformation of mud into gold. Mud is a natural resource in Dalit villages: mixed with powdered rocks and cow dung it is used to build stronger walls for their homes; mud and clay are used to make earthen pots; it is a significant ingredient to create idols of gods to place in Dalit temples or just under a tree. The singer converts such mud into gold, a transgression which suggests that to a Dalit mud is as precious as gold in its utility and meaning. This could suggest that in the singer's imagination, a subversion of the ideology of the polluted infecting the pure takes place. A Dalit woman arms herself with mud, normally considered dirty and worthless in a caste community, and converts it to gold which is considered pure, desirable, and valuable.

Singing for strength

Doubling or sameness of the person and material heightens the purity of the product—gold. Despite being Dalit herself and therefore commonly rendered powerless, she transforms herself repeatedly into a power-exerting being. The singer again reverses the idea of the polluted fated to further pollute into an agent of purification. Through imaginative words, a Dalit singer gives life to a boy with magical powers. Like fire that purifies gold, the woman's determination to change things leads her to create magic among the younger generation who represent a better future for her. She seems hopeful that in the action of the future generation, there will be a reversal of situations. Perhaps the young boy who walks on the road of gold with an air about him displays the confidence that emerges from his mother's ability to transform the characters of matter and being. If the boy is from a caste community, he could be a reminder of the continuity of exploitations of the hard labor of Dalit women—walked upon and taken over. I, however, aspire to envision him as an embodiment of a Dalit child who walks with confidence.

The following song praises the deity *Yellamma* as the provider who owns wealth and lives in royal comfort as she protects the community's territory.

Song 6, Singer: Ratinam from the village of Vallarpirai

One liter of grain I measured, O *Yellamma*, One lakh liters of gold I measured

For the girl did I do all this? O *Yellamma* it is all yours

You wear all splendor like a king, you are all splendor like a
queen
While she bathes head to foot, you guard her head specially

Two liters of grain I measured, O *Yellamma*, Two lakh liters of
gold I measured
For the girl did I do all this? O *Yellamma*, it is all yours
You wear all splendors like a king, you are all splendor like a
queen
While she bathes head to foot you guard her head specially.
(The song continued to seven liters of grain)

The possibility for the singers to enter fulfilling relationships relies on the reciprocity of giving and receiving. The circular motion of life could be the center
in offering gifts of gold and grain to *Yellamma* so that she in turn will provide a
good life to the daughter of the singer. The women look up to her as the one
who protects, purifies, and sustains their female identity as she blesses the ritual of the bath water that purifies the body of the daughter. Ratinam confirms
that material wealth is used for the girl who needs *Yellamma* for both economic
and spiritual security. For this purpose, the mother who looks out for her
daughter's needs is able to significantly increase the number of measures of
gold because of her relationship with *Yellamma*. The unending nature of the
song could suggest the limitless possibilities that the partnership with *Yellamma* can produce as the mother figure who will faithfully continue to nurture
Dalit women for generations to come.

Song 7, Lead singer: Maniamma from the village of Karunguzhi

O you one eyed Kungumma, one-and-a-half-eyed Sambamma,
Sprinkle the *saanthu* [holy powder], spread the
saambraani [frankincense].
The powerful *Muthumaari* [god] is arriving for the *golu* [festi-
val of lights]

O you two eyed Kungumma, two-and-a-half-eyed Sambamma,
Sprinkle the *saanthu* [holy powder], spread the
saambraani [frankincense]
The powerful *Muthumaari* [god] is coming for the *golu* [festi-
val of lights]
(The song continued into ten-eyed Kungumma and ten-and-a-
half-eyed, Sambamma)

In this annunciatory song, Maniamma announces the divinity of Dalit female body. She invites Kungamma and Sambamma to represent specific communities of Dalit women and to join in the worship of *Muthumaariamman* who resides in the community. During *Navarathri* [93] (*Nava*=nine, *rathri*=nights), a festival of lights celebrated primarily among caste communities, *golu* [94] is a significant part involving a display of dolls representing various gods who are honored at this festival. India, as a land of tradition and culture, celebrates numerous festivals to keep alive the ancient, ritualistic, traditional celebrations passed on from one generation to another through oral tradition.

Traditionally, *Navarathri* is celebrated for nine days and nine nights. During this celebration, neighbors are invited to an exhibition of a collection of idols and to a sharing of the legends of the gods through songs and dances. It in-

---

[93] Nemani lives in Hyderabad, India and hails from a progressive Brahmin family who are against the practices of caste-based and religion-based discriminations. Their family and extended family include members from a diverse caste and religious background made possible through marriages. The Nemanis are an exemplary family. Nemani provided the following information: The first three days of *Navarathri* are celebrated in praise of goddess *Durga* (a form of *Kali* acknowledged among the upper-caste communities), the goddess of strength who destroys evil. The next three days are celebrated for the goddess *Lakshmi*—the goddess of spiritual and material wealth. The last three days of *Navarathri* is celebrated to praise goddess *Sarawathi*—the goddess of wisdom and education. The foremost significance of *Navarathri* is to remember goddess *Durga* (also known as *Shakti*) who slayed a Demon *Mahishasuran* in a nine-day battle. Since the other gods could not match up to his power, they call upon goddess *Shakti* who slays the demon. It was in this battle that *Shakti*, the female power transforms herself into the fierce *Kali*.

[94] In a personal interview Nemani stated, *Golu* is celebrated as part of *Navarathri* to invoke gods into a home. During the nine days of *golu*, *puja* (worship rituals) are done in the morning and evening for dolls of gods and goddesses displayed in a home. The display consists of dolls from the supreme gods to insects, animals, and plants as a way of way of remembering creation and respecting all beings. Such celebration helped the local artisans who made these dolls to be able to sustain their traditional talent. During this celebration, women and children from the neighborhood are invited to view the display of dolls through which children would learn about the stories related to the dolls displayed. Women and girl children who are invited home are treated and respected as goddesses. *Kunkum (red powder)*, *turmeric (yellow paste)*, and *sandalwood* paste are applied to them as marks of respect. Sweets and savories are shared with the welcomed guests. The entire house is decorated with flowers, incense, and banana plants indicating festivity and prosperity. Some dolls displayed would include Dasavatharam (ten incarnations of Lord Vishnu), Krishna Leela (stories of Lord Krishna), Rama Parivaram (family of Lord Rama), Shiva Parivaram (family of Lord Shiva), Mahishasura Mardhani (goddess *Shakthi*). During *Vijayadhasami*, the ninth day of *Navarathri* celebration signifying the power of good over evil, people start getting involved in any good deed or activities such as enrolling in a fine arts class or school, or starting a business enterprise.

volves a sharing of food, especially sweets. Dalits are excluded during these occasions, and it is therefore noteworthy that the singer invites the community of Dalit women to a *golu* where *Muthumaariamman* is displayed. The song reveals the transgressive courage of the Dalit woman to not only take part in the *golu*, but to create the *golu* and invite other Dalit women to participate.

A reminder on the *Amma* or *Amman* (mother) aspect of deities such as *Yellamma* and *Muthumaariamman* is significant in the singer's usage of a mother figure to express a closeness between herself, her people, her mother, and goddesses—*Maniamma* desires a merging of identities of the people with that of their *Amman*. This song elevates the social status of Kungamma, Sambamma, and other mothers in adding them to an array of spotted goddesses. Significantly, these goddesses are one-eyed and one-and-a-half-eyed, and the number of eyes increases according to the stanza. The augmented presence of numerous eyes in these women could be a reference to the power that they derive from *Muthumaariamman*. Dalit women in this song, who eventually possess innumerable eyes, start with less than what they should have: one eye. The close association with *Muthumaariamman* counters this deficiency by endowing her with more eyes; and as women are surrounded with many eyes, they are protected as well as elevated to the status of a god. The consistent adding of the eyes is transfigurative and a transgression where a Dalit woman is a goddess. Traditionally, Dalits are not allowed inside certain temples of the upper caste; they stand outside the temple without a *dharisanam* (vision of the god). In addition, the increased number of eyes could suggest a subversion of a denial of vision; now, a Dalit woman in the song is able to participate in the worship of spotted goddesses. *Maniamma* grants this wish for herself as she calls forth eyes into being, possessing creative power to validate her female identity through this annunciation of divine characteristics in her body.

Song 8, Singer: Jothi from the village of Irusaamanallur
> There were sugarcanes, sugarcanes in thousands;
> I will come and give you gold
> To round up the ship.
> Won't the ship crash, O lady?
> Won't the road crash?
> Somewhere the parrot is singing a lyric for the ship.
> Gooseberries from the green groves, green groves, broken groves of pearl.
> The best variety of vegetables load up onto the ship;
> Move out, move out, but won't the ship lean on the water?

Jothi evokes an abundance to reverse poverty into prosperity large enough to fill a ship. It is possible that the singer has not seen a ship but knows that it is something big. The ship is the largest container (in her imagination) to hold loads of cargo, and the woman imagines her wealth as not only that which can fill the ship but cause it to lean due to excessive weight! The presence of an internal voice in the poem raises the doubts and questions in the mind of the woman, revealing a sense of fear and excitement at the prospect of abundance. She claims ownership of the ship that would sail far away beyond the horizons carrying her wealth as a part of herself. She does fear that it might tip and disappear into the sea; nevertheless, she seems to enter that risk to transport her wealth, a symbol of her well-being. Though the question arises on where she wants to send her cargo, she assumes a role representing her temporal female authority as provider, making it clear that her wealth is drawn from nature. The song of the parrot echoing the song of the narrator seems to assure the safety of the ship, an assurance from nature herself that she will protect the abundant wealth.

Functional Transgress-sing and Dance-gressing

The few examples of songs by Dalit women carry with them the character of traditional expressions of Dalit female identity in the experiential, yet authoritative roles in which Dalit women present themselves as power, provider, and goddess. Trawick claims:

> The meaning (*porul*=substance) in a word is likened in some Tamil poems to the light in the eyes, the heat in the fire, the scent in the flower, the spirit in the body – a subtle power guarded by the form, hidden by it, difficult to grasp. Thus, much of high Tamil poetry is not straightforward; its perceptible surface is a play of illusions, it seems to be saying many different things, and no one can know for sure what is inside. (196)

As evident in the songs presented, the key to a close reading of the singer's imaginative universe lies in the meaning hidden in her use of words, body, rhyme, and rhythm. Singers conjure limitless possibilities in marrying meaning and rhythm to represent an earthy humane partnership with nature, sharing sustainable creativity, love, and nurturing abundance. They sing of relationships and the significance of strong human bonds. Fecundity of the singing process and songs is nursed by the participation of the community in the world of the transgressive imagination of the singer. As mentioned earlier, the whole community of women participated in the singing, either by singing along, repeating, dancing, or just nodding or clicking the tongue. The most popular ways in which the listeners participate are by repetition of lines and refrains. Repetition provides substance for equally repetitive transgressive expressions confirming the connections among singers, experiences, meanings, and protests.

In addition, repetition asserts experience as a cycle, an endless action and endless transformation; and with each slight variation, it enacts the process of building upon words, plot, and action. The refrain is used to enhance repetition; a specific word or a conglomeration of sounds serves to provide the beat and rhythm for the song or dance (I have indicated most phrases that are used as refrains in italics). The refrains are an invitation for the community to participate in this process of proclaiming the strength and identity of the community, and repetition reaffirms the collectivity of experiences narrated in these songs and the effective subversion of meanings. The significance of an experience is attested in repetition, which allows unlimited possibilities to flow through. Thus, a singer can imagine the creation of an unlimited length of a road of gold from mud, which testifies to the limitless powers of transformation that the singers possess—a way of naturalizing an unnatural phenomenon. The singer's supernatural powers of transforming objects and images are normalized by such repetition where the process takes on a magical quality of ceremonial language. This enables the singer to transform situations and images by carrying them into transgressive spaces, both actual and actualized in the imagination. This transformation into a larger consciousness happens spontaneously among a group of women in circular spaces creating a vision of collectivity to bring alive the communal context in which transgressive strategies take root.

Earthy images and symbols in these lyrical narratives subvert the negative stereotypical images of Dalit women. They convey a deep sense of spirituality through familiar natural phenomena such as water, trees, flowers, animals, and familiar experiences of work and family life. The effect is a transcendence of the victimized and exploited bodies of the singers, where Dalit women in their knowledge, beauty, strength, and magical qualities reverse negative situations and project themselves as powerful celebrants of their identity and as creative transgressors. The songs reveal an affirmation of female consciousness of Dalit women as providers and sustainers of relationships with people, nature, and goddesses. Trinh T. Minh-Ha in *Woman, Native, Other* (1989) interprets the emergence of female marginal voices in terms of the transmission of a displaced tradition within dominant cultures. This tradition is constantly modified by new contexts and changing situations, and the storyteller functions as the living memory of her time. Minh-ha perceives indigenous women singers and storytellers as women warriors who break a spell. Likewise, Dalit singers preserve tradition as they break maiming spells, as they call themselves and their community into being to celebrate the gift of life. The singers dispel vicious and imprisoning stereotypes and liberate themselves—songs are danced with and heard as a process of healing the maimed images associated with being polluted and rejected. Dalit cultural expressions authoritatively make and re-make, and claim and reclaim specific experiences that are central to their community's day-to-day life. This happens in imaginative confrontation, protest, and transgression that in turn culminate in changing the social conditions that oppressively dictate their lives; such an active role of Dalit women is evident in the chapters describing Dalit women's leadership.

Postlude: As I mentioned in the beginning of this chapter, my responses to these songs are influenced by various factors: my academic background, teaching experiences, activist involvements, relationships with Dalit women and young girls, and—to some extent—my own experiences, emotions, and thoughts related to my Dalit identity. As much as the songs are embedded with ambiguity and open-endedness about Dalit female power and Dalit female vulnerability in physical, emotional, and intellectual spaces of various activities, my processes of engagement are varied and ambiguous as well. I acknowledge that I dive into an intimate relationship with these songs as they immerse me in an interplay of rhythms, music, intonations, dances, and gestures where I experience both a gentleness and a fierceness in this relationship. On the other hand, I wrestle with questions: "How much of these interpretations are elicited, and how much are simply assumed? Do my responses reflect the daily news stories on atrocities against Dalit communities, especially upon Dalit girls?" Based on the occasions of these songs and the experiences of women in these communities, I aspire to find meanings. Perhaps I am too eager, impatient, and maybe even too loud at times. These songs have been enunciated in spaces and times that are private to a village community and most times, just to women who are not expecting interpretations beyond what these songs live as in their natural spaces. I am grateful that I am welcomed into those proximal spaces to hear sacred voices of a transforming beauty that they cradle and are cradled by and their audacious desiring of social change. I grasp the singers to feel and enter untouched and unknown spaces that are life-giving and identity-binding. These lyrical narratives burst in merging beauty, audacity, and an awareness of danger as punishment for transgression, and yet they are daring in the act of trans-gress-sing and dance-gressing in body and mind.

CHAPTER EIGHT

Bama's Critical-constructive Narratives: Visible Bodies and Audacious Voices as TEXTure for Dalit Women's Freedom

In this chapter,[95] I discuss the works of Bama (1958-), a Dalit writer from Tamil Nadu, widely recognized for her contributions to Dalit literature as she presents the otherwise invisible world of Dalit women from her village of Pudupatti in South India to the larger public. I interweave various forms of her narratives that include her written texts and personal interviews along with casual conversations. These narrative TEXTures present her community to a larger world, interwoven with all its vulnerabilities and resistance, strengths and weaknesses, determination and dilemmas, rebellion and submission, ignorance and awareness, and confrontation and acceptance. Dalit women are part of a communal sphere where a hierarchical structure composes, forces, and judges their behavior. In that space, Dalit women who dare question the primacy and self-assumed sexual prerogatives of the land-owning male sector are demoralized. Dalit female presence in Bama's narratives embodies the looming existence of a moral ambiguity where voices who claim identity and human dignity amid dehumanization and victimization of their bodies, are silenced and made visible only as disposable objects of immorality.

The voices in Bama's works are testimonial in nature bearing witness to interlocked cultural institutions and eliciting a cross-sectional analysis of a social structure that has long been kept in place by longitudinal authoritative constructs of gender, class, and caste. Bama's narratives present oppressive social codes put in place by these constructs that are held fast by tensions that feed the seeming stability of power. Tensions include confrontational collectivization of power—economic, psychological, moral, cultural, spiritual, and political—and of established traditional cultural practices and resistant Dalit communities. Such narratives expose existent tensions as they loosen and threaten such structures of authority that hold traditional cultural practices in place, especially those that involve women's bodies and voices. My analysis of Bama's narra-

---

[95] This chapter is a second version of my essay "Bama's Critical-Constructive Narratives Interweaving Resisting Visible Bodies and Emancipatory Audacious Voices as TEXTure for Dalit Women's Freedom." Sathianathan Clarke, Deenabandhu Manchalla, Philip Vinod Peacock, eds. *Dalit Theology in the Twenty First Century. Discordant Voices, Discerning Pathways*. Oxford University Press: New Delhi, 2009.

tives establishes that rather than only focusing on the invisibility of Dalit women, Bama highlights the *selective visibility* of Dalit women as they are sought after in their state of invisibility for exercising dominant power in and around Pudupatti. As a mark of subversion, she chooses to provide visibility to the Dalit female body as a celebrative space. She breaks through stereotyped images of Dalit women and indulges in revealing their individual and cultural strengths. From among Bama's written works, I will draw from experiences she describes in *Sangati* (*News* or *Events*), first published in Tamil in 1994 and translated by Lakshmi Holstrom in 2005. I will include Bama's earlier narrative *Karukku* (Palmyra Leaf, 1992) and her oral narrative, which is my personal interview with Bama.

In her narrative *Sangati,* Bama recollects the strengths as well as the everyday struggles of Dalit women in her village of Puduppatti in Tamil Nadu. In detail, she exposes the exploitation of Dalit women by the "dominant caste masters" and by the faithful Dalit male servants of the landlords who replicate their masters' violent authority over women. Bama describes the processes by which gender, caste, and class collude to cast Dalit women into a "subgendered" status. However, Bama galvanizes Dalit women as socio-political actors in their demand for justice and in their expression of resistance. She creates a persuasive methodological process that interweaves non-dominant, silenced voices and discourses: Dalit women and men, resistant young Dalit girls, older experienced women, Dalit songs and rituals, and narratives emerging from forced silences and coerced internalization. Her narrative carries an intermixing of the voices of Dalit Hinduism and Christianity as both oppressive and liberating. The alternative teachings of a liberating Christianity are opposed to the misappropriation of such teachings by exclusive oppressive sectors in Christianity. Such interweaving of voices renders Bama's narratives as stories that are durable and rich in their lending of various layers of the complex lives of Dalit women.

In her work, *Karukku*, Bama exposes the ways in which both Hinduism and Christianity control the lives of Dalits in her village. She describes her experiences as a Catholic nun and the prevalence of caste differences in the nunnery that hurt her so deeply that she needed to leave. Bama articulates the failings of the ancient religious tradition of Hinduism and the failed promises of Christianity, the so-called liberating religion, in the metaphor of the double-edged sword of the palmyra leaf, reflecting her inner struggles. Like the interlocked knife-like edges of the palmyra leaf, *karukku,* Bama highlights the interwoven layers of caste, and religious and gender structures that keep Dalit women locked within their fears and stifle signs of assertion and subjectivity. Bama blames the portrayal of Dalit women as silent not on an inability to speak, but rather on the deafened ears of the oppressor and the seeming liberator, Christianity, as she reveals these complex dynamics as a necessary reality of daily life in Pudupatti. She reveals the frailty of her hopes in the Catholic Church to lift her out of her identity as an untouchable and enable her to emancipate other Dalits from their state of untouchability.

Situating Bama

Bama is one of the first Dalit women to question social issues directly related to caste through her writings, which are used widely today in universities around the world. Bama discusses the necessity and potential of Dalit women to forge a positive identity despite limitations and distortions imposed upon them, and she employs her literary skills to subvert traditional images of Dalit women as imperfect objects in caste imagining. Writing in Dalit Tamil inflected by colloquial particularities of the *Paraiyar* community, Bama rejects hegemonic versions of Brahminized Tamil (a revered version of Tamil spoken by the highest caste, Brahmin) in Tamil literature. Commenting on her use of Dalit Tamil in writing, Bama says,

> Each medium has its own language such as cinema and likewise. Dalits need their own language to assert a separate category of language. Language is a symbol of dignity. Dalit people's language has always been said to be impure just like their bodies are assumed to be. I want to prove that it is good. I have proved it to be a successful medium of communication. Dalit language is a new genre.[96]

Claiming a separate identity for the Dalit language, Bama views her own identity tied into this separatism from dominant modes of institutionalization of language, thought, and action. She does not attribute her awareness of inner self to a foreign religion that she was born into but to the inherent characteristic of a Dalit woman. In her interview, Bama states this clearly:

> Yes, I am Christian, but I do not really practice it. But spiritually I believe in Jesus. I like his teachings, his values, and the way he stood up for the oppressed. This is my choice and not because I was born into a Christian family.... My sense of identity comes from being a Dalit woman. I value resilience as my strength from my culture. This is where my inner strength comes from. This is very, very important in a Dalit woman. She keeps going against all odds. The undaunted spirit of the Dalit woman guides me.

---

[96] All quotations above are from a personal interview with Bama on July 17, 2002.

Bama joined the Catholic order of nuns in her twenties in the hope of serving Dalit communities, but she was soon disillusioned by institutional Christianity. Yet, Bama highly values ideals drawn from the life and teachings of Jesus, whom she considers a radical reformer; Jesus' teachings inform a spirituality that allows her to practice the ideals of peace and justice. Bama speaks of the experiences of religious conversion in the *Paraiyar* community and of her own grandparents in the early twentieth century as a move towards a claim for justice and dignity. She states two reasons why Dalits became Christians: the first was economic reasons since the missionaries provided work, food, and education that dominant culture denied Dalits; second, Dalits gained a social status and dignity within Christianity that they did not experience in Hinduism. Bama, however, points out that the Church, both Catholic and Protestant, bought into the caste paradigm that created inequality. Ironically, despite the perpetuation of caste paradigms, Dalits found their voice, dignity, and respect affirmed in Christianity within their own church territory where they did not have to be in contact with Christians from caste communities.

Dalit Women's Voices in Bama's Works

In our interview, Bama was insistent that Dalit women are not silent women, they have been speaking in their cultural languages as they tell and retell their stories in songs, folk tales, dances, and laments. Instead, due to their fear of authority, they are "silenced" voices who continue narrating their discourses of resistance to those who will listen:

> As you see, Mariamma in *Sangati*, she speaks and the women with her speak. Dalit women have always been speaking, questioning injustice among themselves, but have never been heard by an outside world…. Dalit women have been representing themselves. This is not a new phenomenon. It has always been so, but only now are they being recognized to a certain extent. A Dalit woman must continue claiming her rights. Anyone who is likeminded is welcome to join the struggle. Questioning is an inborn trait among Dalits. This is not acquired. But certainly, education helps to make larger connections and compare current situations with alternatives.

Among the various significant voices we hear in *Sangati,* Bama's grandmother, or *Patti* (Tamil=grandmother) is the most significant. She is the voice of tradition, the authoritative questioning voice from the margins who has unwarily internalized caste reality, and she is silenced outside of her realm of Dalit women. In the argumentative voices of Bama and her *Patti,* the tensions and ambiguities that define the daily lives of Dalit women in Pudupatti are evident. For *Patti*, Bama represents a restless generation that grabs every chance to criticize aspects of Dalit life, especially of Dalit women; for Bama, *Patti* represents a generation that holds onto tradition with a non-questioning acceptance. Bama elucidates and provides visibility to the fact that holding onto tradition through rituals, as displayed in the role of *Patti*, is an affirmation of the Dalit female body and voice.

Patti represents unadulterated indigenous strategies of survival that remain within cultural specifications that inform her consciousness of a life controlled by social hierarchy within which she learns that she must continue to speak and be heard by other Dalit women to share in a discourse of survival. *Patti* often singles out formal education as the reason for Bama's inquisitiveness and her audacious hopes to overturn conventional patterns of Dalit life, especially that of Dalit women. The grandmother's way of life is quite unlike Bama's: her discourses are made up of songs, stories, lamentations, and rituals. Through these, she reinstates the authority of men over women and the cultural practices that a girl child enters. Within such a hierarchy, however, she learns that it is her responsibility to continue to speak so that other Dalit women will be encouraged to share their cultural narratives—whether it is singing in the fields to keep themselves from reeling under the long and hot hours of the day, or lamenting aloud to cope with the untimely or unjust deaths in their community. Dalit women are hired as mourners, and in their laments, they celebrate the life of the deceased in a refusal to conform to their ritualized segregation as polluted beings. For Bama, such cultural practices are enduring cultural elements that should be recognized by Dalit women as their strength and be transformed into active elements for change.

When *Patti* reminds Bama about the practice of women eating after the men in the house, Bama questions, "So what is wrong if we change the practice and make the women eat first?" *Patti* answers, "Wrong? You'll end up like that Ananthamma of West street, who was thrashed soundly and left lying there, that's all" (30). *Patti* knows of a woman who tried to break the practice of women eating last and was severely punished for it. She sings a folksong that narrates the consequences of a pregnant wife who ate crab curry before her husband could eat:

> Crab, O crab, my pretty little crab
> Who wandered through all the fields I planted,
> I pulled you off your claws and put you in the pot
> I gave the pot a boil and set it down.
> I waited and waited for him to come home
> And began to eat as he came through the door.

He came to hit me, the hungry brute
He pounced at me to kill me
He struck me, he struck my child
He almost crushed the baby in my womb
He beat me until my legs buckled
He thrashed me until my bangles smashed. (30)

As the song states, the pregnant woman who ate the crab curry was brutally beaten to death by her husband because she did not wait for him! Effectively, the song dramatizes an instilled fear that is an ominous presence in the lives of women even within the safety of their home, in the form of certain cultural practices that reinstate the authority of the male—loud voice and violence. The culture that Bama envisions for her community of women transforms such instances of naturalized or slave-like acceptance as she insists on women speaking up for themselves and establishing their rights as equal human beings, refusing to accept denial of basic physical and emotional needs.

Body and Visibility

I use the word "visibility" in reference to Dalit women's bodies to qualify the corollary of their state of invisibility tucked away in invisible social and physical spaces. As mentioned before, Bama writes about the ways in which invisible and untouchable Dalit women become highly visible and touchable as readily available bodies for purposes of revenge, pleasure, or to make a strong public statement. First, Bama believes in providing visibility and sexuality as a celebration of Dalit female bodies, meticulously detailing Dalit cultural practices and rituals, and presenting her body as a positive cultural construct and a visible marker of subversive discourses that reject dominant traditional images of Dalit bodies as polluted, immoral, and dispensable. Second, Bama details ways in which Dalit women are objects of "selective visibility" subject to "selective touchability" as targets for sexual pleasure and attack for the oppressive powers that surround them. (This theory of visibility is in relation to their immediate surroundings, and I do not, however, undermine their state of invisibility to the rest of the world.) Bama simultaneously reveals as well as tills new grounds where Dalit female identity can and will thrive through active resistance to sanctioned, imposed identities upon their bodies versus a mere irksome coping.

In *Sangati*, Bama interweaves depictions of the Dalit female body and voices in the stories of young girls. One such story is about the victimization of Mariamma, her fifteen-year-old cousin, who makes a living by working in the fields as a laborer. As Bama narrates, Mariamma stops to collect some firewood on her way home from work in the fields, and she passes by a water pump shed (normally situated in the middle of the fields). Her landlord, who happens to be in the room attached to the water pump shed, tries to force her inside. Mariamma escapes and runs into her colony and tells about the incident to her close friends who advise her to remain "silent" because this incident would stigmatize her as immoral.

> "Mariamma," they said, "it is better if you shut up about this. Even if you tell people what actually happened, you'll find that it is you who will get the blame; it's you who will be called a whore. Just come with us quietly, and we'll bring away the firewood that you left there. Hereafter never try to come back on your own when you have been collecting firewood. That landowner is an evil man, fat with money. He's dominant caste as well. How can we ever try to stand up to such people? Are people going to believe their words or ours?" And so they went together, picked up the bundle of firewood, sold it and then went home. (20)

For young Dalit girls, silence becomes their only protection from further harm; and their "silencing" is a form of discourse as a testimony to the knowledge of caste power and their helplessness. The event twists fatefully when the landlord, fearing blemish to his name, reports to the Dalit village headman that young Dalit girls who pass his fields are indulging in immoral behavior. He alleges that he saw Mariamma physically intimate with a young lad, Manickam, and demands that Mariamma and Manickam appear before the village council. The council, made up of Dalit men, is forced into an irrational judgment where the primary aim is to stigmatize the woman—they bring Mariamma to trial and publicly accuse her of misconduct. The council forces her to beg forgiveness by falling at the headman's feet and to pay a fine of two hundred rupees. At the trial, the landlord who is not physically present, imposes himself as vitrifiable just by the fact that he is a caste male and that he is a landlord. Mariamma tries to speak for herself as she is questioned, and she concedes, "What that Machaan states is true [in reference to Manickam's statement of self-defense]. When I was gathering firewood with a few others, he said a word or two to me, in fun. I came away before the others left." Bama recalls, "If Mariamma had said anymore, she would have burst into tears. She finished speaking, wiped her face with her sari, and stood there, her head drooping" (23).

Unconvinced, the council insists that she fall at the feet of the headman, beg forgiveness, and pay the monetary fine. If she would not comply, her father would have to pay a lot more money as *thendam* (penalty). As her father forces her to beg forgiveness, she maintains her innocence, saying, "'Ayya, (Sir) I never did any of that. It was the *mudalali* (landlord) who tried to misbehave with me. But I escaped from him and ran away.' She began to weep loudly" (24). Mariamma speaks to defend her honor and dignity, but the highlighted inscription on her body of blame, shame, and humiliation speak louder than her actual attempts to speak, throwing her into a state of silence but highly visible as a silent victim. Her submissive body carries a powerful message to the rest of the community: her body is used to both blame the victim and to redeem the village of Pudupatti through forceful acceptance of that blame. Though she is aware of the dynamics of the situation, and knows that her silence will not redeem her but will redeem her village, she chooses to break her silence and speak the truth. But truth is not emancipatory or edifying; instead, truth is defeated as a self-justifying ploy. This incident leads us beyond dual conclusions into a reading of multiple meanings.

Mariamma falls at the feet of the headman, bent by the weight of caste, patriarchy, and class. She breaks and finally falls in submission under these structures, expected to perform her culturally sanctioned, original, natural definition as polluted and immoral.[97] While this victimization unfurls in its crude details, the landlord is in his home sheltered among the paraphernalia of caste and class power structures. In Mariamma's embodiment of a culture of defeat and shame, the landlord re-establishes a pattern of the visibility of defeat and the hypervisibility of his sovereignty. She is surrounded by Dalit men who make up for their emasculation by accusing her because they fear losing their ties of servitude to the landlord. But at the same time, Mariamma is surrounded by the physical presence and rebellious voices of Dalit women, voices that they dare not raise among men which provide the moral affirmation that Mariamma needs. But when they do speak, their voice is invalidated. Anandamma, who is a woman from the village, testifies: "It was the *mudalali* who tried to rape her. She was scared out of her wits, refused him, and ran away. Now he has turned everything around and told a different tale. I actually went with her that evening to fetch the firewood that she left behind" (24). Susaiyamma says, "What can you say to these men...there's no way of convincing them.... But it is only to us that they'll brag. Ask them just to stand up to their *mudalali.* They'll cover their mouths and their backsides and run" (24). The women do not accuse the men openly but only in muffled whispers, as Bama recalls; and although they are fully conscious of Mariamma's victimization, the women dare not speak out of fear of both Dalit and dominant caste men.

Mariamma stands still and silent in front of the accusing audience when her father slaps her repeatedly; Mariamma must accept this accusation so that the

---

[97] Bending of the body is a common cultural practice in most parts of South India, as a mark of submission to higher authorities based on caste, class and gender.

colony may be spared the threats of violence if they let her go unreprimanded. One Dalit woman says, "And none of them has the brains to find out whether it wasn't the *mudalali* who was doing wrong in the first place" (25). Another woman responds, "That's a good one! Suppose these fellows go and question dominant caste men. What if those rich men start a fight, saying, how dare these *paraiyar* dare be so insolent? Who do you think is going to win? Even if the mudalali was really at fault, it is better to keep quiet about it and fine these two eighty or one hundred. Instead you want to start a riot in the village?" (25). Dalit patriarchy is sustained by fear, and because of the seemingly inextricable cycle of oppression that they are caught in, the members of the colony accept the workings of the system and move on. Finally, it is Mariamma who stands stigmatized, humiliated, and morally mutilated as yet another dispensable, immoral Dalit woman.

The practice of displaying Dalit women's bodies or parading them naked is not a rare occurrence in rural India: every time Dalit women's bodies are invaded, the caste-based patriarchal systems of authority are reinvoked. Therefore, as texts, bodies of Dalit women are sites of power struggles, sites of traditional and emerging caste ruling orders, and sites of political and cultural demarcation. Hence, in the very process of creating Dalit women's bodies into sites of violence, a deep sense of collectivity of voices, though silenced, proves to be the strength that subverts the dominant notion that their bodies can be formulated as texts of violence to make a statement to the community. Within the purview of power, their bodies morph into billboards that carry a terrifying message to warn their larger community where a public statement is made in punishing their bodies and making them a highly visible public spectacle.

Remaining within one's defined space is crucial to prove one's obedience to a set of rules. When women cross over their gendered spaces as active agents to claim their rights or dignity, it is unacceptable to the authoritative structures and should be punished. It is the meanings of boundaries and markers that one wrestles with in such situations, where interactions between communities are solely based on power equations. The undercurrent that informs these interactions is complex, but nevertheless, the consequences of non-compliance to boundaries are straightforward.

Bama reflects, "I could never forget the way Mariamma was humiliated in front of the entire village" (28). It is this public memory of injustice against a Dalit woman that Bama recollects and rearticulates as testimonial literature. Disappointed in her grandmother's silence, she says, "*Patti*…after all, you are a big woman in this village, why couldn't you have gone and spoken the truth that day?" (28). The grandmother replies,

From your ancestors' time it has been agreed that what the men say is right. Don't you go dreaming that everything is going to change just because you've learnt a few letters of the alphabet...whether it is right or wrong, it is better for women not to open their mouths. You just try speaking out about what you believe is right. You'll only get beaten and trampled on for your pains. It is the same throughout the world, women are not given respect. (28-9)

Bama says,

"Look, she talks as if she's been around the whole world," I thought to myself. But I didn't actually say this to *Patti*. I took some of her betel mixture and began chewing it too. "It's you folks who are always putting us down." I told her. "From the time we are babies you treat boys in one way and girls in quite another. It's you folk who put butter in one eye and quicklime in the other." (29)

The grandmother normalizes her acceptance of gender oppression to assert that there is no respectable status for women anywhere in the world. Bama interestingly reveals the ambiguity in her grandmother, for her reaction to Mariamma is very different from her argument with Bama: "When the fellow pulled you into the shed, why couldn't you have kicked him in the balls then and there? Now you've been hauled unfairly in front of the whole village, given a bad name, and made to pay a fine..." (61). The novel *Sangati* grapples with the conundrum of the various states of ambiguity of women, caught between the nexus of fear and resistance, safety and honor, and passive peace and conflict.

Later, when Mariamma is forced to marry Manickam, an alcoholic, Bama states:

When I thought of Mariamma's life history I was filled with such pain and anger. Because of some dominant caste man's foolishness, she was made the scapegoat, and her whole life was destroyed. If a woman is slandered that's always her fate. People won't consider whether the accusation is true or not, nor will they allow the woman to speak out. They'll marry her off to any disreputable fellow and wash their hands of her, not caring in the least whether she lives or dies. I was disgusted by it. I wanted to get hold of all those who had brought her to this state, bite them, chew them up, and spit them out (42).

Bama resists the colonizer's discourse of conquest even as she acquiesces that she is surrounded by a culture of forced acceptance of defeat and, even more, by a culture that internalizes defeat. She recalls Mariamma's forced acceptance of defeat publicly by falling at the feet of the village headman and begging for forgiveness, despite her innocence. In this, Bama points out male arrogance and authority as forces that lead women to believe in their continued defeated state of existence: "Even here, it is the man's maleness and power that takes precedence. A woman's body, mind, feelings, words and deeds and her entire life are all under his control and domination.... But if only we were to realize that we too have our self-worth, honor, and self-respect we could manage our own lives in our own way" (68). When acceptance is not a choice, resistance surfaces only when these women's lives are sifted through a close analysis; Bama provides an opportunity for her readers to take such a close look.

Bama recounts extremely violent scenes that are part of the daily life in the village of Pudupatti wherein women are subject to extreme forms of violence by their male family members. They are subject to this violence for reasons such as not providing money to purchase alcohol, not feeding them on time, wanting to marry a boy from another Dalit community, *et cetera*. Bama narrates a powerful incident in which a woman Rakkamma, about to be hit by her husband, pounced on him with filthy language and screamed curses upon him: "Ayayoo, he's killing me. Vile man, you'll die, you'll be carried out as a corpse, you low life, you bastard, you this, you that..." Bama continues that Rakkamma would not leave him alone, and when he threatened to hit her, she yelled, "Go on da, kick me now, let's see you do it, da, let's see if you are a real man. You only know how to go for a woman's parts. Go and fight with a man who is your equal, and you'll see. You'll get your balls burnt for your pains. Look at the fellow's face! Thuu,' and she spat on him" (61). The infuriated husband dragged her, pushed her down, and kicked her, but Rakkamma got up and cursed him some more and in front of the entire crowd gathered there, she lifted her sari and exposed her naked body! It worked. The shocked Pakkiaraj left her alone and walked off. While everyone stared, Rakkamma said, "Why don't you lot go and mind your own business? It is I who am beaten to death every day. If I hadn't shamed him like this, he would surely have split my skull in two, the horrible man" (62). In recalling the incident, Bama notes that her immediate reaction was disgust, though she condones Rakkamma's clever strategy of resistance and self-protection in subverting the use of her body and her voice to shame her husband: "I realized that she acted in that way because it was her only means of escape" (62). The body of a Dalit woman, usually used by men to enact revenge and abuse is now used by a Dalit woman to bring shame upon the man who claimed ownership of the body. What the body receives as punishment despite the lack of crime, the self is expected to silently appropriate as its lot in life. But Rakkamma defies this passive acceptance.

Bama observes:

> The position of women is both pitiful and humiliating really. In
> the fields they have to escape from dominant caste men's mo-
> lestations. At church they must lick their priest's shoes, and be
> his slaves while he threatens them with tales of God, Heaven
> and Hell. Even when they go to their own homes, before they
> have had a chance to cook some kanji or lie down and rest a lit-
> tle, they have to submit to their husbands' torment (35).

Amidst such physical and emotional battering that these women endure, Bama
strives to establish a renewed self and awakening within Dalit women by drawing on their cultural strengths and raising self-consciousness amongst them.
Emerging from a recalling of the experiences of silenced and victimized bodies
in Bama's writings, in that same recalling of experiences, Dalit women's consciousness and awareness of their state of being, girded by their communal
experience of being Dalit women who take pride in their sense of collective
identity, cause a reversal of social expectations and strategies that keep Dalit
women at the bottom. Speaking on the strength of Dalit communities, Bama
reiterates this sense of collective identity: "It is definitely the collective identity, 'kuzhu unarvu.' If you review the European history, all social rebellion
starts from within oppressed communities. We are fighting for human rights
against a religious order grounded on inequality. We are a collective voice." It
is such a sense of collectivity that keeps Dalit women strong within a unifying
bond held together by the commonality of their experiences of exploitation and
victimization.

The Catholic Church figures problematically for Dalit women because—
despite some of the tangible benefits it initiated—it took away the few liberating possibilities. Providing thoughts on divorce, Bama notes that the internal
Paraiyar law allows for any man or woman to live separately based on reason-
able doubt; the council legally separates them, and both are free to remarry.
Unlike her Christian upbringing that forbade divorce, Bama finds the non-
Christian *Paraiyar* law liberating based on her observances of the violence
around her because the law offers the possibility that a woman can choose to
leave her husband and escape from domestic violence. She notes that the Catholic faith curtails the freedom, voice, and assertion of *Parachi* women through
its sacrament of marriage, which forces married Dalit women to accept their
state of exploitation. Thus, their bodies are forced to accept violence and stay
bound by religious law. Furthermore, Christianity domesticates Dalit women
through silencing their voices; they are ordered not to vocalize their emotions
and to stop yelling and crying. This is done to instill modesty, silence, and
moderation through Catechism as ideals to be emulated by women; but such

church-enforced constrictions silence Dalit women's expressions of their true self. The cycle of meanings laid upon women's bodies and voices, even in another form of institutionalized gender oppression foreign to the land, continues to reappear without the need for much reformulation or renegotiation. Religious sanctions on bodily comportment connive to resettle on their bodies, depriving them of emotional or physical outlets for both joy and pain.

In their quest for a new social status in conversion, the *Paraiyar* who convert to Christianity find themselves in a more vulnerable position. While Bama's ancestors became Christians in the hope of access to formal education, she observes that they were not all educated, and their hopes were never realized. To make matters worse, their new religious identity as converts deprived them of access to government issued benefits. Thus, Bama feels doubly cheated that Dalit's ignorance has been manipulated, and she feels less secure in the society that she is in now because she should constantly prove herself as a productive human being against the suspicions that caste people still carry about converts and specifically, Dalit converts. While human dignity was the reason for many Dalit conversions, they were not aware of the limitations of a colonial charity.

As an educated Dalit woman, Bama senses a heightened scrutiny by values of the dominant caste. While she struggles with the memory of her tortured self as a Dalit woman and the imposed images of two colonizing structures, both Christian and Hindu, she looks for her adequacy in a new self that she finds in her voice. This new self, she says, can only rise from a situation where a Dalit woman is independent of male dominance, of caste, and of moral expectations. In her attempts to remind her readers and Dalit women of their capacity to liberate their bodies, Bama re-enacts cultural ceremonies and rituals as an integral part of a new self-understanding. Her detailed description of the ways in which a girl who comes of age is celebrated, revered, and initiated into a culture of care is an integral part of validating Dalit female identity. She strategically precedes her narration of Mariamma's state of victimization with the celebration of her body, when—just a few days prior to her public humiliation, Mariamma comes of age—which is widely celebrated as a community event.

The entire village is invited to the ceremony for Mariamma when she is decorated with colorful clothes and flowers and is presented to the village as a girl who has now become a woman, adorned with a sari that women wear, as opposed to the long skirts that girls wear. The elderly women in the community start the ritual of bathing her in milk and turmeric, as if she were a deity (*Sangati* 16). She is then made to sit in a small tent erected for her which brings in a new meaning to being set apart: her body that has come to fruition is isolated so that she is celebrated. In a process of positive selective visibility, Mariamma is affirmed by her feminine beauty and sanctity. One cannot help but be re-minded how *Mariamman* is ritually bathed, decorated, and prepared for the viewing or *darshan* by devotees. Bama's emphasis on the celebration of the Dalit female body and its potential to reproduce reverses the stigma on the untouchable, polluted woman. *Patti* sings at Mariamma's celebration:

> On Friday morning, at day-break
> she came of age, the people said
> Her mother was delighted, her father too—
> Her uncles arrived, all in a row—
>
> Opened the Cloth shop and chose silk and gold
> Went upstairs to find the silk of their dreams
> The lower border with arrow of swans
> The upper border with a row of clouds.
>
> The mountain wind can touch her if she bathes in the river
> The chill wind can touch her if she bathes in the pond.
> So bathe her in water that is drawn from the well
> And wash her hair in a tub made of illuppai flowers.
>
> Shake her hair dry and comb it with gold
> Toss her hair dry and comb it with silver,
> Comb her hair dry with a golden comb,
> And women, all together, raise a kulavai. (Bama 17)

This song ceremoniously leads the young Dalit girl in grandeur into woman-hood; even in their poverty, the close relatives of the girl make sure that she is clothed in new silk-like clothes (not necessarily pure silk as is the custom among the wealthy). The caring ways with which she is bathed in a tub of flowers, clothed, and decorated are specific, necessary subversive acts that revise her body which has traditionally been rejected, ridiculed, mutilated, and easily dispensed with as in Soorpanakha in the *Ramayana*. The use of gold and silk combs in the song help by expressing the emphatic desire for the abun-dance of wealth in the young girl's life and the desire that she be treated like a queen. *Kulavai,* the ululation raised by Dalit women in honor of the girl, further heightens Bama's emphasis on community and family as foremost in the for-mation of a sense of a Dalit female identity that has the power and authority to subvert authoritative sanctioned identities, thereby elevating the status of Dalit women's bodies; once again, we witness the working together of voices and bodies in Bama's narrative as she provides visibility to Dalit women.

Initiating a New Culture

In the culture that Bama seeks to reinstate, cultural strengths drawn from the community's beliefs and practices testify to a personal sense of identity that resists dominant culture. Where Hindu religion inscribes slavery as an inborn requirement of one's karma, recovering Dalit women's voices and bodies will overturn their karmic acceptance of servitude. Bama seeks to tap into the cultural strengths that the grandmother and other Dalit women embody. She depicts through her act of recollection that this can happen only when Dalit women make the conscious decision to replace humiliation, a sign of defeat, with a sense of pride and dignity in their existent multifarious roles that include sustenance of a Dalit culture made up of ceremonial rituals enacted by and on voices and bodies.

The envisioned new culture calls for naming specific forms of exploitation and identifying specific ways of resistance and change. The reality of exclusion and exploitation and its passive acceptance by the *Paraiyar* community infuriates her. In *Karukku*, we read about a community caught between two invasive structures: the colony and Christianity. Bama juxtaposes both these structures in her narrative as proofs of the possible permanency of a slave identity for her as a *Paraiyar* woman. As a voice of revolt and rebellion against structures of injustice, Bama declares the failings of seemingly iterative structures towards liberty like Christianity. In her works, she credits her Dalit roots rather than religion for the acquired benefits of a culture that questions the ethos of subjugation as she reveals the fact that Dalit women speak and raise questions about exclusion from within their small communities. In the culture that Bama seeks to reveal, these voices will be heard as strong voices. She establishes that where slavery has traditionally been inscribed as an inborn requirement of one's karma, recovering Dalit women's voices will overturn their karmic acceptance of servitude.

Bama has maximized the autonomy of Dalit female bodies and voices through this powerful form of testimonial narrative where she presents and interprets specific dynamics and institutions that threaten physical survival. This process of conscious resurgence and contestation subverts dominant stereotypes that categorize oppressed bodies as weak and vulnerable, and redefines them in the context of specific economic, religious, and gender-based alienation that arises from circumstances that she specifies. In this discourse involving bodies and voices, Bama re-members and re-inserts Dalit women into their culture and into the public mind in a reversal of their demonization in traditional discourses. Bama instates Dalit women's resilience, determination, cultural production involving songs, dances, folktales, humor, and an untiring work ethic. Her narratives serve as resources of organic systems of knowledge, lifestyle, and praxis while revealing a claim to human dignity. Bama has proved that Dalit women can define their own identity even within limited horizons; they can rearticulate discourses that have so far defined them and their needs, and by self-determination, Dalit women can forge a culture where human dignity becomes a force in its own right. To this end, education must be both formal and consciousness-raising so that Dalit women recognize their strengths and assert themselves with dignity. Voices of Dalit women, which through such discourses carefully embrace a sense of collective identity that surfaces in a sifting of memories, become voices of collective deliverance in a culture that has been denied even the conceptualization of a shared humanity.

In Bama's vision for new social configurations, she takes us through the conflicting experiences of pain, struggle, work, survival, and cultural expressions amidst the stifling circularity of systemic violence. Yet her stories boldly engage the structures and systems of oppression to unsettle what many have accepted as traditional behavioral patterns normalized upon Dalit women's bodies. Creative explorations of meanings inscribed on bodies reanimate the silences and reinstate existent cultural strengths that are transformed from mere survival strategies to life-affirming possibilities pointing towards the existence of a productive resistance.

Excerpts from Personal Interviews and Conversations with Bama between 2002 and 2016

Roja: Who in your family first became Christian and why?
Bama: My great grandparents, in the late nineteenth century. Missionaries from France converted them. They became Christians primarily for a few major reasons: First of all, it was for economic reasons. They were offered better jobs than working in fields… Even though they were small jobs. Secondly, for the sake of social status. Other people from outside started treating them with respect. This was important for them. It was for self-dignity. They were also offered the opportunity of education. At that time, what they did was right because education is important for independence, both political and for economic power.
Roja: What is your understanding of Marx?
Bama: Marx's theories are not applicable to caste. Economic liberation is not sufficient for us Dalits. You need social emancipation: "Podhu udaimai kolgai." Common wealth for all is not enough because caste identity is deeper than economic necessity.

Roja: Can you comment on your use of Dalit language in your writings?

Bama: Each medium has its own language such as cinema *et cetera*.... likewise, Dalits need their own language to be a separate category. Language is a symbol of dignity. Dalit people's language has always been said to be impure like the people. I want to prove that it is good. I have proven that it is a successful medium of communication. Dalit language is a unique genre.

Roja: Do you consider yourself Christian?

Bama: Yes, I am Christian, but I do not really practice it. But spiritually I believe in Jesus, I like his teachings, his values, and the way he stood up for the oppressed. This is my choice and not because I was born into a Christian family.

Roja: Where does the essence of your identity come from?

Bama: My sense of identity comes from being a Dalit woman. I value resilience as my strength from my culture. This is where my inner strength comes from. This is very, very important in a Dalit woman. She keeps going against all odds. The undaunted spirit of the Dalit woman is what guides me.

Roja: What is the social dynamics of your life now, living in a small town amidst caste people?

Bama: I have no deep relationships with people, but I have an everyday courteous reaction from others. Of course, there is a lot of suspicion because I am a Christian, I am single, *and* I am a Dalit woman. But there is no room for outright discrimination here in my town.

Roja: When and how do you think Dalit women have started speaking?

Bama: As you see in Mariyamma in *Sangati,* she speaks and the women with her speak. Dalit women have always been speaking, questioning injustice among themselves, but have never been heard by an outside world. Through my writing, I have gained visibility and I am able to promote visibility to invisible issues and also let the voices of Dalit women be heard to a larger public. Dalit women have been representing themselves. This is not a new phenomenon. It has always been so but only now are they being recognized to a certain extent. A Dalit woman must continue claiming her rights. Anyone who is likeminded is welcome to join the struggle. Questioning is an inborn trait among Dalits. This is not acquired. But certainly, education helps to make larger connections and compare current situations with alternatives. Awareness of situation is of course made possible by education.

Roja: What was your family's reaction to *Karukku*?

Bama: My parents were upset. They said, "Why write about our family? Why expose things about our village? Why degrade?" The villagers were also upset with me.

Roja: What is the strength of the Dalit community?

Bama: It is definitely the collective identity: *Kuzhu Unnarvu.* If you see the European history, all social rebellions start from within oppressed communities. We are fighting for human rights against a religious order grounded on inequality. We are a collective voice.

(2014)

Roja: Advice for me?

Bama: Why are you writing about ancient scriptures and all of that? You need that framework, sure. But write more about what Dalit women are doing today. We are changing history and challenging Indian society. We are breaking out of our stereotype mold. We are changing our lives and the lives of our community. Give visibility to that. Us, educated Dalit women can do that.

Roja: Do you or how do you perceive the character of Dalit feminism?

Bama: See, the way we see feminism is very different. We experience it in our everyday life. As Dalit women, we don't need special rights as other feminisms would like to see happen in women's groups. We demand equal rights as that which we deserve, as we deserve. Yes, we are vulnerable as Dalit and as women, but we are just not stuck in that place of being vulnerable. We demand equal rights with every other human citizen of this world and of this nation. We are constantly stereotyped as if we are stuck in that vulnerable place as Dalit women. We are most certainly not. Dalit feminism is different because we have more and different problems that are unique to us. Our response and reaction is different as well.

Roja: So how would you explain the character of Dalit women? Is there an innate character?

Bama: Of course! There is a human value in us. Those values that are most significant are resistance and resilience. We are not lying low and taking beatings of shame. We fight. We protest, we rebel—this is who we are. We defeat our problems like that. We act from faith in our culture and in ourselves. We value our life style. We don't see it as worthless as others see it.

Roja: In what ways are Dalit women and culture intertwined?

Bama: As you have written, I have said it all in *Sangati.* Dalit women and Dalit culture are inseparable. We are the creators and sustainers, and we maintain Dalit culture. Any ceremonies or rituals, nothing happens without us. We provide all the wisdom that has been handed to us from our foremothers. Values and beliefs are very important to us. We maintain that human value in and through Dalit culture that we constantly breathe as our life. We value and respect our village life or anywhere we are. We work hard. We value our work ethic and the cultural beliefs we have. We are proud of who we are. We see beauty in our life, our community, in one another, within ourselves, and in our body. Our songs, dances, and stories are very important to our inner core. They form us as we form them. Our character is born in our culture and vice versa.

CODA

My Story: Embracing Dalit Identity

This is my story. I was twenty-six years old when my Dalit roots found me. My husband knew about it before I did! I returned to my hometown in August 1991—Tambaram, a suburb of Chennai in Tamil Nadu, India—after completing a year's study in Richmond, Virginia, USA. I met my husband-to-be in July 1991 in Chennai and was married two months later. We settled in the town of Karunguzhi where my husband served as a priest in the Church of South India. I was young and aspiring with the bling tag of a "US return." My religious identity as a Christian was important to me at that time more as a religious sentiment and less as a social meaning related to liberation in my Dalit cultural context which I came to realize later. At that point in my life, my parents and most of my relatives were economically well placed, educationally accomplished, and socially respected, and there was no circumstance (at least in my life) when the caste question was raised. My parents hid our Dalit identity from all of us children; I was angry about this at first. Some of the details I present here clarified and answered my questions and calmed my anger as to why my parents decided not to speak about our Dalit heritage and identity.

Life in Tambaram

I was born in Vellore, Tamil Nadu, and our family moved to Tambaram when I was three. As I reminisce, growing up in Tambaram was filled with complex intricacies which did not seem so then. I grew up with two older brothers, my father was a college professor of Tamil Literature in the Madras Christian College (MCC), and my mother was a middle school teacher in Corley High School (a Church of South India institution). We lived on Sharma Street in a part of Tambaram called Ganapathipuram. My parents enrolled me in Kindergarten in the Christ King Convent School run by the Carmelite nuns where English was the medium of instruction. They were very proud of the fact that they had the economic status to do that—attending such an "English medium" school was a mark of social status; I completed my twelve years of school education there. Interestingly, during this time in school, I recall no experiences of discrimination because of my caste. In fact, my father's position as a college professor and my mother's teaching position earned us social respect in the church, among neighbors, and from our regular grocers. I grew up with no awareness of social divisions of caste, but we were well aware of how the "poor" were treated. I heard nuns use the term "poor children" often in my Catholic School.

The only detail that I can remember close to social divisions was when during lunch break in school, we would sit under trees on the school grounds and eat our lunch. Noon to one-o-clock was a segregated time: boys and girls (strictly binary) ate separately, friends formed their own cliques, and the Brahmin children would form their own lunch circles. My awareness of a Brahmin identity was only about them being vegetarian Hindus; there was nothing more to it in my child-mind and awareness. Later, I attended the Women's Christian College in Chennai for my Bachelor's degree and MCC for my Master's and my M. Phil degrees, all in English literature. These years went by without mention of caste at home, school, or college. The only distinctions that I remember about my peers were whether they were rich or poor, Christian or Hindu, Brahmin Hindu (those Hindus who did not eat meat) or non-Brahmin Hindu (meat eating).

I grew up privileged indeed and sheltered from the social realities that were just around the bend from Sharma Street. Dalit families (this realization came only later) lived in a *ceri* community close to my home. When I was eight, our house maid's ("servant") daughter Kuppu and I became close friends; she was a couple of years older than me. Kuppu lived in the *ceri* which is a segregated living area where only Dalits lived. Since Kuppu and I played a lot together, one day I went to her home in the *ceri.* That was my first exposure to a *ceri* community where she lived in a hut primarily made of mud. Another maid, Gramini *Aayya* (respectful, affectionate term for an older woman), lived in the *ceri* as well, and when she saw me there, she furiously yelled at Kuppu for bringing me into the *ceri.* The next day she informed my mother about seeing me in the *ceri,* and I remember that my mother just smiled. I remember the smile because it came as a surprise to me when I expected to be scolded.

The beginning of my interactions with the *ceri* community in Tambaram started then. I visited there more frequently with Kuppu; we would sit under the *murungai* tree in front of her home and play "house"; Kuppu would always be the mother and I would be the child. We would walk holding hands to Sunday school sessions on Sunday afternoons led by mesmerizing storytellers from the organization of the Scripture Union. These Nadar (Shudra) Christians narrated Bible stories with the aid of felt-board and paper figures that stuck to the board. They never entered the *ceri,* but held these sessions just outside the *ceri* in a street corner. I would sit with all the children from the *ceri* to listen to how Jesus was with the despised!

Kuppu and I excitedly skipped along with other children whenever the candy man showed up with the sticky, stretchy pink candy on a long stick on which stood a clay lady doll with rosy cheeks and red sari. The Hindu Nadar seller adorned little hands that held five paisa, with candy bracelets and watches; little "*ceri*" hands without five paisa just stretched in and out in empty hopes. Amma gave me ten paisa and both Kuppu and I enjoyed magical candied moments; we lifted decorated wrists to our mouths in candy-delight. Our dark skins were transformed into the pinkness of the candy as the lady atop the candy stick blessed—only outside the *ceri*. Little did I know that Kuppu and I shared more than candy-delight, gender identity and dark skin color.

When I was about ten years old, we moved into the gated community of MCC campus very close to Sharma Street, where the families of college faculty lived. Kuppu's mother continued to work in our home, and sometimes Kuppu would come with her. Later, my mother hired a live-in helper, and I saw less of Kuppu. I was sucked into the pretensions of sophistications in this "elite" gated-campus community, and I did not want to be friends with Kuppu anymore. The *ceri* dwelling in Tambaram became more invisible and alien to me. I began to feel ashamed and embarassed whenever a child I knew from the *ceri* would identify me in a public space and come running to me or call out my name; I would turn away, pretending not to know her. I changed, and my parents patted themselves on their backs for their achievement in raising their social status.

My world turned different. The MCC campus faculty community was unique in its religious and linguistic diversity; people from various parts of India and one family from the USA resided there. The Christian community formed a niche defined by church activities, and being Christian became a caste equalizer—or so I thought. My close friend's family was originally from Kerala. She lives in Maryland (USA) now, and in our recent conversation, I asked her if she was aware of caste dynamics while we were kids. She did remember that some of her parents' colleagues would not eat or drink water in her house, which she later realized "was a caste thing." As far as I can remember, our family and one other family were the only Dalit families on campus (as I realized many years later). There were many other family-oriented campus activities that brought all castes, religions, and languages together. Looking back, the only caste-based behavior I can remember is when our Brahmin neighbor would turn back when he saw one of our family members walking towards him. Years later, my father laughingly commented that the Brahmin neighbor would pretend that he had forgotten something. The other instances were when my father reminded me of the many times when his Brahmin colleagues would come to visit in our home but would not eat or drink in our home. They held a deep respect for my father's scholarship but were quite rigid in following caste-based religious practices. My father spoke of discriminatory moments and deeply hurtful comments from the evangelical Christian Nadar preachers (Shudra) than Hindu Brahmin colleagues; they found his scholarly biblical discourses threatening.

After my father retired from MCC in 1984, we moved back into a neighborhood close to Sharma Street. I attended elite Women's Christian College for my undergraduate studies as a residential student. I moved back with my parents in 1987 and attended MCC for my Master's program in English Literature. I started reconnecting with the *ceri* community and with Kuppu who was a mother of three by then. I started Sunday school sessions on the terrace of my house for the children from the *ceri*. I still just placed "the poor" in the *ceri*, not knowing the vicious role of caste at play in the lives of those like Kuppu.

Partnering with Identities

I completed my M. Phil Degree in English Literature in MCC, and after teaching in the Lady Doak College in Madurai, Tamil Nadu, I came to Richmond, Virginia, USA in 1990 to secure a Master's Degree in Christian Education. The reasons for me leaving India were many. At the time we lived in Madurai, Tamil Nadu, I became highly aware of a certain distancing and discrimination by the Christian communities belonging to the Shudra community. They openly expressed their disapproval of our family's participation in church activities because we were not from their communities. I grew up with the idea that we were some kind of a mixed group of people who were clearly not from specified communities such as Nadar or Vellalar. I was not aware that rigid caste identities existed. I had Brahmin schoolmates whom I associated with an orthodox Hinduism, and I knew of Nadars whom I associated with those hailing from the Southern region of Tamil Nadu.

I was twenty-five and well past marriageable age when we lived in Madurai; a few families who were scheduled to visit us to explore possibilities of matchmaking withdrew when they found out we were not from their caste community of Christians. Another main reason was that our family was against the practice of dowry. Rejection by these families was hurtful and affected my self-worth; I was disgusted with society and with namesake Christians for whom caste identity and money mattered more than who I was. I wanted a break from this society where caste, money, and possession of gold and property seemed to be of primary concern. My cousin Christopher helped me secure admission in a Master's Program in Christian Education in Richmond, Virginia. It was hard for my parents to let me go; it is common now for unmarried girls from India to move to the USA, but not in the 90s. My mother saw that I was not happy in

India; she spent all her retirement money on sending me to USA. What a sacrifice!!

In the year 1991, I returned to India for summer break and through a close friend met my husband who is from the Christian Nadar community on the caste scale, but was not particular about marrying a Nadar girl (this community only marry within their caste and demand high dowry); surprisingly he was against the practice of dowry. He did not seem real at first! Marrying this Prince (that is his actual name) was the beginning of a meaningful life journey of social awareness regarding Dalits and discovering my Dalit identity. Though Prince was against the practice of dowry, such a tradition showed its fangs in disguised language from other relatives during the wedding plans. My father tearfully hung his head and told me that he was afraid for me; he was right. "Brought-no-dowry" would be a haunting reminder and an opportune "dowry-redress" would be justified. Prince stood (stands) different in his values of non-materialism and his compassionate social activism among those ostracized by society; my family and I love/d him for it. We were married in October 1991 in Chennai. My life would get exciting and complicated at the same time with beginnings of claiming a Dalit identity; the "prove-myself" pressure was on.

"I Knew Your Grandfather"

Prince and I started our life together in the village of Karunguzhi (translates as "black pit" in Tamil) in the Chengalpattu district of Tamil Nadu, where he worked as a priest with the Church of South India serving Dalit communities. Interestingly, Prince had known about my Dalit identity even before we were married because he served in the villages where my ancestors lived. I learned about my Dalit identity in the very first week that I lived in Karunguzhi when an older person from our church congregation started making kind enquiries about my father and grandfather and stated that he knew my grandfather as a catechist (evangelist) who travelled by foot in the villages in the Chengalpattu region preaching the gospel. He further informed me that my ancestors converted to Christianity like many other Dalits in the area due to missionaries from the Church of Scotland. It was then that I came to know that many of the people there knew my family, and I discovered my Dalit roots. I was a bit perplexed as to how I should react to this discovery of my Dalit roots at twenty-six; I was bewildered by a sense of shame and denial. I remember walking into the kitchen to bring more tea for the parishioner and found myself suddenly gasping in tears! The word Dalit did not come up then but only the sudden realization that my ancestors were "untouchables." My feelings turned into anger as I wondered why my parents would hide this fact from me.

My husband was involved with social justice movements that addressed the struggles of Dalit communities and urged me to be proud of my Dalit identity and not run away from it. In talking with him and Paul Divakar (whose mother was murdered in caste-based violence in Andhra Pradesh) and his wife Annie Namala, who are Dalit rights activists, I was exposed for the first time to the social hierarchical practices of the caste system and the systemic injustices meted upon Dalit communities. I came to realize that Dalit families had embraced Christianity not as just a matter of convenience but as a social statement against a sect of Hinduism that kept them apart as the unclean and outcaste people. To protect their families from the knowledge of a shameful identity, most Dalit Christians continue to hide this identity from their children. This conversion created a protection from open discrimination and from low self-worth in the larger society, and protection from a knowledge that could deter their children's sense of confidence. The appalling realization for me was the fact that I could live twenty-six years of my life not knowing about Dalits and daily struggles specific to them. The caste system was not part of our school curriculum.

As I engaged more with Dalit people who were mostly farmers in this region—simple, selfless, and earthy—and they embraced me with an unconditional love, I accepted a peace that came from a deep sense of belonging. I had lived my life only knowing that we were Christians and that we were not a Shudra Nadar or Vanniyar. This new sense of belonging to a specific community was a confusing, nervous, shy, and thrilling feeling. The little Vespa scooter that my husband and I rode around into the villages to get to village church gatherings, bumped down the narrow paths that my grandfather used to walk as a traveling catechist, and that realization was exciting enough for me!

Meanwhile, just as many young married girls in India, I found myself caught between the sharp edges of trying to satisfy traditional expectations of families we marry into and a pretentious magnanimity of modern progressive families, societies, and individuals. My dark skin color, no-dowry status, bold claims to my Dalit identity, and more, placed me at the bottom of the family and social scale. For the first time, I felt it. My personhood sunk along with my confidence due to such derision. Suddenly, material "gifts" had to be prioritized over prayerful blessings from my father (many others sought my father's prayers); my parents stood "different" from materialism and that was sufficient reason for derision. Soon, my protected worlds on MCC campus, my education, my circle of friends, my church group security would all be terrifyingly interrupted by the sudden non-mingling of who and where I now was, after marriage, with my new-found Dalit identity. Growing up, I was sheltered, cared for, and loved very much by my immediate and extended family. My extended families through marriage were kind to me whenever I visited them but I knew that I would never be a choice for their sons, especially since I was dark, not from their caste community, and I "brought-no-dowry." I felt vulnerable and afraid for the very first time in my life as I chose to embrace my Dalit self. My husband stood with me on this. I was in a unique situation, and I did not know what to make of it. Everything was changing rapidly: my inner self and forced behavioral changes would not merge.

The Magic of "Visibility"

I began to feel the pain of being Dalit, and I understood now why my parents protected me. I kept seeing the face of Kuppu (I have now reconnected with her, still in the same *ceri*), and in my mind, I saw the clay smile on the candy lady prettied with pink cheeks ominously changing. I discovered that I was expected and supposed to be invisible even in a modern society because I was a woman, dark, Dalit, and Christian. Several months after I discovered my Dalit roots, I held a certain amount of guilt within me that I had managed to master the magic of visibility, while Dalit people I met in the villages were still living the reality of being invisible. (Of course, my idea of visibility and invisibility changed for me as I discuss in the Introduction section.) Now, I was faced with the choice of whether to continue to ignore a shameful past or be outspoken. A selective anonymity came in handy just as it had helped my parents. I was trying to dance between rain drops; I had to choose carefully when I should reveal my Dalit identity and when I should hide it. In the villages where I was with Dalit people, I was outspoken and excited about being Dalit; and among family or friends in the urban areas, I felt abhorrence and I would downplay that excitement. My awareness and pride of belonging to the Dalit community became stronger in my husband's passion to work with Dalit communities as well. The more I was vocal about my identity, the more I felt push-back from family, even my own. I decided to embrace a Dalit identity first as an activity of celebrating my Dalit femaleness as positive and as an act of resistance to the cultural norm of deriding Dalits. I slowly learned the complexity of the lives of Dalits which was not only about gender and caste; it was much more complex. The educated and land-owning Dalits threw a superior attitude at Dalits who did not possess those assets. Women and children from other castes, especially the Shudra communities, expected a slave-like servitude from Dalit men and women. I wondered if my claims to be a feminist, which only went as far as resisting dowry and male domination, was sufficient to be inclusive of addressing the diverse nuances of power entities that determined and dictated the lives of Dalits.

My connections with Dalit women led to building a consciousness within me that looked up to the strengths of Dalits, and women in particular. They worked hard; took pride in their capacity to earn money; nurtured their family and community by providing food and care; and boldly held various community relationships together. I found my own confidence amongst such an audacious and indelible energy that simply refused to be put down. In the lives of these simple women, I saw the crude intersections of not just caste, class, and gender (which we saw plainly), but more complex layers of vulnerability at play in structuring both perceptions and actions around women in these rural areas.

Sadly, my husband and I left the Church of South India due to strong criticism from the first Dalit Bishop of the church (once power comes into play, educated Dalits exercise authority) because of our involvement with social justice issues in standing up for Dalit women's rights. The Bishop was friends with a wealthy Dalit family whose son had sexually victimized a Dalit housemaid. After ensuring that justice would be brought to the young girl, we moved out of the village. We came to the United States in June 1993 with our seven-month-old son, Nivedhan, so that I could complete the Masters' degree I had begun in Richmond, Virginia before we were married. Our involvement with the Dalit community grew stronger after we moved to the USA.

Embracing a Dalit Identity in the USA

During my time in the USA before and after my marriage, non-Indians would ask me about the caste system. I knew nothing. Upon my return to the US after living among Dalit people and discovering my own Dalit roots, I could speak with authority about the situation of Dalits. Mid 1990s onwards, Prince and I were invited to speak in colleges, universities, and churches about injustices meted out to Dalits, and very soon we built a large support group in New Jersey and New York from non-Indian communities, mostly Caucasian and African-American. Most Indian Christian "friends" told us that we should stop talking about an ancient practice in India and that we must stop shaming our country.

I developed a deep sense of pride in my Dalit identity but along with this new-found enthusiasm came difficulties. Both my husband and I soon realized we were taking the risk of losing some of our friends and family in the USA who had moved from India and worked very hard seeking a better life here for their children. Immediate families on both sides, visiting from India, would not take part in public events related to Dalit rights that we would organize in New York City. It became very clear to me that no matter how well-educated or highly cultured I was or our family was, my open voicing of my Dalit identity would remain a problem and would affect close relationships. We brushed these concerns aside in our enthusiasm and excitement over the energy we had created in various communities in New Jersey and New York. Despite open insults and accusations, my husband and I continued to write statements against caste practices that were featured in newspapers and on the local television channel in Morristown, New Jersey. I felt a deep sense of fulfillment as well as a responsibility both to embrace my Dalit identity and to create awareness in whatever way possible so that changes could happen in the lives of Dalit people I had lived with.

I cannot paint only a rosy picture of my life here in the USA. I deal with the baggage that comes along with being a woman, a South-Asian woman, a dark South-Asian woman, and a dark South-Asian Dalit woman. I can keep adding to this game of Jenga, but where do I begin to deconstruct? I must carefully and safely dismantle my identity while being careful not to topple the security I have built for myself and my family here with great difficulty through my education, church, children, and close friends while financially supporting our families in India. I have finally reached the age when I can tell most of my students that I have lived longer in the USA than they have! I am not sure if I am desperately claiming an "American" identity to downplay my South-Asian identity that I cannot hide. I can, however, hide my Dalit identity because no one associates being Dalit with holding a Ph.D. This is when my strategic choices matter: I decide with whom I would talk about being Dalit, with whom I would discuss caste politics, with whom I could be proud of my Dalit identity, and how far I should carry these conversations. Yes, in a white crowd, I can talk all I want about being Dalit and about caste; for some it provides a good commercial break from dwelling on racism, sexism, heterosexism, ableism, ageism, and all other -isms here in the USA, but most of them truly engage with the caste issue. When I do allow my Dalit identity to surface, I can converse about caste most comfortably with non-Indians, and then with some comfort with close Indian-American friends who are Hindu, and least comfortably with Christian Indian-Americans. My progressive Hindu friends in Rochester tell me that they are ashamed of the caste system. We have formed close bonds with families from the so called "dominant castes." Select universities with South Asian studies programs provide conferences on caste-based social analysis of Indian society where I can engage academically.

I realized that being openly proud of my Dalit identity, without facing violent consequences, is a privileged position. For my family, anonymity was more desirable than a shameful identity because they wanted to forget shameful experiences. When my father was in his late seventies, we openly discussed his childhood as a Dalit for the first time. In one of his letters to me, he painfully recalled a time when he once bent down to pet a puppy on a leash that a caste boy was holding, and my father's "untouchable" outcaste hand accidentally touched the boy's leg; he was beaten by the caste bystanders for that. It became clear to me why many Dalit Christians hid in that anonymous social space starting in the early late 1800s and into the late 1900s when the missionary movement produced educated Dalits who aspired to break free from centuries of cultural bondage and leave their deprived cultural spaces to live in a culture of privilege. Their anonymity was a lived identity made real in a relationship shared with one another as the privileged Dalit mass that could get by day to day without having to encounter their Dalit identity as they did when they or their ancestors lived in the villages.

When my parents left their villages to study in Christian boarding schools, they were encouraged by their parents to escape their shameful identity and grab onto any chance to move up into different social and cultural spaces that only education and economic self-sufficiency could make possible. For my parents, education was a tool to be able to flee a cultural identity that had heaped degradation and shame upon their childhood. Today, as an educated Christian Dalit woman, I can lean on supportive structures that are now in place: national Dalit organizations, an international Dalit solidarity network, mentors who dared to embrace their Dalit identity in public spaces and arenas, the Episcopal Church and friends from various faith and caste communities, Dalit leaders, Dalit scholarship, and strong Dalit female voices.

My "Hindu" Ancestors Convert to Christianity[98]

Paulraj Dayanandan in his research on one-hundred-years of history of Dalit Christians in Tamil Nadu provides me with insights that deepen my understanding of why my ancestors embraced Christianity. [99] For the first time, my Dalit ancestors were noticed as human beings by missionaries, and they were

---

[98]Since both my parents have passed on, I rely on family members as well to fill me in on details of my ancestors. My oldest family member on my father's side, his niece, Dorothy who is eighty, is one of my main informants along with my cousin John Raja-dorai (Rajan, as we call him, gathered a lot of information from his mother who was my father's sister before she passed on). Both Dorothy and Rajan live in Tamil Nadu. Christopher Solomon is my oldest cousin on my mother's side living in New York who provided me with some information on my mother's family.

[99] Dayanandan is a noted Dalit scientist in India, and has become a historian now. He knew my parents well as we all lived on the same college campus where my father and Dayanandan taught. In his research article, "Dalit Christians in the Chengalpattu area in Northern Tamil Nadu" (2002), Dayanandan traces the history of the Christian missionary movement in Tamil Nadu, especially in regions around Chennai and Chengalpattu districts.

treated with dignity and provided with education and responsibilities denied to them for centuries. Dayanandan argues that in comparison to upper caste homes, the life of the *Paraiyar* was much more egalitarian when gender-based oppressive practices were not the norm. They were not bound by a marriage or dowry; men and women shared equal life skills. They were not bound by obligatory religious rituals, nor were they dependent on their temple priests for mediation with the gods. Already possessing a rich cultural heritage, it must have taken a lot of consideration on the part of Dalits to convert. Mostly—observes Dayanandan, from what his family told him—it was the idea of a god who suffered, who was tortured and killed, but who rose above all of this, that appealed to them. This god was not very different from their *Mariamman* and other goddesses who are similar in their vulnerability and power (Dayanandan "Dalit Christians," 26).

Both my parents attended and taught at mission schools: Anderson High School (Conjeevaram also known as Kanchipuram) and Columbas' High School (Chengalpattu). Dayanandan records that Anderson converted many students in these schools who later became priests and teachers, worked alongside missionaries, or secured jobs in government offices (15). Developing an understanding of Dalit Christian identity from oral narratives of his ancestors, Dayanandan affirms that Dalits sought a "new identity" as "active agents of a protest movement" through missionary involvement. He states, "The religion of a white man who touched the untouchable and nursed the afflicted and gave a decent burial to those who perished in cholera or famine must surely have love and truth. The anger and pain of endless oppression can now be ignored and their energy and time diverted to this new religion of love" (Dayanandan 26). I can boldly claim this identity now as a positive identity from a privileged position as I am secure in my social and economic place and in my family life, where my husband and my two sons are enthused about their connection to a Dalit identity through me.

Another interesting dimension that Dayanandan points to in his research is the fact that missionaries were divided in their actualization of their "mission": changing Dalit lives and catching elite caste souls.[100] Some catered to the needs of the already wealthy caste communities who would pay handsomely to acquire a quality, English-based college education. Without the finances to attend college, both my parents taught in mission schools in Kanchipuram (which they could do with just a high school degree and a two-year teacher training certifi-

---

[100] Dayanandan reports that Adam Andrew, John Anderson, and J. H. Maclean served Dalit villages in the Chengalpattu district and in the Northern Coasts of Tamil Nadu between the years of 1870s-early 1900s. Others like William Miller, on the other hand, saw conversion among the dominant castes as an accomplishment.

cate). My father did not give up on earning a higher degree and while teaching in high school, he enrolled in correspondence education (through mail) and secured a college education. Then, while teaching in colleges, he obtained his Doctoral degree. My mother, however, did not pursue higher education but dedicatedly and responsibly settled into her school teaching job and taking care of the family. Tireless work by missionaries like Adam Andrew has indeed resulted in Dalit Christians moving ahead in society, leaving segregated lives and shameful identities, and entering more common grounds with other caste members.[101]

Deborah Premraj et al. in their fieldwork-based research published in *From Role to Identity: Dalit Christian Women in Transition* (1998) confirm that two aspects that deeply influenced Dalits, especially Dalit women in their conversion, was first and foremost the "genuine friendship" and counsel offered by missionary women and the Bible women (35). They were nurtured by the acceptance and relationship they developed with missionary women. My mother very often spoke fondly of her missionary teachers in Northwick School in Chennai. For both my parents, as I recall, the respect and love they received from missionary families made them happy in attaining a sense of fulfilment. I remember that these relationships were deep, mixed with an awe and affection.[102]

Analytical explorations on life stories of Dalit Christian Women in Tamil Nadu inform us that the "Dalit tradition and Christian tradition together offer some alternative role expectations as well as nurture her [Dalit woman] sense of personal worth and equalitarian attitudes" (Premraj et al. 55). These stories relay the dedication with which these women value their faith that is rudimental to their self-image and identity. They claim a higher social status through their Christian identity. I observed this confidence among the Christian Dalit women in the villages surrounding Karunghuzhi as well.

---

[101]Dayanandan identifies Andrew as one who combined spirituality with social and economic realities of the oppressed. He initiated inventions that would support Dalit communities and other farmers to lighten their work and increase food production. He started entrepreneurial small businesses among Dalit peoples. He unearthed ancient irrigation tanks and established banking systems in the villages. Andrew ensured the passing of the "Panchama Magna Charta," a Government Order of 1893 that provided for grant-in-aid for the education of Paraiyar students and the supply of land to outcastes for cultivation and settlement. He earned the affectionate title, "Pariah Andrew" (15).

[102] Several missionaries have stayed in our home as my father taught them Tamil, especially the noted theologian Bishop Leslie New Begin (1919-1998) from Britain who served as the first Bishop of the Church of South India.

On the other hand, educated Dalit Christians who are economically well-placed act superior to non-Christian Dalits and those Christian Dalits who are not formally educated and still live in villages in servitude. This happened among Dalit Christians in Karunguzhi who employed poorer Dalits from villages as servants and would expect submission and servitude. As mentioned earlier, a young Dalit man from our church raped a Dalit girl who worked as a domestic servant in his house. It was hard to gain justice for the victimized girl because of the economic advantage of the boy's family.

My cousin Dorothy informed me about my grandfather Ponnusamy, a first generation Christian Dalit who treated non-Christian and poor Dalits with scorn. He served as a catechist (an official title provided by missionaries to men who were trained to carry on the teaching of the Bible in villages) and travelled to several Dalit villages, but he did not get close to Dalits, says Dorothy. Dalit Christians meticulously severed ties with Dalit villages and peoples as soon as they could. They found ways to hide their socially-imposed identity and were eager to merge into the larger society as educated Christians. The sudden change into a new social role and privilege caused an escape mechanism blended into scorn for their Dalit identity.

My great grandfather converted to Christianity in the early 1800s responding to missionaries from the Church of Scotland. His son, my grandfather Ponnusamy received mission education and worked as a teacher in a small mission school near Arakonam (Dorothy lives here), Tamil Nadu; later, he became a catechist. My father attended Christian mission schools as well. On my mother's side, her father Henry served as a catechist in many villages near the Kanchipuram area (known earlier as Conjeevram). According to Dayanandan, church records indicate his catechist work and teaching in the Vedal village mission school where my uncle George was baptized in 1918 (Dayanandan 8).

My mother was born in 1928 in the village of Melrosapuram close to Vedal. She studied up to fourth class in the village school and then attended the Northwick Boarding school where a lot of Christian girls (especially from Dalit communities) attended high school. On completing her high school education, with the help of other missionaries she attended the St. Christopher's Teacher's Training College in Chennai. She became an elementary school teacher in a mission school in Little Kanchipuram (also spelt as Conjeevaram). She met my father who was teaching at the Anderson High School; they were married in Kanchipuram in 1951. Both my brothers were born in the Kanchipuram mission hospital. My father secured a lecturer position at Voorhees College, Vellore, and the family moved in 1963. I deeply admired the fact that my father was a self-made man in his pursuit of higher studies and his knowledge of Tamil Literature. He was a prolific writer and a lay preacher. He excelled in

Carnatic music as a vocalist, which is a classical form of South Indian music traditionally only learned, taught, and performed by the Brahmin community. He learned the techniques of this complex music structure just by listening to Thyagaraja Bhagavadar, a famous Carnatic music singer, on the radio. He became a professional performer of this music set to Christian theme lyrics in various parts of Tamil Nadu. His songs have been included in the collection of songs published by the Church of South India and used nationwide and internationally.

My mother taught in a Christian high school, Corley where she excelled as a teacher among other castes and religions who held her in high regard. She received a state award as "Best Teacher." Even though my mother was a quiet and a gentle-spirited woman, she was confident about herself. In my recollection, I can say that her sense of a Dalit female identity was defined by her work and family. Even if she did not articulate it, she was proud of what she was in society. Later, in her sixties, when she met with an old high school classmate of hers who held a Ph.D. degree and was teaching in a seminary, she stated that if her parents had the money they would have sent her to the same college that her classmate went to. She did not overlook the connection between caste and class—it surely remained a festering realization. She was well respected by the large Christian Community in Tambaram and by her students and colleagues, including members of the caste communities. When she visited me in the USA in 1994, one of her former eighth grade students who is a Brahmin came to visit her out of deep respect and affection.

Tambaram was our home for nearly twenty-four years. My parents were active in the local Church of South India congregation. Their faith was important to them, the social and religious significance of which I only learned later. Most of my relatives were educated in schools and colleges started by missionaries in Tamil Nadu and excel as teachers, doctors, and priests (with the CSI-affiliated institutions). My older brother taught at the Madras Christian College. Open competition in other arenas of jobs where caste individuals were preferred was unthinkable. My second brother excelled in his studies in the Coimbatore Agricultural College as a university gold medalist and later worked with the Indian Overseas Bank in the loans section for over nineteen years. He was provided with minimal pay increase and promotions while those from dominant castes would gain speedy professional and monetary recognitions. He retired at the earliest opportunity and is now the Chief Financial officer with World Vision where he is happier, well respected, and recognized for his work excellence. Now, the next generation of my nieces and nephews possess education, skills, and confidence and are accomplished in areas of work and art other than that provided by the church circle.

Since the larger Indian society stigmatizes Dalit identity, I recognize Dalit female identity as a life-giving energy in which I take pride. It takes time to work myself into a socially secure position both economically and culturally before crossing over from hiding an identity to embracing and publicly acknowledging a heritage. Stories of Dalit women crossing over into that space of security to be able to shake off their anonymity and boldly proclaim their identity requires another space—a social and familial space of acceptance of oneself as a Dalit woman. One does wonder if such spaces of economic and cultural security, the mental spaces of confidence, and the social spaces of acceptance have been in place long enough for us to be able to hear Dalit women's voices. Dalit voices in this book are compelling storytellers who have surely placed themselves at risk in their own immediate social surroundings. But risk-taking among such Dalit female voices is now (in the past decade) being discussed in academic literature that honors diversified experiences. Due to the risks involved, Dalit women have the need to reconcile a freed sense of self with the immediate consequences. I do fear losing my sense of security that my ancestors have carefully built for me. Often, my immediate and extended family members who have learned the skills of camouflaging a life of a sustained anonymous identity are threatened by open declarations of a Dalit identity, especially as this affects marriage prospects for girls in our family, who otherwise would be able to "marry up" into the social hierarchy of caste. I am afraid that even this narrative of my open declaration of my Dalit identity will cost the security and social freedom that my nieces now enjoy as their mothers hail from Brahmin and Vanniya caste converts into Christianity.

Dalit women's voices are only active at the dangerous risk of being subject to scorn, ridicule, and resentment for exposing or highlighting a shameful identity. We can feel it but cannot say it out loud! What would make Dalit women who are agents of change be more acceptable as respectable, credible scholars and women is the ensuring of the strengthening and sustained longevity of spaces of security. This could be safeguarded by the strength in numbers of Dalit female voices and by the recognition of Dalit female expressions. Practices such as transnational feminism harbors the preservation and re-generation of voices within experiential lived discourses rooted in an *earthy humanness.*

WORKS CITED

Ambedkar, Bhimrao Ramji. *Annihilation of Caste.* Verso, 2014.

Anzaldua, Gloria. *Borderlands La Frontera: The New Mestiza.* Aunt Lute Books, 1987.

Arumugam, Kalaimagal. Personal interview. 3 August 2006.

Arumugam, Kalaimagal. Personal interview. 29 July 2007.

Arumugam, Kalaimagal. Personal interview. 26 July 2007.

Arumugam, Kalaimagal. Personal interview. 12 July 2010

Arumugam, Kalaimagal. Personal interview. 24 November 2012.

Arumugam, Kalaimagal. Personal interview. 25 November 2012.

Arumugam, Kalaimagal. Personal interview. 29 May 2014.

Arumugam, Kalaimagal. Personal interview. 27 December 2015.

Ashcroft, Bill, et al., eds. *The Post-Colonial Studies Reader.* Routledge, 1995.

All India Dalit Mahila Adhikar Manch. National Campaign for Dalit Human Rights.www.ncdhr.org.in/aidmam/aidmam?searchterm=dalit+women. Accessed 25 August 2013.

Aloysius, G. *Nationalism Without a Nation in India.* Oxford UP, 1997.

Arumugam, Kalaimagal. Personal interview. 3 Aug. 2006.

Bagwe, Anjali. *Of Woman Caste*: *The Experience of Gender in Rural India.* Stree, 1995.

Bama. Personal interview. 17 Jul. 2002.

Bhaware, N.G. "Dalit, Woman and Writing" *Eve's Weekly.* Dec 29-Jan 5. J.C. Jain, 1980.

Chandra Roy, Pratap. *The Mahabharata of Krishna-Dwaipayana Vyasa: Translated into English from Original Sanskrit Text.* Dutta Bose & Co, n.d.

Chandrika. Personal interview. 20 Jul. 2002.

Chatterjee, Partha. *The Nation and Its Fragments.* Zed Books, 1992.

Chatterjee, Partha and Pradeep Jeganathan, editors. *Community, Gender and Violence: Subaltern Studies XI.* Permanent Black, 2000.

Chaudhuri, Maitrayee. *Feminism in India.* Zed Books, 2005.

"Child Marriage – Fact Sheet Nov 2011." UNICEF. www.unicef.org/india/Child_Marriage_Fact_Sheet_Nov2011_final.pdf/.

Sumi, Cho, et al. "Toward a Field of Intersectionality Studies: Theory, Applications, and Praxis." *Signs* 38.4 (Summer 2013): 785-810.

Clarke, Sathi. *Dalits and Christianity*: *Subaltern Religion and Liberation Theology in India.* Oxford UP, 1998.

Constitution of India, (1950). Art. 15:1, 17:7. www.india.gov.in/sites/upload_files/npi/files/coi_contents.pdf/.

"Dalit Rights Situation," *National Campaign for Dalit Human Rights*, 22 Jan 2015. www.ncdhr.org.in/ncdhr2/aboutncdhr/.

"Dalit Women – Facing Multiple Forms of discrimination," UN Special Rapporteur on Violence against Women, International Dalit Solidarity Network, www.idsn.org/.

David Philips, trans. *"The World of the Untouchables:" Paraiyars of Tamil Nadu.* By Robert Deliège. Oxford UP, 1997.

Dayanandan, Paul. "The Life and Teachings of Rev Adam Andrew." Church of South India Department of Christian Education, 2007.

___ "Dalit Christians in the Chengalpattu area in Northern Tamil Nadu" Oommen, George and John C.B. Webster editors. *Local Dalit Christian History.* ISPCK, 2002.

De Beauvoir, Simone. *The Second Sex.* Knopf, 1953.

Derrida, Jacques, *Writing and Difference.* U of Chicago P, 1978.

Dirks, Nicholas. *Castes of Mind: Colonialism and the Making of Modern India.* Princeton UP, 2002.

Divakar, Paul. Personal Interview, 17 August. 2002.

Doniger, Wendy and Brian Smith, trans. *The Laws of Manu.* Penguin Books, 1991.

DA Profile. Jeyam P, 2010.

Dutt, C. Romesh. *The Ramayana and the Mahabharata Condensed into English Verse.* Dutton and co, 1911.

Dumont, Louis, *Homo Hierarchicus: The Caste System and its Implications.* U of Chicago P, 1980.

Edmonds, I.G. *Hinduism.* Franklin Watts, 1979.

Elmore, W. T. *Dravidian Gods in Hinduism.* Asian Educational Services, 1995.

"Ending Child Marriage – A Guide for Global Policy Action." International Planned Parenthood Federation and the Forum on Marriage and the Rights of Women and Girls. United Nations Population Fund.
www.unfpa.org/sites/default/files/pub-pdf/endchildmarriage.pdf/.

Forgas, David, *A Gramsci Reader.* Lawrence and Wishart, 1988.

Fowler, Jeaneane. *Hinduism: Beliefs and Practices.* Sussex Academic Press, 1997.

Frye, Marilyn. "The Necessity of Differences." *Signs* 21.4 (Summer 1996): 991-1010.

George, Sarath. "We converted for quota benefits." *The Hindu* 23 Dec. 2014, 1.

____. "30 Christians converted in Kerala: VHP" *The Hindu* 22 Dec. 2014, 1.

Gilmartin, David. "Rule of Law, Rule of Life: Caste, Democracy, and the Courts in India." *American Historical Review* 115.2 (2010): 406-427.

Goldenberg, Maya. "The Problem of Exclusion in Feminist Theory and Politics: A Meta-physical Investigation into Constructing a Category of 'Woman." *Journal of Gender Studies*, July 2001. 139-153.

Gosh, G.K and Shukla Gosh. *Dalit Women.* APH Publishing, 1997.

Government of Tamil Nadu *Abolition of the Bonded Labor System.* Government of Tamil Nadu, 2001.

Govindarajan, Saraswathy. "Caste, Women and Violence." *Dalits and Women: Quest for Humanity.* Ed. Devasahayam V., Gurukkul Summer Institute, 1992.

Grace Neelaiah. Personal Interview. 5 July, 2002.

Green, Marcus E. "Rethinking the Subaltern and the Question of Censorship in Gramsci's Prison Notebooks." *Post-colonial Studies.* 14. 4 (2011): 387-404.

Grewal, Inderpal and Caren Kaplan "Postcolonial Studies and Transnational Feminist Prac-tices." *Jouvert,* vol. 5, no. 1.
english.chass.ncsu.edu/jouvert/index.htm/.

Hameed, Sadika, et al., "Human Trafficking in India: Dynamics, Current Efforts, and Inter-vention Opportunities for the Asia Foundation." Stanford UP, 2010. www.asiafoundation.org/resources/pdfs/StanfordHumanTraffickingIndiaFinalReport.pd f/.

Hannah, Stephen. Personal interview. 23 August 2013.

"Human Rights in Tamil Nadu – 2009," People's Watch, Chennai, 25 Jan 2014. www.peopleswatch.org/monitoring.php/.

Holstrom, Lakshmi, translator. *Sangati.* By Bama, Oxford UP, 2009.

India Tribune. "Over 60 Million Child Laborers in India." *India Tribune*, September 2013. Web. September 30, 2013.

International Dalit Solidarity Network, "Caste Facts" www.idsn.org/.

___. "UN Principles and Guidelines."

Irudayam, Aloysius, et al. *Dalit Women Speak Out.* The Institute of Development, Education, Action and Studies, 2006.

Jayshree, P.M, et al., eds. *Dalit Human Rights Violations: Atrocities against Dalits in India.* National Campaign on Dalit Human Rights, May 2000.

Joffres, Christine, et al. "Sexual Slavery without Borders: Trafficking for Commercial Sexual Exploitation in India." *International Journal for Equity in Health* 7 (2008): 1-11.

Jolande, Jacobi. *Complex Archetype and Symbol in the Psychology of C.G. Jung.* Princeton UP, 1959.

Jordan, June. "We are the Ones We've Been Waiting for." "Poems for South African Women." August 9, 1978. www.junejordan.net/poem-for-sout-african-women-html/.

Kanmony, Cyril. *Dalits and Tribes of India.* Mittal, 2010.

Kaplan, Caren, et al., eds. *Between Woman and Nation: Nationalisms, Transnational Feminisms, and the State.* Duke UP, 1999.

Karuppaiah, Rani. Personal interview. 3 August 2006.

Keer, Dhananjay. *Dr. Ambedkar: Life and Mission.* Popular Prakashan, 1962.

Kinsley, R. David. *The Sword and the Flute: Kali and Krsna, Dark Versions of the Terrible and the Sublime in Hindu Mythology.* U of California P, 1975.

Kinsley, David. *Hindu Goddesses.* U of California P, 1986.

Kumar, Radha. *The History of Doing: An Illustrated Account of Movements for Women's Rights and Feminism in India, 1800-1990. Kali* for Women, 2002.

Lal, Shyam and Saxena, K.S. eds. *Ambedkar and Nation Building.* Rawat Publication, 1998.

Lanjewar, Jyothi. Personal interview. 19 August 2002.

Linda J Craft. *Novels of Testimony and Resistance from Central America.* U of Florida P, 1997.

Lourdusamy, S. "Village Deities of Tamil Nadu in Myths and Legends: The Narrated Experience" *South Asian Folklore Studies* 66.1/2 (2007): 179-199.

Mani, Lata. *Contentious Traditions: The Debate on Sati in Colonial India.* U of California P, 1998.

Mari Marcel Thekaekara. *Endless Filth: The Saga of the Bangis.* Books for Change, 1999.

Marudai, personal interview. 1 June 2014.

"Ministry of Labor and Employment: Government of India" labor.gov.in.

Mittal, J.P. History of Ancient India: Vol 1, From 7300 Bb to 425 Bc. Atlantic P, 2006.

Mookerjee, Ajit and Ajit Khanna. *The Tantric Way.* New York Graphic Society, 1977.

Moon, Vasant, ed. *Dr. Babasaheb Ambedkar: Writings and Speeches.* Vol. 12. Education Department, Government of Maharashtra, 1993.

Narayan, R.K. *The Ramayana: A Shortened Modern Prose Version of the Indian Epic.* Viking P, 1972.

Narula, Smita. *Broken People: Caste violence Against India's Untouchables.* Human Rights Watch, 1998.

National Campaign for Dalit Human Rights. ncdhr.org. Accessed 25 August 2013.

Neelaiah, Grace. Personal interview. 5 July 2002.

Nemani, Kamala. Personal interview. 31 May 2014.

Nyrop, Richard. *Area Handbook for India.* American UP, 1975.

Oommen, George and John C.B. Webster, editors. *Local Dalit Christian History.* ISPCK, 2002.

Omvedt, Gail. *Dalits and the Democratic Revolution: Dr. Ambedkar and the Dalit Movement in Colonial India.* Sage Publications, 1994.

___. *Dalit Visions.* Orient Longman, 1995.

Oppert, Gustav. *On the Original Inhabitants of Bharatvarsa or India: The Dravidians.* Asian Educational Services, 1988.

Palagummi, Sainath. *Everybody Loves a Good Drought: Stories from India's Poorest Districts.* Penguin Books, 1996.

People's Watch. "Human Rights in Tamil Nadu–2009." Chennai, 25 Jan 2014.

Periasamy, Rani. Personal interview. 3 August 2014.

Piggot, Stuart. *Prehistoric India to 1000 B.C.* Cassell, 1950.

Premraj, Deborah, et.al. *From Role to Identity: Dalit Christian Women in Transition.* ISPCK, 1998.

Racine, Josaine, and Jean-Luc Racine. "Dalit Identities and the Dialectics of Oppression and Emancipation in a Changing India: The Tamil Case and Beyond." *Comparative Studies of South Asia, Africa and the Middle East* 18.1 (1998): 5-20.

Radhakrishnan, Sarvepalli. *Indian Philosophy* I. Macmillan, 1923.

Raheja, Gloria. "Women's Speech Genres, Kinship and Contradiction." *Women as Subjects: South Asian Histories.* Stree, 1994. 49-80.

Ragozin, Zenaide A. *The Story of the Nations.* G.P Putnam's Sons, 1895.

Raj, M.C. *Dalitology.* Ambedkar Resource Center, 2001.

___. *From Periphery to Center: Analysis of the Paradigm of Globalization, Casteism and Dalitism.* Ambedkar Resource Center, 1998.

Rajagopalachari, C. *Ramayana.* Bharatya Vidya Bhavan, 1990.

Reed, Jean-Pierre, "Theorist of Subaltern Subjectivity: Antonio Gramsci, Popular Beliefs, Political Passion, and Reciprocal Learning." *Critical Sociology* 39.4 (2013): 561-591.

Rege, Sharmila. "Dalit Women Talk Differently: A Critique of 'Difference' Towards a Dalit Feminist Stand Point." *Economic and Political Weekly.* 33. 44. (1998): 39-46.

Renou, Louis ed. *Hinduism.* George Braziller, Inc. 1961.

"Report of the Committee on the Elimination of Racial Discrimination," Committee on the Elimination of Racial Discrimination. Seventieth Session, Seventy First Session. United Nations, 2007. www2.ohchr.org/english/bodies/cerd/docs/A.67.18%20English.pdf/.

"Reworking Gender Relations, Redefining Politics: Nellore Village Women against Arrack." *Economic and Political Weekly* 28.3/4 (1993): 87-90.

Richman, Paula, Ed. *Many Ramayanas.* U of California P, 1991.

Roy, Arundhathi. *Confronting Empire.* Porto Alegre, Brazil, January 27, 2003. www.sikhnet.com.

___. *War Talk.* South End P, 2003.

___. *The God of Small Things.* Indiaink, 1997.

Sadika Hameed, et al. "Human Trafficking in India: Dynamics, Current Efforts, and Intervention Opportunities for The Asia Foundation." Stanford UP, 2010.

Safai Karmachari Andolan,

www.safaikarmachariandolan.org/docs/Report%20to%20the%Working%20Group%20o
n%20Safai%20Karmacharies.pdf/.

Saminathaiya, V. trans. *Puranaanooru*. Kabir Press: Chennai UP, 1955.

Sangari, Kum Kum, ed. *Recasting Women: Essays in Indian Colonial History*. Rutgers UP, 1999.

Singh, Jebaroja. "Purity and Pollution: Dalit Woman within India's Religious Colonialism." SAGAR. Houston, 2005.

Singh, Prince. Personal interview. 24 September 2013.

Susairaj, Bama. Personal interview. 17 July 2002.

Susairaj, Bama. Personal interview. 2 January 2015.

Susairaj, Bama. Personal interview. 10 October 2016.

Staff Reporter. "11 Muslims Converted to Hinduism, says VHP" 25 Dec. 2014, 2.www.thehindu.com/news/national/kerala/11-muslims-converted-to-hinduism-says-vhp/article6723375.ece/.

Sunderajan, P. "Sushma pushes for anti-conversion law" *The Hindu* 22 Dec. 2014, 1.

Sunderajan, Rajeswari. *Real and Imagined Women*. Routledge, 1993. *Praxis: Theory in Action: Critical Transnational Feminist Praxis*. Eds. Amanda Lock Swarr and Richa Nagar. State University of New York, 2012.

The Hindu. Chennai. India. www.thehindu.com. September 18, 2012.

www.thehindu.com/news/national/other-states/dalit-woman-makes-history-in-rajasthan/article3910333.ece/.

Thekaekara, Mari. M. *Endless Filth*. Bangalore: Books for Change, 1999. Print.

Trinh, T Minh-ha. *Woman, Native, Other: Writing Post Coloniality and Feminism.* Indiana UP. 1989.

Trawick, Margaret. "Spirits and Voices in Tamil Songs." *American Ethnologist* 15 (1998):193-215.

___. *Notes on Love in a Tamil Family*. Oxford UP, 1996.

Trafficking in Persons Report. United States Department of State, 2011. www.state.gov/documents/organization/164452.pdf/.

"Universal Declaration of Human Rights." www.un.org/en/documents/udhr/index.shtml/.

Venkatasan, Radha. *The Hindu,* Sunday, October 20, 2002.

Venkateswarlu, Davuluri. "Seeds of Child Labor–Signs of Hope–Child and Adult Labor in Cottonseed Production in India." India Committee of the Netherlands, 2010.

Viramma, Racine, Josiane and Jeanne-Luc Racine. *Viramma: Life of an Untouchable.* Verso, 1997.

Webster, John C.B., et al. *From Role to Identity: Dalit Christian Women in Transition.* ISPCK, 1998.

Wolpert, Stanley. *A New History of India.* Oxford UP, 1989.

Zenaide, A. Ragozin. *The Story of the Nations.* G.P Putnam's Sons, 1895.

Zelliot, Eleanor. *From Untouchable to Dalit.* Manohar Publications, 1996.

INDEX

ABOUT THE AUTHOR

Roja Singh teaches Interdisciplinary Studies at St. John Fisher College, New York, with a major focus in Sociology, Anthropology and Gender Studies. Her ongoing human rights involvement and field work is among Dalit communities in the Chengalpattu and Pudukkottai districts in Tamil Nadu, India. She holds a doctorate in Comparative Literature—with a focus on women in indigenous cultures—from Rutgers University, New Jersey, USA. She has authored essays on caste and gender for book volumes and journals on human rights, comparative cultures and literatures. Singh is President of the Dalit Solidarity Forum in the USA.

Contributions to Transnational Feminism

edited by Dr. Silvia Schultermandl (Graz) and Dr. Erin Kenny (Drury University)

Tegan Zimmerman
Writing Back Through Our Mothers
A Transnational Feminist Study on the Woman's Historical Novel
For the first time in the literary tradition the contemporary woman's historical novel (post 1970) is surveyed from a transnational feminist perspective. Analyzing the maternal, the genre's central theme, reveals that historical fiction is a transnational feminist means for challenging historical erasures, silences, normative sexuality, political exclusion, and divisions of labor.
"The international scale and scope of this comparative project is extremely welcome, as is the explicit focus on post-1970s feminist historical fiction. This is still a neglected area with an ever-growing body of historical novels which, as the introduction states, have not been adequately recognized or studied." – Diana Wallace, author of *The Woman's Historical Novel*
Bd. 5, 2014, 280 S., 34,90 €, br., ISBN 978-3-643-90560-4

Maria-Sabina Draga Alexandru; Mădălina Nicolaescu, Helen Smith (Eds.)
Between History and Personal Narrative
East European Women's Stories of Migration in the New Millennium
This book presents a broad spectrum of studies focusing on fiction, graphic narratives, photography, online forums and interviews.
The contributions engage with important aspects of women's mobility and migration in the aftermath of communism. Thus the book covers untrodden ground in Eastern European studies, feminism and transnationalism, and is a highly welcome intervention in the field of transnational feminism.
The essays in this collection focus on a wide variety of fictional and non-fictional East European women's migration narratives (by Dubravka Ugrešić, Slavenka Drakulić, Vesna Goldsworthy, Iva Pekárková, Ioana Baetica Morpurgo and Marina Lewycka), multimodal narratives by migrant artists (Nina Bunjevac and Svetlana Boym) and cybernarratives (blogs and personal stories posted on forums). They negotiate the concept of narrative between conventional literary forms, digital discourses and the social sciences, and bring in new perspectives on strategies of representation, trauma, dislocation, and gender roles. They also claim a place for Eastern Europe on the map of transnational feminism.
Bd. 4, 2013, 296 S., 29,90 €, br., ISBN 978-3-643-90448-5

LIT Verlag Berlin – Münster – Wien – Zürich – London
Auslieferung Deutschland / Österreich / Schweiz: siehe Impressumsseite

Samuel Veissière
The Ghosts of Empire
Violence, Suffering and Mobility in the Transatlantic Cultural Economy of Desire
This experimental ethnography set against the background of nighttime encounters in the rough streets of Salvador da Bahia, Brazil, explores how such transnational characters as textit gringos, putas, and street children are at once co-constructed and reinvented through the legacy of Conquest and the global inequalities of late-capitalism. Theorizing the desires that drive these encounters as forms of colonial violence *and* sincere emancipatory strategies, Veissière's gaze travels outward across the Atlantic and the historical violence of Empire, and turns back inward to revisit the violence of his own White colonial desires.
The Ghosts of Empire "lays bare the questions we cannot answer and the doubts that we push to the side about how transnational forces distort the personalpolitical, internal external dimensions of everyone's lives. Veissière's story-telling is powerful and timely." Stephanie C. Kane, Indiana University
Praise for The Ghosts of Empire
"Veissière has written a book that lives transnationality. He confronts us with the importance of everything most of us leave out of our published writings. The Ghosts of Empire lays bare the questions we cannot answer and the doubts that we push to the side about how transnational forces distort the personal, political, internal, and external dimensions of everyone's lives...
Veissière throws himself into fieldwork about street people to an extraordinary degree [and] takes participant observation in night life to an almost unbearable extreme. His story-telling is powerful and timely. This is a courageous work that, if used in the classroom will shock and surprise students and professors out of their complacency; outside of the classroom, it may well be read for pure pleasure."
Stephanie C Kane, Indiana University
Bd. 3, 2011, 192 S., 19,90 €, br., ISBN 978-3-643-90080-7

Silvia Schultermandl; Şebnem Toplu (Eds.)
A Fluid Sense of Self
The Politics of Transnational Identity
In this era of increasing global mobility, identities are too complex to be captured by concepts that rely on national borders for reference. Such identities are not unified or stable, but are fluid entities which constantly push at the boundaries of the nation-state, thereby re-defining themselves and the nation-state simultaneously. Contemporary literature pays specific attention to internal and external notions of belonging ("Politics of Motion") and definitions of self resulting from interpersonal relationships ("Politics of Longing"). This collection looks at texts by authors who are British, American, or Canadian, but for whom a self-definition according national parameters is insufficient.
Bd. 2, 2010, 256 S., 24,90 €, br., ISBN 978-3-643-50227-8

Silvia Schultermandl
Transnational Matrilineage: Mother-Daughter Conflicts in Asian American Literature
Transnational Matrilineage offers a novel approach to Asian American literature, including texts by Maxine Hong Kingston, Amy Tan, Mei Ng, Nora Okja Keller and Vineeta Vijayaragahavan, with particular attention to depictions of transnational solidarity (that is the sense of community between women of different cultures or cultural affiliations) between Asian-born mothers and their American-born daughters. While focusing on the mother-daughter conflicts these texts portray, this book also contributes to ongoing debates in transnational feminism by scrutinizing the representation of Asia in Asian American literature.
Bd. 1, 2009, 240 S., 29,90 €, br., ISBN 978-3-8258-1262-1

LIT Verlag Berlin – Münster – Wien – Zürich – London
Auslieferung Deutschland / Österreich / Schweiz: siehe Impressumsseite